SECRETS OF A SUCCESSFUL TRAINER

A Simplified Guide for Survival

CLARK LAMBERT

A Wiley-Interscience Publication
JOHN WILEY & SONS
New York • Chichester • Brisbane • Toronto • Singapore

This publication is designed to provide accurate and
authoritative information in regard to the subject
matter covered. It is sold with the understanding that
the publisher is not engaged in rendering legal, accounting,
or other professional service. If legal advice or other
expert assistance is required, the services of a competent
professional person should be sought. *From a Declaration
of Principles jointly adopted by a Committee of the
American Bar Association and a Committee of Publishers.*

Library of Congress Cataloging in Publication Data:

Lambert, Clark, 1931–
    Secrets of a successful trainer.

    "A Wiley-Interscience publication."
    Bibliography: p.
    Includes index.
    1. Technical education.   2. Employees, Training of.
I. Title.

T65.3.L35   1986   607'.15   85-22596
ISBN 0-471-80143-7

Printed in the United States of America

10 9 8 7 6 5 4 3 2

To the three "J's" who entered my world—

with each teaching me
more about love
than could ever be learned
from a singular experience.

And to the good ship IRCLA,
with crew past and present
maintaining a steady course
through the unpredictable sea
called life.

The teacher is like the candle

which lights others in consuming itself . . .

RUFFINI

PREFACE

Secrets of a Successful Trainer is a factual guide based on proven techniques involved in the skill of classroom instruction. Writing especially for platform instructors, I have focused on both illustrating and reinforcing the specific skills required to impart knowledge to others in an industrial classroom setting. While many of the techniques featured can successfully be used in both undergraduate and graduate schools, the primary thrust of this book is to aid trainers in business and industry to teach more effectively in the classroom.

The material offers a wide range of benefits. For the newly placed instructor with limited platform skills, the book will provide a step-by-step framework of simplified teaching techniques that can aid in the delicate transition from novice to expert. For the experienced trainer, the book will furnish a viable bench mark against which current techniques can be realistically measured. For students of communication, the topics explored provide a practical down-to-earth guide in the vital task of presenting material to other people in classroom environments that are often less than ideal.

Mastering a new skill is not always easy, and the art of successful training is no exception. It demands personal effort and dedication. The student must have the motivation to learn, coupled with liberal and repeated doses of old-fashioned determination and patience. Applied learning requires constant practice and positive reinforcement.

For many students, the journey along the road to skill mastery usually proves a bit bumpy; at times it may seem both discouraging and tedious. It is precisely at this point that less motivated learners could falter. Perhaps the greatest challenge facing the trainer is to insure that even when obstacles arise, original learning objectives will be met and failure avoided.

Training is certainly no easy task, but for the true training professional, the rewards are well worth the time and effort expended. The demand for experienced classroom trainers has never been stronger than it is today. Whether this book is used as a basic guide for new trainers or as an additional resource for established teaching professionals, the principles outlined throughout the chapters should aid them in developing more effective teaching skills.

How to Use This Book

Secrets of a Successful Trainer has been geared specifically to active learning. Each chapter begins with a summary of learning objectives, or what the reader should reasonably expect to learn from the unit. The main body of the chapter highlights key elements of the particular skill being discussed. Following this is a summary of the main learning points. Each chapter then concludes with either a case study (including discussion points) and/or thought questions that have been designed to challenge the reader in translating the principles learned into actual practice. Where appropriate, suggested reinforcement exercises are also included.

CLARK LAMBERT

Huntington, New York
December 1986

ACKNOWLEDGMENTS

No book based on actual experience can be created within a vacuum. Effective writing, like good teaching skills, always requires a collaborative effort.

For the past twenty years I've been in the fortunate position of both designing and conducting training programs for the educational and business sectors. This book could never have been written without the continued enthusiasm, cooperation, and valued input of the thousands of students throughout my teaching career. In one form or another, I learned more from each class than one could reasonably hope for, with each teaching experience continuing to build into the bank of self-satisfaction that money could never buy. From Singapore to Syracuse, from Geneva to the Grand Bahamas—though the language and cultures may be somewhat different, the desire of participants to learn coupled with the motivation of the instructor to teach effectively provide a climate that is difficult to match in any other profession.

A continuing note of thanks is due to Citicorp and their high dedication to ongoing training and education programs for employees on a worldwide basis. Their high standards of training expertise offer an enviable record for the industry to follow.

Acknowledgments would not be complete without a very special note of appreciation to my family who, once again, patiently endured the writing of this book, the fourth in a planned series for business and industry.

C.L.

NOTE TO THE READER

Writing a text on effective instructional techniques is a difficult undertaking. This complexity arises from the nature of training organizations today and the correspondingly varied roles of the person called the "instructor." In very large organizations this individual can be one whose sole function is to *teach*. While this in itself is a crucial task, it frees the instructor from the very large job of doing the required needs analysis, development, design, production, and follow-up. In small companies just the reverse may hold true. Here, one individual could be responsible for *all* program logistics, *including* the platform teaching role.

Over the years I've been in both situations and have experienced the advantages and disadvantages associated with each, along with the many variations in between. The challenge in writing this book, therefore, was to aim mainly at supplying the teacher with *specific teaching tools* to use within the classroom but also to provide an overview of some design elements that are essential to program development. It's my opinion that the more a platform instructor knows about how a course was developed, the more effective he or she can become in front of the class.

I'm also a strong believer in the crucial role that the instructor plays in the total success or failure of the program itself. Experience has repeatedly shown that a good instructor can take a mediocre program and turn it into a dazzling success. But the reverse also holds true. A course that is well designed in every respect can fail miserably solely because the instructor lacked the required platform skills to conduct it properly.

In effect, then, a training program effort represents a partnership among all concerned—designer, writers, researchers, administrators, facilitators, instructors, and of course, the participants. If everyone does their job well, chances for success are good. However, a weak link anywhere in the chain greatly increases the risk of failure.

In many respects the entire process can be compared to an airline flight. The passengers (participants) who have experienced a good flight will probably remember the check-in ground personnel and the baggage service (administrators). Most of all, however, they will probably have the most vivid memories of the flight attendants (facilitators) coupled with the most significant memory of all—their exposure to the pilot (instructor). Quite understandably, they have little appreciation of the crucial supporting role played by others associated with the airline, but who remain behind the scenes. Starting with the designer of the aircraft and reinforced by a host of others, such as meteorologists, mechanics, and flight-scheduling personnel, the passengers never see these people—but their flight is directly affected by the efficiency with which the behind-the-scenes people do their work.

So the perennial question remains as to the added value a superb instructor can lend to a given offering. While I personally believe it's highly significant, one should never forget the back-up personnel who also made an important but unseen contribution to the success obtained.

In the final analysis, however, it's the instructors who put themselves "on the line" every time a program begins. Regardless of how an instructor might personally feel that day, the "show must go on," and the truly professional instructor puts everything else behind and concentrates solely on doing the best job possible in front of the participants.

To me, it's one of the most rewarding occupations one can enter, and I am proud to be in the field.

CONTENTS

1. **TRAINING AND THE ORGANIZATION**   1

   Learning Objectives   1
   Background   1
   Securing Management Commitment   3
   Manager's Role in the Training Process   6
   Training's Role Within the Organizational Structure   10
   Learning Based on True Needs   15
   Summary   26
   Chapter Questions   26

2. **ADULT LEARNING METHODOLOGIES**   29

   Learning Objectives   29
   Overview   29

Barriers to Learning   31
Principles of Learning   36
Positive Reinforcement   37
Adult Learning Guidelines   42
Summary   46
Case Study: I'm in Trouble, but Who Cares?   46
Case Study Questions   47
The Next Step   48

3. INSTRUCTIONAL COMMUNICATION SKILLS   49

Learning Objectives   49
Background   50
The Communication Cycle   53
Communication Cycle Components   55
Frame of Reference   63
Effective Listening   69
Listening Roadblocks   70
Active Listening   75
Summary   79
Case Study: The Problem with Martin   80
Case Study Discussion Points   82
Chapter Questions   82
The Next Step   82

4. DEVELOPING THE INSTRUCTOR'S GUIDE   83

Learning Objectives   83
Overview   83
Instructor Guide Components   87
Common Traps   97
Common-Sense Guidelines   101

Summary   102
Case Study: "Time Is Money, or Haven't You Heard?"   103
Case Study Discussion Points   106
Chapter Questions   106
The Next Step   106

5. PRECLASS LOGISTICS   107

Learning Objectives   107
Overview   107
Facilities Review   110
Daily Activity Planner   129
Pitfalls to Avoid   134
Summary   136
Case Study: "Can I Help It If I Get Sick?"   136
Case Study Discussion Points   144
Chapter Questions   144
The Next Step   145

6. AND WHAT DO YOU SAY AFTER YOU SAY HELLO?   147

Learning Objectives   147
Rationale   147
Sequential Teaching Steps   150
Summary   169
Case Study: "In Our Opinion, This Whole Thing Is a
Waste of Time!"   170
Case Study Discussion Points   172
Chapter Questions   172
The Next Step   172

7. EFFECTIVE PRESENTATION SKILLS   173

Learning Objectives   173
Introduction   173
Observable Techniques   175
Presentation Framework   176
Presentation Notes   192
Presentation Planner   193
Audio-Visual Aids   202
Video Presentation Guidelines   205
Summary   207
Chapter Questions   208
Chapter Exercise   208
The Next Step   208

8. CLASSROOM GAMES THAT WORK   217

Learning Objectives   217
Background   217
Introduction   220
Game Features   221
Game Cautions   222
Four Classroom Games That Work   223
Summary   238
Chapter Questions   239
Chapter Exercise   239
The Next Step   239

9. TEACHING STRATEGIES   241

Learning Objectives   241
Introduction   241

Use of a Facilitator   243
Characteristics of a Successful Facilitator   243
Instructional Roles   247
Role Playing   249
Strategy for Role Playing   250
Handling Class Disruptions   258
Summary   265
Case Study: "Teachers Aren't God, You Know"   266
Case Study Discussion Points   268
Chapter Questions   268
The Next Step   269

10.   EVALUATING TRAINING RESULTS   271

Learning Objectives   271
Background   271
Evaluation Biases   272
Evaluation Techniques   275
Sample Criteria   276
Cautions   282
Summary   284
Chapter Questions   285
The Next Step   285

11.   THE TRAINING/ORGANIZATION PARTNERSHIP   287

Learning Objectives   287
Overview   287
Partnership Foundations   288
Building the STARS Team   291
Summary   296
Case Study: "So, What Are Friends For?"   297

Case Study Discussion Points   300
Chapter Questions   300
The Next Step   300

12. QUESTIONS FREQUENTLY ASKED ABOUT TRAINING   303

Learning Objectives   303
Training and the Organization   303
Adult Learning Methodologies   305
Instructional Communication Skills   306
Developing the Instructor's Guide   308
Preclass Logistics   309
And What Do You Say, After You Say "Hello"?   311
Effective Presentation Skills   312
Classroom Games That Work   314
Teaching Strategies   315
Evaluating Training Results   317
The Training/Organization Partnership   318

13. EPILOGUE   321

The Opportunity   322
The Bench Mark   323
Parting Guidelines   323
Finale   325

SELECTED READINGS   327

INDEX   331

1

TRAINING AND
THE ORGANIZATION

LEARNING OBJECTIVES

Upon completion of this chapter, you should be able to:

Define the role of a trainer.

Have a better understanding of the manager's role in the training process.

Describe training's role within the organizational structure.

Discuss the needs-analysis process and its relationship to program development.

BACKGROUND

Within this first chapter we will examine some of the basic concepts of training and see how this function should be closely integrated within the strategic framework of the organization. Although this book will continually em-

1

phasize the more practical aspects of the overall training process, it is in no way meant to reduce the importance of the role involved with adult learning theory. Successful application of classroom instruction relies heavily on the instructor's knowledge of how participants absorb material and retain it. At the same time, however, it is the trainer's primary responsibility to process the flow of learning within the classroom—bringing each participant up to the stated learning objectives for the session. The trainer requires high levels of skill, knowledge, stamina, and versatility to transmit learning to each student in the most practical manner possible.

Training most likely originated with primitive man. One can only imagine the thrill of self-discovery when the basic essentials of survival were unearthed. The simple act of rubbing two objects together to start a fire for warmth and cooking or tying a crude rock to a stick to form a primitive knife or ax for hunting and self-defense formed the basis of applied learning *at that point in history*. Without any prior knowledge of learning fundamentals or classroom theory, one individual passed on the techniques of rudimentary fire-building and weapon construction to another. We can only guess how this "training" came about, but it is fairly safe to assume that a combination of fundamental elements was operating:

A definite need was present.

An individual perceived the need and discovered a vehicle for fulfilling that need.

The "student" had a high motivation to learn.

The information (skill) was transmitted from one person to another.

Results were measureable and satisfied a need.

Many thousands of years have passed, but the basic principles of applied learning are equally applicable to today's instructor conducting classes in an air-conditioned facility and employing the most advanced training techniques. The *level* of sophistication has changed dramatically over the years, but today's trainer can still be described as one who *identifies, evaluates, and transmits the appropriate knowledge that aids individuals in performing assigned tasks*. Specific responsibilities can vary widely depending on the size and complexity of the organizational structure, but they will generally include several of the following duties:

Evaluating need for specific programs

Determining effectiveness of current course offerings

Designing programs

Managing outside consultants where applicable

Conducting classroom instruction

Acting as a resource facilitator in matching individual training needs to applicable programs

Evaluating training results

Assisting individuals in transferring newly acquired learning skills to the job

Being a viable resource for and constantly being responsive to *line needs*

Supporting and building on management's commitment to the training effort

These listed duties will be interwoven throughout the book, and the last two points will be *constantly* highlighted. In my opinion the *degree* to which they are astutely carried out will directly relate to the eventual success or failure of the training function within the organization.

SECURING MANAGEMENT COMMITMENT

In many respects the term *management commitment* is a misnomer. It is never automatically given, nor is it suddenly withdrawn on a whim. In effect, it is a relationship between the organization sponsoring the training function and the perceived value of the activities that make up the function.

Like any other relationship, its foundation is built around certain basic principles where:

Mutual trust and respect have been earned.

Performance consistently matches stated expectations.

Nothing is taken for granted.

Maintenance of status quo is never tolerated, and new levels of expertise to meet changing needs are continually being sought.

Let us briefly look at each of the principles involved and relate them to the required commitment from management.

Mutual Trust and Respect

Commitment is a pledge to support the fundamentals within a relationship. Regardless of the activity being performed, the cardinal rule to remember is that trust and respect are intangibles that always must be *earned*; they are never automatically granted. Once earned, they must be constantly maintained. Further, these "ingredients" are rarely inherited by the trainer, even when an ongoing and highly successful training department is taken over from a competent individual with a proven track record. In fact, in this situation, it's even more likely that the new trainer will encounter difficulties due to the high expectations already established.

Finally, mutual trust and respect never magically occur overnight. As in all relationships, they build slowly over time. We should never forget that whenever we are building relationship, the element of fragility remains ever-present, and *nothing* can ever be taken for granted. In other words, what was true yesterday does not necessarily hold true for today—and certainly not for tomorrow.

Performance That Matches Expectations

No misunderstandings are ever tolerated here. Expectations for training and the classroom experience are initially set by the line with input and consultation from trainers. This results in a mutually agreed-upon set of performance criteria that *must* be obtained as a result of the time, money, and effort expended by the training department.

In effect, a "contract"—not a written document, but more of a verbal agreement—is drawn up between the line (those managers directly responsible for the profits of the organization) and the trainer in charge. The training effort is fully expected to produce the anticipated results within pre-established time frames and allocated budget. Going a bit further, the truly successful trainer is *never* content merely to achieve the stated expectations but works to *exceed* them wherever possible. The pursuit of excellence has never rested on attaining the minimum goals, but strives to go beyond the established norms. Training is certainly no exception to the rule.

Nothing Taken for Granted

Unlike a typical line operation, training deals with more intangibles than other segments within the organizational structure. The basic act of teaching others a new set of skills by necessity involves changing attitudes, introducing new learning concepts, and encountering varying degrees of uncertainty. It demands high degrees of patience for all concerned. Under these conditions, it's all too easy to make two unwarranted assumptions.

The first of these is to assume that *all* students within a classroom are eager to learn, highly motivated, and receptive to whatever is being taught. Not only is the assumption *incorrect*, it's also highly misleading and will usually lead to eventual failure—or, at the very least, to students with insufficient skill levels to perform a desired task. Figure 1, The Expectation Iceberg, shows how misleading the mere presence of a participant in a classroom can be. It is precisely because the participant has a *variety of motives* that the instructor must constantly probe the class as a continuing check on his or her version of reality.

Students who are indeed motivated usually learn easily. It is the ones who are not that provide the real challenge to the instructor's skill. We can assume, of course, that the program content being presented is at least reasonably valid. If not, even the most knowledgeable and versatile teacher will be able to achieve little more than marginal results.

The second unwarranted assumption is a *continuing* organizational commitment for training. Even experienced trainers in their long-term planning

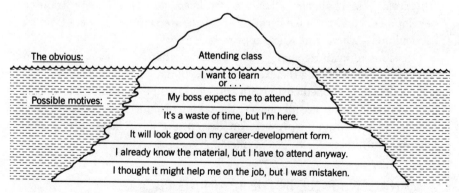

Figure 1. The expectation iceberg.

effort can mistakenly assume that, since training was heavily supported in the past, it will *always* have ongoing support. As with everything else in life, times continuously change. Management has a definite right to examine the value of the training effort on a *year-to-year basis*. Last year's departmental approach to training may have been effective, but it in no way guarantees that organizational commitment will continue in view of a slowly diminishing performance record for the current year. Support from top management can be taken away as quickly as it may have originally been granted. This organizational fact of life applies not only to the training function but to every component within the company.

Maintenance of Status Quo Is Never Tolerated

In securing and retaining management commitment, the trainer must act as a catalyst for innovation—yet at the same time strive for a reasonable balance between proven techniques and advanced theory. The trainer operates and must continually succeed in a very delicate environment.

Let's look at an example. Certain fundamental programs developed several years ago might still be quite efficient—they remain simple in content, very easy to administrate, and continually reach the assigned learning objectives. Although programs of this type should be periodically reexamined to determine if they can be further improved, they should *never* be discarded merely because they are a few years old. On the other hand, the trainer should be continually exploring a wide variety of possible applications for today's host of new training technologies, such as computer-assisted instruction. The challenge, then, is to keep abreast of new training developments and to make certain that these are included in new training curriculums—where and when appropriate.

Decisions to institute changes in training methods are never simple and usually involve blending the excitement and potential of a new technology with plain old-fashioned cost justification and feasibility studies. Nothing is ever gained without risk taking, yet the taking of unnecessary risks to continually prove "training prowess on the cutting edge" is simply a poor management practice.

MANAGER'S ROLE IN THE TRAINING PROCESS

Much has already been written about the total training and development process, yet due to its complexity, some uncertainty still remains as to the specific activities involved. Figure 2, The Training Process, displays a typical functional structure in use today. Let us take a closer look at each of the activities, then discuss the interrelationships involved from both a macro, or overall, and micro, or specific, viewpoint.

To start, let's clarify the relationship between the *size* of a training staff and the *functions* involved in the training process. There is no ideal number of people required to fulfill a training and development function. The number of people employed is generally based on the following:

Size of the organization being served

Training expectations from line management

Budget available for training

Stated management priorities

How training is viewed by the organization (its perceived value)

Depending on the relative importance of each factor, a training department's personnel could easily run to over 100 people or, by comparison, be

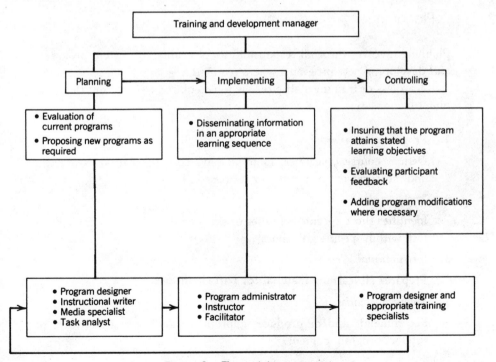

Figure 2. The training process.

staffed with a single person! Further, the number of people employed within the department should never be used as a measure of training potential or efficiency. For example, let's look at two similar companies that have a total training budget of $400,000 each—which includes departmental salaries and overhead expenses. The training department within the first organization employs a manager and a staff of eight training specialists. In view of this large staff, no budget is available for use of outside consultants, and all tasks are required to be done "in-house." The second employs only a manager and one secretary, but budgets more than $300,000 for outside consulting help each year. Now, you be the judge. Which training department performs the more useful function? Most likely you would say that this is difficult to answer because of the many variables involved—and you would be entirely correct!

Using this premise as a base, let's first look at the role of the *training and development manager*. This job encompasses responsibility for the planning, implementation, and control of all training and development functions within the organization.

Planning

Planning involves the dual responsibilities of evaluating current programs *and* developing new programs where required.

Regardless of training staff size, the jobs required to carry out the planning function are:

1. *Program Designer*

    Defines course objectives, methodology, content, learning sequence, and measurement of results for proposed program.

2. *Task Analyst*

    Identifies those specific activities or skills necessary to perform a given task within specific guidelines.

3. *Instructional Writer*

    Prepares all learning material for participant use.

4. *Media Specialist*

    Recommends and/or produces appropriate audio-visual software to support program content.

Implementing

During implementation, the actual program is conducted in a planned learning environment. The course material is presented in an appropriate sequence and concludes within the scheduled time frame—having met the stated learning objectives.

Depending on the complexity of the material being taught, several roles will usually be filled.

1. *Program Administrator*

   Works with line management, identifies appropriate participants, is responsible for notifying them of all course details (time, place, and program logistics). The program administrator plays a supporting role to the instructor in selecting classroom location, setting up the room, and insuring that all course material is ready, food and beverage service (where applicable) have been ordered, and all required audio-visual support material—flip charts, pads and pencils, video and assorted projectors—are on hand and *already checked out*.

2. *Instructor*

   Responsible for disseminating the program information to participants in the most applicable learning sequence—to insure fulfillment of stated learning objectives. The instructor carries the responsibility of actually conducting the class and usually has the final word in any major decision affecting the program within the classroom setting.

3. *Facilitator*

   Assists the instructor in "facilitating" the classroom instruction via such methodologies as leading participants into small group exercises, role plays, and various learning games, including the task of providing feedback to the class at the conclusion of the exercise. Depending on the size and resources of the training organization, the facilitator may also act as the program administrator. As noted, however, while both roles can be quite demanding, the facilitator must always have the added skill of being able to work effectively with small groups on simulations of all types. As we shall see later on in this text, that is a crucial skill, and one that can either enhance or diminish the work being done by the instructor.

Controlling

The final step in the training process is the "reality check" to determine the total effectiveness of the program just completed. Regardless of the evaluation form used, the key elements here are the unbiased critique of the participant feedback and the development of any appropriate remedial action necessary to improve the program.

The ultimate responsibility for the control step rests with the *training and development manager*, although its function is usually assigned to the *training specialist* responsible for the course. When an outside consultant has been employed to create the program, responsibility for making the necessary changes to content and structure fall within the domain of the consultant, and the changes are made without additional charge to the training department.

As we saw in Figure 2, The Training Process, each of the major responsibilities are interconnected to insure the required continuity from the program preplanning stage through to the controlling phase. A break or weakness in any of these segments will usually result in an inferior program or, at best, one that falls short of its stated learning objectives.

TRAINING'S ROLE WITHIN THE ORGANIZATIONAL STRUCTURE

As a traditional staff function (not directly responsible for the profits of a business segment), training has been occasionally exposed to the "bottom line" fluctuations of the organization. During periods of prolonged recession, it's only natural that management will take a long, critical look at *all* staff functions to determine where cost reductions can be instituted—and training is no exception.

The key to the training function's success within the organizational structure is to display a continuing track record as a cost-efficient unit that satisfies the needs of the business both on a proactive and reactive basis. Put another way, the training department must maintain constant liaison with the line units to provide programs that achieve mutually agreed-upon learning objectives and to suggest new learning technologies and methods that will improve the efficiency of the training delivery system.

Continuous, effective communication with line management paves the way for increased levels of mutual trust and commitment. To develop this premise further, I offer my own view of how the reporting structure of the training department should be organized—and one which may well provoke a great deal of controversy.

In most organizations, training has traditionally been a function of personnel, with the manager of training generally reporting to the manager of the personnel group (see Figure 3). Using this organizational structure as a base, one can reasonably assume that training is a *function* of personnel—or put a bit differently, an extension of that department. It's precisely at this point that I take exception. In my opinion, personnel should *not* control the training activity. Instead, it should become a client (or user) of the programs created by training to fulfill specific needs of *all* units within the organization. The rationale for this viewpoint is simple—when training reports to personnel, the ultimate responsibility for programs that should originate from personnel can easily get shifted over to training since it becomes a "natural fit."

A common case that comes to mind is the responsibility for the typical orientation program that many organizations offer to new employees. Whether it be several hours or days in duration, the program formally in-

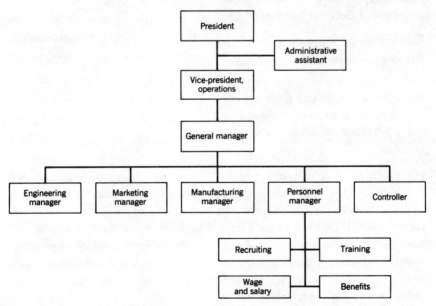

Figure 3. Common organizational training relationships.

doctrinates the newcomer in the firm's philosophy, history, structure, and procedures. Typically, training both *designs* the orientation program, then as part of its training responsibility, *conducts* it on a regular basis. The point to consider here is the somewhat fine line between where training's responsibility begins and ends. In the case illustrated, I would suggest the following roles of both training and personnel:

Training Responsibility	Personnel Responsibility
Initial needs analysis	Input to training department on all phases of program development, where required
Determination of program objectives (based on input from personnel and the line)	
Program design	Selection of members of department to be trained as instructors
Production of materials (handouts, audio-visual aids, notebooks, etc.)	Review and approval of all program material (as the client)
"Dry run" (conducting program for personnel staff)	Notifying participants of program logistics
Rewrite of material where required	Conducting program (after completion of pilot)
Instructor training (for selected members of personnel department)	
Conducting pilot program	Arranging for room facilities, coffee breaks, meals, and related logistics
Rewrite of material, where necessary	Maintenance of ongoing program evaluation
Monitoring first program (personnel staff teaches; a member of the training department critiques at the conclusion)	

Note that from a macro viewpoint the training function was assigned responsibility for all phases encompassing program development, including the actual conducting of the pilot and monitoring of the first regular offering. Using this philosophy as a base, I believe the necessary ingredient of keeping training solely occupied with its primary responsibility of program development can be easily attained. Naturally, this line of reasoning would not be applicable for very large organizations who can afford to maintain separate training departments for each major segment of the business.

At this point, I offer my own view as to a more efficient reporting structure for the training function. Figure 4 shows the training function reporting directly to the marketing manager. To understand this rationale, let's delve a bit into the philosophy of marketing and its relationship to the success of the business. A true marketing-oriented company is one where *all efforts and resources of the business are directed towards satisfying the customer.* Accordingly, in this type of organization, the role of marketing management becomes a key catalyst in the success of the overall effort in directing the firm's total resources in customer need satisfaction. Since the role of training and development is to support these efforts by fulfilling the needs of the organization it serves, the natural organizational tie-in should become apparent. Skeptics might argue that training, because it reports to the marketing manager, would then become heavily "market-driven" and perhaps lose its focus. My answer to that would be, the more market-driven, the better! Again, let's not lose sight of the fact that there is a direct ratio between training's involvement with the line and its credibility throughout the organization!

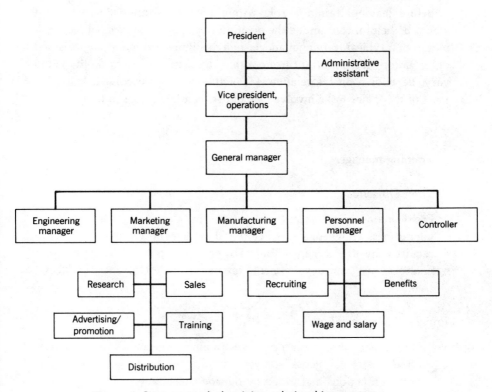

Figure 4. Recommended training relationship structure.

The truly successful training function will be closely involved with marketing management in the development of:

The strategic business plan

Yearly organizational goals

Operating plans

The training approach to be employed in achieving the stated goals

Training strategies that will be used to support the operating plan

Implementation procedures with stated milestones of accomplishment

In effect, then, through the close working relationship between marketing and training, the organizational goals of the business and the efforts of training forge a working, successful partnership, providing a vital link in the future growth of the organization—any way viewed, a relationship worth striving for!

Before leaving training's role within the organizational structure, it would be helpful to examine the position objective and principal responsibilities of a typical training manager in a medium-sized marketing-oriented organization. It's important to note that the *scope* of responsibility could vary, depending on the relative size of the company involved. However, most of the major tasks involved should remain fairly constant.

Title:

Training manager

Position Objective

Provide consulting services, training design, and management skills, using business knowledge to develop and implement training programs as required by the organization. To be accomplished through needs analyses, program development, instructional design, and administration.

Principal Responsibilities

1. Recommend, design, and manage training projects. Develop training models, perform needs analyses, implement training requests, and manage functions performed by outside consultants.

2. Work with line management to identify opportunities for improving practices and upgrading personal performance to increase productivity within the organization and enhance service to clients.

3. Negotiate and initiate projects dealing with marketing practices, product knowledge, client relations, management, communications, technology, and other practices, including both consulting and training services.

4. Create long-range plans and design training courses and job programs for upgrading old skills and developing new ones.

5. Manage professional training staff.

6. Develop and manage project budgets, evaluations, tracking mechanisms, and quality control.

7. Serve as liaison to corporate and other organizational counterpart services, to coordinate mutually beneficial resources and programs.

8. Actively market the staff services to line management and potential participants, informing both of appropriate objectives for an approach to job and career development.

9. Provide technical assistance for all video projects and monitor quality of production.

Again, while specific responsibilities could differ slightly, the key point here is that the objective of a training unit is to always completely support the organization's continuing needs. To accomplish this, the training manager must always stay close to the line and be attuned to its requirements. As the reader will note in subsequent chapters, this theme will be continually reinforced, since it remains a key element in the ultimate success—or failure—of training's role within the organization.

LEARNING BASED ON TRUE NEEDS

We have already seen that for a training program to become truly effective, it must be based on a real need from a particular client segment within the organization. In this sense, the "client" is any functioning unit within the firm that requires assistance from the training department.

Unfortunately, due to time pressures and other factors, it is not unusual for an organization to inadvertently rush headlong into program design before determining two critical factors:

1. Is this a real *training* problem (or challenge), or should the problem be addressed in a different manner?

2. If a training problem (situation) is indeed present, what needs must be addressed to solve it?

Let's take a closer look at each of the factors.

Attempting to separate those situations that can be resolved by training and those that *cannot* is one of the most difficult challenges facing the training department. To accomplish this, one must always keep in mind the cause-and-effect relationship of situations that occur in a business environment. Figure 5 displays this both on a social and "real-world" occurrence. It's very important to note that a symptom (effect) can easily be confused with the underlying problem (cause). In Situation one, when a headache occurs, most people simply take a few aspirin and the pain is quickly relieved. Consider the following office dialogue between a supervisor and a key employee:

Supervisor: What's wrong, Frank? You look terrible.

Frank: Guess it's my headache. It started this morning, and now it seems to be a lot worse.

Supervisor: Well, we can fix that problem! Here, take a few aspirin. They're the new kind, with lots of pain reliever built in.

Frank: Thanks! I'll take them right now.

ONE HOUR LATER

Supervisor: You look much better Frank! Pain all gone?

Frank: You bet! Thanks to you, my problem is gone. Now I can really get back to work.

Supervisor: Glad to be of help. If you need any more aspirin, just let me know.

Has Frank's real problem (the true cause of the headache) now been solved? Only time will tell. But the real warning signal of an ongoing problem would be that the "simple headache" kept recurring. To treat the "problem" with more aspirin without seeking medical advice would not be an appropriate solution.

Let's now focus on Situation two. A serious situation has developed in the Telephone Customer Section. The section has 20 telephone operators who respond to a wide variety of customer inquiries each day, ranging from an incorrect billing to an apparent error in a customer's monthly statement. A careful record is kept as to the *number* of calls each representative handles per hour, and the supervisor occasionally monitors an actual call.

Cause (real problem)	Effect (symptom)	Action taken (remedy)
Situation one (social environment)		
Simple tension *or* Lack of sleep *or* Glare from the sun *or* Requires glasses *or ?*	Have headache	Take two aspirin
Situation two (business environment)		
New incentive compensation plan introduced eight weeks ago *or* Department had to relocate to new quarters last month *or* Influx of new hires into department *or* Heavier use of temporary help—less overtime now for full-time employees *or* New telephone equipment installed recently may be reducing efficiency *or ?*	Telephone customer service reps handling 20% fewer calls over past two months	Meet with training department to "solve problem"

Figure 5. Cause and effect relationships.

As noted in Figure 5, the volume of calls answered has fallen and a definite drop in the efficiency of the representative's responses to customers has been noted. Obviously, corrective action must be implemented as soon as possible. Since the organization's training department has earned an excellent reputation, it is viewed as a reliable source for "quick cures." Let's now listen in on a brief conversation between the customer service section's head and the training manager. It's 4:00 P.M. on a very busy Friday afternoon.

Supervisor: Glad you come come on such short notice, Neil. Sit down and let me tell you about a real problem that's developed here.

Neil: Sure. Be glad to help, if I can.

Supervisor: It's quite simple. Our volume of responses has dropped close to 20 percent over the past two months, and we've got to correct this fast. Know what I mean?

Neil: Okay, but I need to know more about the situation. Have you discussed this with any of your key people? Has anything unusual occurred within your department during the past eight to ten weeks?

Supervisor: Well, a few things, but I'm sure they are unimportant.

Neil: Like what?

Supervisor: A few things. We put in a new compensation plan a while ago, but I think everyone liked it. And, as you probably noticed, they moved us to the other side of the floor. Personally, I think we have a nicer space now.

Neil: Anything else?

Supervisor: Minor things. We hired four new people a few weeks ago, and we now use our temporary help for most of the overtime that's required.

Neil: Don't you also have new telephone answering and display equipment? Could that be posing a problem for your staff?

Supervisor: That's it! Glad you could spot the problem right away. I knew that you could be counted upon to clear everything right up. Now, how about starting a training program next week to make certain that everyone is using the new equipment properly?

Neil:	I don't think that's the right approach.
Supervisor:	Why not? I thought you were here to help.
Neil:	I am. But we definitely need time to explore the situation further. For one thing, after we really look into it, you may find that the cause of the volume drop-off isn't really a training problem.
Supervisor:	That's hard to imagine. Give me an example.
Neil:	Well, for one thing, you mentioned that "temps" now get all of the overtime.
Supervisor:	So what? It's a less expensive way to run the operation, and no one seems to mind.
Neil:	Are you certain of that? Approximately how much weekly overtime did each of your regular staff earn over the past six months?
Supervisor:	About forty to fifty dollars. Plus, their regular salary averages out to four hundred dollars a week.
Neil:	You mean many of your full-time people have taken a drop of almost 10 percent in their weekly paycheck? Your problem may not be training but applied compensation.
Supervisor:	Never thought of it that way. So what's the first step?
Neil:	We'll begin by asking a lot of questions. As a starter . . .

Neil astutely avoided the "trap" of immediately attempting to apply a training "band-aid" to a problem that called for a different approach. But not all line supervisors are so understanding! During periods of extreme pressure (both on the training department *and* the line), it's all too easy to quickly introduce an array of programs—hoping that one of them will cure all the ills present.

On the other hand, let's assume that after closer examination of the facts, it appears that some type of training would be appropriate. It's precisely at this point that a *needs analysis* would be brought into play. Let's take a few moments and explore what *needs analysis* is, the various approaches that can be employed, and the assumptions that can be drawn from it.

The Needs-Analysis Process

Figure 6, Needs-Analysis Process, displays a typical sequence in the preparation of a needs analysis for a possible new program in supervisory training. Let's review each of the segments and their interrelationships with one another.

1. *Reviewing Elements of Skills and Performance Requirements of the Job.* In the first segment, a trained job analyst (a person trained to identify key performance skills for a given task) conducts a thorough investigation into the main elements of the job. For illustration purposes, let's assume the function under review is the job of a first-line supervisor.

In this case, the job analyst would most likely interview not only a representative group of supervisors but, in addition, would also visit with both

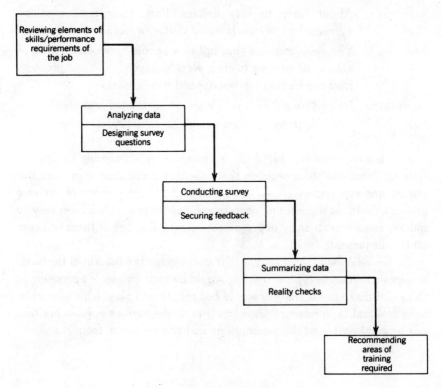

Figure 6. Needs-analysis process.

managers and subordinates of these supervisors. The reasoning for this is quite valid on two counts. First, interviewing employees on a vertical management scale has the added benefit of bringing out supervisory task requirements that may not be evident to the job incumbent. Conversely, talking with the supervisor's subordinates gives the same benefit at the opposite end of the hierarchy scale. Second, by interviewing several employee layers within the organization, a much higher numerical sampling is obtained, which always proves advantageous in analyses of this type.

All job analysts have their own individual approaches, but the objective is always the same: *To identify the skills necessary to perform the job at reasonable levels of expectations*, it's especially important to note that the interviewer *never* focuses on any one individual (for this might introduce some type of bias from the respondent), but always directs the conversation to supervisory requirements on a broad scale. Here are some typical questions that might be asked from each level:

From the Supervisor

In order of importance, what are the ten most important skills required to do your job?

What special skills are required, and how often do you use them?

From the Supervisor's Manager

From your viewpoint, what are the key performance requirements for the supervisors who report to you?

What special qualities are needed to make a truly outstanding supervisor?

Is there any one factor that causes a supervisor to fail?

From the Supervisor's Subordinate

Please tell me about traits that you believe make a supervisor an excellent boss.

In your opinion, what are the important skills that a supervisor in your section must have?

Note that these interviews are usually conducted on a face-to-face basis (although they can be supplemented with a written questionnaire), and are always completely *confidential*. If at any time the interviews are perceived as any less—even inadvertently—they become completely invalid.

2. *Analyzing Data and Designing Survey Questions*.   In this phase of the process, data from each of the three groups interviewed are ranked both separately and collectively. For example, if an organization has 30 first-line supervisors, the survey sampling would attempt to collect data as follows:

First-line supervisors	30 (if possible)
Managers (of these supervisors)	10
Subordinates (of these supervisors)	40
Total respondents	80

The 80 respondents would be analyzed as a total group, and in addition, each group would be totalled individually. The objective here is not only to uncover key elements of the job but to note correlations or variances regarding key skills required for the supervisor's job. Any significant variances noted here are highly important, since it's a clear signal to the job analyst that *perceptions* of required supervisory skills are present and will probably have to be considered in the forthcoming program design. Common areas where perceptions of skill importance differ among levels have been:

Degree of recognition given to effective coaching

Level of skill necessary to communicate effectively

Importance of building and maintaining high trust levels

Importance of the supervisor's role in performance appraisal

Once all data has been collected and reviewed, the next step, actual survey design, can begin. In general, the survey attempts to gather information in these broad areas:

1. Determination of the importance of the skill in question, in relation to the effective performance of the supervisor's job.

2. The degree of confidence the respondent has that he or she is using the skill properly.

3. How much the respondent devotes to this skill each day in relation to the other skills necessary to accomplish the job.

In other words, for each of the identified skills to be listed in the needs-analysis questionnaire, the respondent is asked how important it is, the "comfort level" involved in using it, and finally, how often it is used. For each area, a range of responses is offered. Let's take the skill of *interviewing job applicants*, for example. The first question might read: "How critical is this skill to the effective performance of your job?" The range of responses, on a scale from 1 to 6, could be:

6 Vital

5 Extremely important

4 Very important

3 Moderately important

2 Slightly important

1 Not at all important

Depending on the complexity of the needs analysis, it's not uncommon to probe for responses in 50 or more areas, including specific skills together with personnel policy and procedure questions. Again, while procedures can vary among job analysts, the questionnaire is usually designed to be completed by the same three levels of representative groups who were originally polled. Only a slight rewording of the needs analysis is required to obtain separate questionnaires for each group, and the results are well worth the effort.

3. *Conducting the Survey and Securing Feedback.* If the first two steps in the process were done reasonably well, the actual conducting of the survey should go smoothly. The survey form can be simple in design. It usually consists of a cover page that explains the purpose of the questionnaire, plus a statement reinforcing the confidentiality of the responses. In addition, it would ask for the person's job title and group or division.

Those surveys aimed at a manager or supervisor would also request such facts as the number of people supervised and length of service with the organization. This background data (which naturally *excludes* the respondent's name) serves a very useful purpose in the summarizing data phase. As just one example, the job analyst would certainly look for any significant variations in perceptions among managers regarding a key supervisory skill, then correlate these findings against the longevity of the managers responding. Specifically, it would be significant if managers who were in their jobs for less than a year felt that the ability to communicate effectively was a top priority for a first-line supervisor, but managers with over 10 years of service believed that the same skill ranked only fourth or fifth in importance.

The primary vehicle for conducting the survey would usually be confidential responses supplied by the respondents, answering the questionnaires by themselves. In addition, face-to-face interviews would also be conducted, both to accommodate those who disliked filling out forms and to increase the total number of respondents. It's been my experience that combining the two methods, direct interviews and mail-in surveys, works best. As long as people are convinced that the effort is nonthreatening and highly confidential, the answers will usually be straightforward and honest. Resist the temptation to request the survey back within a short time (such as one or two days). While the survey may be a paramount priority for the training department, it poses an added burden on respondents, and they will resent being pressured. On the other hand, make certain that a *reasonable* deadline is imposed for completion. In some cases a tactful follow-up will probably be necessary.

4.   *Summarizing Data and Reality Checks.*   When a sufficient response base is obtained, correlations are made on each supervisory skill regarding its *importance*, current use effectiveness, and frequency of use. Great care must be taken here to insure the correct interpretation of the data base. In most cases the two key elements sought by the job analyst are (1) the importance of the skill, and (2) how comfortable the respondents are in using that skill.

The final tabulation is usually a cross-blend of the two, with perhaps greater emphasis on *importance of the skill*, but with careful evaluation on the comfort level involved in its usage. Here's an example of two skills with a brief analysis of each. . . .

Skill: *On-the-Job Coaching*

Analysis: 85 percent of all respondents rated skill between "vital" and "very important."

Only 55 percent felt comfortable using the skill in coaching subordinates.

Approximately 20 percent of each day was devoted to this activity.

Skill: *Performance Appraisal*

Analysis: 90 percent of *all* respondents rated skill between "very important" and "extremely important."

85 percent of all *supervisors* responding stated they were very
comfortable in using the skill, but only 25 percent of their subordinates felt comfortable during the appraisal session.

Some interesting comparisons could be made here. Responses regarding
the coaching skill indicated an agreement that this area was highly important and also served as a "red flag" that supervisors required heavy training
in the skill. On the other hand, responses in the area of performance appraisal posed a perception problem. Supervisors as a group believed the
skill was important, and they were confident that the appraisal interview
was being done properly. Not so for their subordinates. Clearly, the subject
of performance appraisal should be included in the development of a supervisory training program, but special emphasis would have to be placed on
the *mutuality* of the process.

Constant reality checks are needed here. As areas of need surface, it's
critical that feedback be obtained from all those affected, and in many cases
the job analyst should do selected follow-up interviews with the original
population of survey respondents. The key here is to remember that while
the data collection process is *quantitative*, much *qualitative* reasoning is
also needed along with liberal doses of old-fashioned common sense!

5.   *Recommending Areas of Training.*   The final step in the needs-analysis process results in a listing of specific skills needed to increase performance effectiveness. A note of caution at this point: This final listing of skill
areas required in the soon-to-be developed program is only one of the many
plateaus to be reached before the course is conducted in the classroom.
Developmental work now required encompasses such specific areas as:

Learning objectives for each skill

Specific content of each module

"Flow" of material

Number of simulations, role plays, and small-group exercises to be
employed

Use of video (where applicable)

Degree of prereading required

Use of tests or quizzes (if applicable)

From a macro view, the needs analysis provides the essential link between perceived needs and concrete areas to be developed. Since the mechanics of program design fall outside the scope of this book, it's sufficient to say that this activity forms the central core of learning effectiveness for participants and is another essential link in the overall learning chain.

SUMMARY

1.　Today's trainer can be described as one who identifies, evaluates, and transmits the appropriate knowledge to aid individuals in performing assigned tasks.

2.　Management commitment for training is never automatically given nor suddenly withdrawn on a whim. It is based on mutual trust and respect, which develops where performance consistently matches stated expectations; nothing is taken for granted and maintenance of the status quo is never tolerated.

3.　Actual size of a training department can vary widely, depending on such factors as the size of the organization being served, training expectations from line management, budget available for training, stated management priorities, and how training is viewed by the organization (its perceived value).

4.　The needs analysis process is a sequential activity encompassing reviewing elements of skills and performance, determining requirements of the job, analyzing data, conducting the survey, summarizing data, then determining areas of training required. The process, therefore, provides the essential link between perceived needs and specific areas to be developed.

CHAPTER QUESTIONS

1.　Since the training function is an integral part of the organizational structure, why then is it common for this function to be heavily affected in periods of budget cuts and downturns in the business cycle?

2.　Training has traditionally reported to the personnel department. The view expressed in this chapter proposes that the function would be more efficiently served if it became part of the organization's marketing structure.

Do you agree or disagree? Remember to include both a short- *and* long-term view in your consideration.

3. All things being equal, do you believe it's beneficial for company instructors to become more involved in the needs-analysis process? Is this really a part of their total responsibility?

4. What are some advantages and corresponding disadvantages of having a needs analysis conducted by an outside consultant rather than a qualified representative from the training department?

THE NEXT STEP

As mentioned earlier, this book has been specifically written for the platform instructor responsible for conducting the actual program in the classroom.

The first chapter was designed to provide an overview of training and its relationship to the organization. As additional background information, Chapter 2 will focus on how adults actually learn—and why in certain situations learning never really takes place, in spite of ideal environments. This background knowledge is vital to every instructor who hopes to become reasonably effective in front of a class.

2

ADULT LEARNING METHODOLOGIES

LEARNING OBJECTIVES

After completing this chapter, you should be able to:

Describe the barriers to effective learning.

Discuss the principles of adult learning.

Integrate the process of positive reinforcement with a real-world application.

Apply adult learning guidelines to a classroom environment.

OVERVIEW

Over the years (and when time permits) I have been teaching one evening a week at a local college. I find it a very rewarding experience since the great majority of students work during the entire day, then despite heavy fatigue, attend classes several nights during the week. The motivation for this effort naturally varies among the students, but most need a steady income and yet have a strong desire for an advanced degree. It is truly an ideal teaching environment for any instructor!

Some interesting observations can be made. While the majority of students are in their early 20s, there's usually a sprinkling of others several years older. Last year, during the first night of class, I noticed a middle-aged woman in the first row who sat attentively throughout the entire lecture, took voluminous notes, and appeared to be completely absorbed in everything I said. Since she was at least 20 to 30 years older than the rest of the class, my curiosity was aroused as to her motives in enrolling in a basic marketing course.

After the class was over, we chatted a bit and I asked her why, after many years, she was enrolling as a freshman in night school. She smiled and quickly replied, "Well, Mr. Lambert, I never had a chance to go to college. I had to get a job right out of high school. I've raised three children, the last of whom is now in medical school. All my life has been devoted to helping my family, and now I feel it's my turn to do something nice for myself. First I'll get my undergraduate degree, then—who knows, maybe I'll even go for a masters."

I couldn't help but be amazed at this woman's motivation for learning and quickly responded, "Do you realize that it will take you at least five to six years of attending school at night to accomplish this?" She thought for a moment, looked straight at me and replied, "Sure. Now, since I intend to get an A in your class, may we review the homework assignment that you just gave? I have a few questions . . ."

Clearly, I had an adult student in my class who was highly motivated to learn (she went on to earn an A!). But what about the rest of the student body, and just as important, how do adults learn? Is there a clear difference in learning attitudes between students on the campus and trainees in a company-sponsored orientation program? Do 20-year-olds have different learning patterns than those in their 40s or 50s?

Since every instructor must be thoroughly familiar with how adults learn, the balance of this chapter will focus on the somewhat gray area of learning methodologies for the adult. While definitions abound for the term *adult*, for instructional purposes I define it as any individual over 18 years of age who (for whatever reason) is attending a class in a training setting.

BARRIERS TO LEARNING

Many roadblocks must be cleared before adults can learn effectively. Further, learning is never a black-and-white situation; that is, learning never takes place either completely or not at all. Rather, various *degrees* of learning take place with adults, depending on the interaction between an individual's *motivational level* and the perceived barriers to the learning process. Let's take a look at Figure 7 as we review this in greater detail.

Motivational Level

Motivation can be defined as *an individual's desire to do something based on a need*. Motivation never remains static; it continually fluctuates on various levels. These motivational levels can be built up, reduced, or enhanced, depending on the stimulus present, and once satisfied, motivation can remain dormant for years.

Some Examples

HUNGER: After a big meal, I may have no motivation to continue eating. Several hours later, the need for food begins to surface. If this need is not

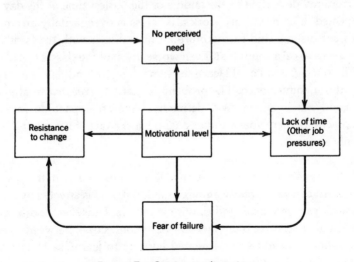

Figure 7. Barriers to learning.

shortly satisfied, the drive (or motivation) will begin to become acute. I eat again, and the level of motivation for food starts to drop sharply . . . until the next few hours. This cycle (for most people) continues with regularity throughout life and is quite predictable.

JOB PROMOTION: I learn of a really good opportunity for a major promotion within my company. Since I greatly value the increased prestige, recognition, and additional money that the new job will bring, my perceived need for the promotion is very high. During the next few weeks when several candidates from my department are being considered, I will work late practically every night, volunteer for extra assignments (but not being too obvious), probably skip lunch with increased frequency to continue working at my desk, and make certain that my image is at its very best. I find myself preoccupied with the thought of this possible promotion, and while my extra efforts will probably take their toll on both my physical and mental well-being, I'm sure the results will be more than worth it. The mere thought of this advancement only serves to drive me on harder.

ATTENDING A TRAINING CLASS: I just signed up for yet another class in product-knowledge training. Personally, I think that most of what's offered by corporate training is a pure waste of time. For one thing, it takes me away from my desk right in the middle of the busiest time of the day—and I'm expected to complete my work after class is over, usually around 5:30 P.M. It's exhausting, and furthermore I'll miss dinner with the family—but no one seems to care about that. Even worse, most of the classes I've attended are really boring, and I could learn the same thing by reading the material at home, at *my* convenience. The problem is that I'm *expected* to attend and get a good grade, and it will definitely have an impact on my career development. So here goes another one. It's just a fact of life around here. If they only knew . . . .

All three examples of motivational levels illustrate that the *perceived need* to learn can vary greatly among individuals and is affected by an array of physical, psychological, and emotional factors. However, as displayed in Figure 7, note that there is an interaction (or connection) between a person's motivational level and several related barriers to learning. How effective learning will be *depends on a barrier's strength*. Specifically, each can have an impact on motivation and on other barriers in the following ways:

No Perceived Need.   Classroom participants can truly believe that:

I already know the material to be presented.

The class will be a waste of time.

I believe that subject-matter knowledge can be more effectively learned on the job.

Very little can be gained from attending that class.

Time would be better spent doing something else (opportunity costs).

The instructor is known to be boring and probably has less knowledge of the subject than I do.

I've already attended a similar class, so what else can they teach me?

As we shall learn later on, the instructor's role is vital when perceived need is low. At the moment that class begins, the teacher has no way of knowing the degree of perceived need that each attendee brings, or the associated motivational level *at that moment*. Clearly, determining the degree of perceived need is a continuing challenge for the instructor, regardless of the subject being taught or the location of the training facility.

   Lack of Time (Other Job Pressures).   Unfortunately, scheduled classes can conflict with other commitments, both on or off the job. Consider these not untypical situations:

Classes must be scheduled during heavy work periods.

Attendance will definitely interfere with a person's travel schedule.

Time spent in class will cause a subsequent problem on the job due to time away from the desk.

A person has been recently promoted, is under heavy job pressures, yet has been scheduled to attend a training session.

Through an inadvertent error, an individual was never notified of a forthcoming class and only learned of it the night before. Unfortunately, he or she has made other business plans, yet is still expected to attend the training session.

Fear of Failure. Failure at training or, for that matter, below-par achievement in any situation, has always been a rather taboo subject—but it does exist and will be continually present to a certain degree with any group of participants. For instance:

An individual has continually exhibited only marginal performance on the job and is deeply worried about any situation that could cause more stress.

A scheduled participant for training had recently been passed over for a sought-after promotion and is now concerned over future career progress.

A participant's closest friend at work has just been fired. Both employees work in the same unit and received a similar performance evaluation report only a week ago.

Resistance to Change. Going beyond a participant's possible fear of failure in the classroom, another barrier to learning is resistance to change. This particular barrier perhaps presents the greatest challenge to the instructor, whether the student openly or inadvertently has a built-in mental set against change—any change—from the current way things are done.

Regardless of program design or content, a certain percentage of the class will perceive a training class as threatening. Most important in surmounting this barrier are the interconnections with the other learning barriers as shown in Figure 7—especially the motivation level of the student a few days prior to the scheduled class. Let's take a hypothetical situation that could come up in a new program for sales managers. As a beginning, use Figure 8 as a guide to possible resistance-to-change thoughts a participant could have *prior* to attending the course. Let's further assume that no formal sales management training had ever been introduced into this company, that the 25 sales managers (representing various levels of management responsibility) eligible to attend training had, on average, over 15 years of service, and that most were elevated to manager as a result of longevity in the field.

It's precisely at this point that many organizations inadvertently blunder. Having assumed that training is *needed*, they further assume that all participants will be receptive to the instruction since it will make them more effective on the job. That's not a safe assumption. In the example of the sales management program, some of the planned audience are very likely to ex-

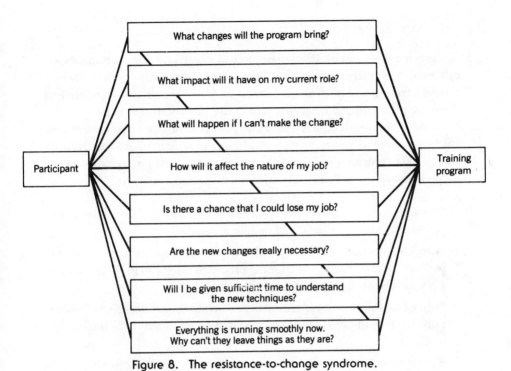

Figure 8.   The resistance-to-change syndrome.

perience the *resistance-to-change* syndrome, especially if any other learning barriers are present.

Reflecting a bit on all of these obstacles to learning, one can appreciate the heavy burden placed on the instructor to deliver the program efficiently. Here is where the typical instructional dilemma occurs. Should the instructor come from "the ranks" and therefore have an effective working knowledge of the participants' "world"? Or should the instructor be a professional from outside the organization, highly skilled in delivery but lacking in the necessary background? Going a step further, the credibility issue has to be faced. Does an outside instructor automatically lend more authenticity to the course, or is the material better presented via someone "from the ranks"? Tough questions—and there are no pat answers. Certainly, every learning situation will be different and must take into account the perceived learning barriers that are built into every organizational climate.

PRINCIPLES OF LEARNING

Just as a manager can positively reinforce or negatively affect a trainee's job experience, an instructor can play a similar role in the classroom. How successful a trainer will be depends heavily on his or her ability to understand the principles of applied learning within the classroom setting.

Broadly defined, learning is *knowledge gained through observation and study, resulting in a modification of attitude or behavior.* As an advanced guide to the principles of learning, and instructor must be cognizant of the following general fundamental surrounding learning activity:

Learning does not start and stop at sporadic intervals. It is a continuous process beginning at birth and ending at death.

Learning generally produces a change of behavior as a result of experience gained; hence, the learning process in itself can breed a degree of stress or discomfort within the individual.

Each of us learns at different rates and with various degrees of absorption—neither of which is directly related to an individual's intelligence level.

True learning cannot take place without some change occurring within the person being taught—even though the person may resist the change.

To be truly effective, learning must be reinforced. It cannot sustain itself in a vacuum—educational, psychological, or otherwise. An unfortunate but common occurrence is to have a participant return to the workplace only to find that the supervisor is "too busy" to reinforce the new skills learned in class. Further, in many cases the participant is psychologically penalized for even attending the class! Consider, for example, what happens when a supervisor does not assign a participant's daily workload to someone else while the class is in session. On returning to the job it's obvious that the participant will have to put in many additional hours, usually under pressure, just to catch up. Admittedly, this situation can happen inadvertently, but it should be avoided wherever possible.

Learning can never be effective without the *complete support* of management. Too often, a person is sent to a training class when there's no definite need. (Perhaps the employee is between assignments.) This should not be allowed to happen. It's unfair to the student, to the instructor, and to all of the other participants.

Stimulation of the senses enhances learning. Participants absorb knowledge more effectively when they not only *hear* the words, but actually *see* a variety of visual effects. Even the most experienced instructor cannot hold class attention for an extended time by lecture alone—the time-tested method of "show and tell" (using such media as 16mm film, video, slides, and overheads) not only offers a better learning environment but a more enjoyable one as well.

"Focused learning" should be employed wherever possible. That is, the training process should begin by having the participants understand the entire process (giving them an overview) of what is being taught. Once this is accomplished, the various "pieces," or components, are more readily understood. For example, referring back to Figure 8 (the case of sales management training), one should start with an overview of the entire sales management system, reviewing objectives, organization, relationships of people within the structure, and learning objectives of the program itself. It's then a relatively easy next step to review components of the program and swing into the first unit to be learned. Having a better understanding of the "big picture" enables each participant to easily grasp the individual modules to be taught and see how they all relate.

POSITIVE REINFORCEMENT

One of the underlying principles of learning is the use of *positive reinforcement*. It enhances the entire learning process, from initial absorption of the material to applied on-the-job skill effectiveness. Used properly by the instructor, positive reinforcement creates an incentive to learn, raises the motivation of participants, and develops their awareness (with corresponding degrees of self-satisfaction) of the new level of skill they have acquired. This is truly a teaching combination worth aiming for in any classroom!

Positive reinforcement is based on the time-tested rule that properly applied, "practice makes perfect." The key here, is the phrase "properly applied." In order to channel behavior in the direction being sought, the instructor must take great care to insure that the positive reinforcement *process* (1) is firmly in place and correctly taught, (2) is perceived as "real world" by the participants and its value is readily discernible, and (3) the newly acquired skill is reinforced within the classroom. To accomplish this, the instructor must lead the class through the following process:

1. Explain procedure.
2. Show positive model.
3. Have participants practice model.
4. Secure constructive feedback.
5. Institute "real-world" reinforcement.

Since the positive reinforcement process is one of the most critical elements in adult learning, let's spend a bit of additional time on the subject and explore it in greater detail via a concrete, applied example: coaching as taught to a class of first-level supervisors. First, we will review Figure 9 (Positive-Reinforcement Process), then we will examine each of the segments in the process individually.

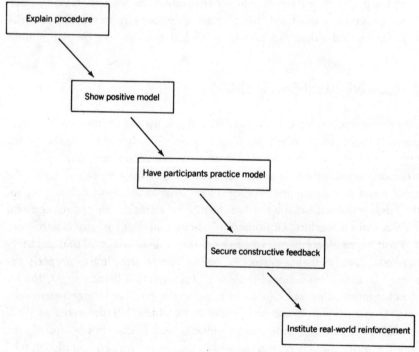

Figure 9.   Positive-reinforcement process.

Explain Procedure

The instructor would first set the stage by illustrating the importance of coaching to supervisors within the organization. The instructor would then illustrate *coaching procedures*, using either a flip chart, overhead transparency, or slide (note the use of audio-visual aids to emphasize the learning process). Let's assume Figure 10, Coaching Procedures, was displayed, then thoroughly reviewed by the instructor. Naturally, as each of the nine steps were outlined, participants would have ample opportunity to both relate the skill components of their own responsibility, and be encouraged via feedback to ask for clarification of any points that were confusing or unclear.

To accomplish this, the really effective instructor will have done the required "homework" *beforehand*. The instructor must thoroughly understand each of the steps within the coaching procedure and be completely familiar with its application on the job—and the supervisor's world. If the class suspects that the instructor is merely talking about theory and not real-life application, the session is in real danger of being doomed from the start.

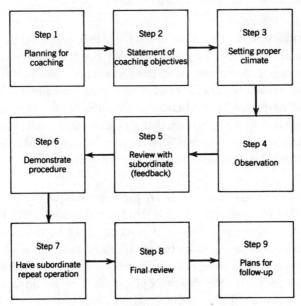

Figure 10. Coaching procedures.

Once again, this harks back to the sometimes difficult choice of selecting either an instructor "from the ranks" (who presumably knows the subject well but may not be an experienced teacher) or a highly skilled instructor who conducts classes well but may lack the necessary work background.

Show Positive Model

The primary purpose of this segment is to illustrate the correct method of applying the skill on the job. Using a real-world example, the instructor demonstrates the model, using any one of these techniques:

1. *Role Play* (Formal)
   While role play is usually effective, the instructor must insure that correct technique is shown to the class. Let's say that the instructor selects two of the most experienced participants to play the roles using a prepared script they were given in advance. While chances are good that they might follow the script reasonably well, there is always the possibility that one of the "actors" will inadvertently begin improvising and perhaps even present a negative example to the class. That is a situation to be avoided wherever possible!

2. *Role Play* (Informal)
   In this situation, the instructor takes the lead role and selects only one participant to play the opposite role. A script may be used, if the instructor wishes. Assuming the instructor is experienced in role play, the scenario stands a better chance of success than the formal role play using two inexperienced participants. Conversely, the instructor must take great care to make certain that a positive skill model is presented, since he or she is performing "live" before the class, and any mistakes will certainly be detrimental to the desired learning.

3. *Video Presentation*
   Demonstration via video is by far the most effective way to show a model. The obvious advantage is that the videotape can be erased and reshot until the desired scenario is reached. If the budget permits, professional actors may be used, but good results can also be obtained using employees who have been thoroughly coached in their roles. The use of line people for the video role playing has an additional advantage of lending more validity to the situation when viewed by the class.

Particpants Practice Model

Once the class has reviewed the model, the stage is set for reinforcement through actual practice. This step gives the instructor an excellent chance to view each participant applying the skill.

Of the many methods available, in my opinion the most effective is the videotaped role play. Here, scripts are prepared in advance, and each student takes a turn at playing the supervisor in a coaching role. As shown in Figure 10, all nine steps of the coaching procedures would be included in the role play, and each participant would be given sufficient time to complete the scenario.

During these practice role plays, the instructor should be well aware of how much experience each participant has had with doing this type of simulation in front of others. For the first-time player, it can truly be a frightening experience, and the instructor should handle it with liberal doses of tact and diplomacy.

Constructive Feedback

Since the primary purpose of the role play is to provide skill reinforcement, constructive feedback from both the instructor and all participants is a must. However, most students dislike pointing out areas for improvement to another participant—most likely for fear of hurting someone's feelings. While this line of reasoning is understandable, it completely undermines the purpose of the role play itself, and often renders it useless. The instructor plays a key role in this process, acting as a catalyst between the observable events in the role play and class feedback.

Done properly, constructive feedback is a very strong reinforcer of skill building since it clearly shows the following key elements:

What was done efficiently

Specific areas for improvement

Suggestions on how the improvement could be accomplished

To be avoided at all costs is the occasional unfortunate incident in which a participant's feedback to a role player is unusually harsh or sarcastic. Nothing whatsoever is ever gained by this, and if left unchecked, the incident can degenerate into an ugly situation. The experienced instructor will *never* allow that to happen under any circumstances.

Real-World Reinforcement

This final step in the positive reinforcement process can sometimes pose a frustrating dilemma for the instructor. Unfortunately, a situation may arise that has the effect of greatly reducing the effectiveness of the newly acquired skill.

Most experts in the field of adult learning agree that if a newly learned skill is to remain viable, it *must* be reinforced on the job. Using our existing example, it would be almost a total waste of time, money, and effort if the coaching skills learned in the classroom were not reinforced by the supervisor's manager. In actual practice, this could happen for several reasons, including a perceived lack of time on the manager's part. Worse yet, it could happen because the manager had never received the proper training to coach the subordinate in the first place! For whatever reason it might occur, the new skill level will most surely diminish, to the frustration of the classroom participant, who sees all his or her effort going to waste.

In some organizational structures, the instructor may have some influence in this type of unfortunate situation. Even when instructors have no direct reporting relationship to the line manager who is not following up with the reinforcement, they do have a responsibility to at least make their feelings known to the appropriate people. Such a situation can require a great deal of tact and patience, but the problem must be tackled.

ADULT LEARNING GUIDELINES

Over the years, much has been discovered about adult learning and how instructors can facilitate it in the classroom. To a degree, these guidelines roughly parallel the principles of learning discussed earlier in the chapter, but whereas the previous segment was based on overall (or macro) learning principles, this section (a microview) concentrates on common-sense guidelines that are *immediately applicable* with participants early in the session.

Guideline 1: Adults Have Options

While there will always be a few people in the class who were told they *must* attend, the majority probably had some choice in the matter. This choice could have been based on deferring the course to a time when a different instructor might be teaching it or perhaps attending the program at a later date. Since they are now in *your* class, you must recognize that you have a special obligation to them. Put another way, the participants have come to your class as a matter of choice—they expect the best, and nothing else can be considered.

Guideline 2: Adults Focus on Relevance

Your class will have high expectations. They will expect the material to be relevant to both their job (short term) and their career and personal development (long term). As such, be prepared for an immediate loss of interest if individual students do not readily see the connection. As we shall see later in this book, the participant's attitude on relevancy will form during or shortly after the instructor has reviewed the learning objectives of the program.

Guideline 3: Adults Have Background and Experience

Participants come to the program with a diversity of work backgrounds and varying degrees of experience from both their business and social lives. As a result, it's important to "build bridges" wherever possible—connecting the material being taught to the participants' frame of reference. For example, you would teach a course in effective communication a bit differently to a group of trainees who were recent college graduates than to a class of first-line supervisors with an average length of employment of 15 years. While you would convey the basic fundamentals of communication in the same way to both groups, your "slant" (or real-world identification with the subject matter) would be different. For the recent graduates you might draw examples from their recent experiences at college, while with the experienced supervisors you would use examples taken from their daily responsibilities on the job.

Guideline 4: Adults Also Experience Fatigue

Just because the class is composed of adults, you should never assume they have more "classroom staying power" than their younger counterparts! Uncomfortable chairs, poor lighting or ventilation, noisy surroundings, and yes, even a boring instructor will quickly take its toll with even the most polite attendees. The typical adult class can experience fatigue *prior to the start of the class* due to work or related pressures. My own experience (shared by many instructors) is that adult classes are usually more receptive early in the morning than in the late afternoon. If nothing else, the instructor must *recognize* and *react* to this factor by providing frequent breaks, using audio-visual aids, and varying both the pacing and intensity of the material being presented.

Guideline 5: Adults Like to Be in Control

Adults can be quite apprehensive when facing a situation they have very little control over—such as attending a class on an unfamiliar subject. Going through each person's mind are such unsettling thoughts as:

Will I like this instructor?

Is the subject matter really relevant?

Are there tests involved?

What if I fail?

Is there a chance that I will look foolish in front of the others?

Will I get bored?

Will the instructor give feedback to my boss on my class performance?

And what if . . .

Once again, it is a direct responsibility of the instructor to reduce these concerns *at the start of the class* through such techniques as a review of the learning objectives, an overview of the program, and a preview of what is expected from each participant. Each student has a right to that information at the outset. If it is not given, the entire class could be headed for failure—or at best, only marginal performance.

Guideline 6: Adults Deserve Adult Treatment

Participants expect the class to start on time—even if not all students have arrived. If they have shown the courtesy of being prompt, then they have a right to expect the same. They expect courtesy and especially dislike it if the instructor is not fully knowledgeable on the subject. They also expect a degree of difficulty in the learning process, and they will not tolerate being "talked down to" or ridiculed, either by expression or implication. Negative backlash will occur when they are made to feel unduly embarrassed (even inadvertently) or when they perceive that attendance at the class is an obvious waste of time. Can you blame them? Would you react any differently?

Guideline 7: Adults Are Generally Gregarious

Once they get to know each other, students like to chat, listen to stories, and whenever possible, have a bit of fun in the classroom. To discourage any type of interaction among participants, relying on straight lecture, is an open invitation to a boring series of interludes. It reduces motivation and brings on varying degrees of frustration and resentment. Note, however, that any large class will always have a few people who are inclined to be on the shy side and need to be drawn out. Here is just one more example of how critical it is for the instructor to treat each person as an *individual* and not as "just part of the class."

Guideline 8: Adults Want to Know Who's in Charge

Participants want to know who will be leading the class so that they can form an opinion about the value of actually attending. An excellent positive reinforcer here is for the instructor to meet with each participant shortly before the class begins. My own technique is to arrive early and greet each person as he or she enters the room. Just a few words of introduction extended here gives each participant a feeling that "someone cares," and that goes a long way in developing positive attitudes about both the course and the instructor.

SUMMARY

1.   Many roadblocks stand in the way of adult learning effectiveness. These can be classified as the motivational level at the time of learning, no perceived need, lack of time or other job pressures, fear of failure, and resistance to change.

2.   Learning can be defined as *the knowledge gained through observation and study, resulting in a modification of attitude or behavior.*

3.   Learning does not start and stop at sporadic intervals. It is a continuous process beginning at birth and ending at death.

4.   Each of us learns at differing rates and with various degrees of absorption, neither of which is directly related to an individual's intelligence level.

5.   To be really effective, learning has to be reinforced. It can never sustain itself in a vacuum—educational, psychological, or otherwise.

6.   The use of positive reinforcement remains one of the underlying principles of learning. Steps in the process (with heavy instructor support) include: explain procedure, show positive model, have participants practice model, secure constructive feedback, and institute real-world reinforcement.

CASE STUDY: I'M IN TROUBLE, BUT WHO CARES?

It was a full 30 minutes before the start of the basic product knowledge class that Jim Beal was going to instruct. Following his normal routine, he had arrived in the classroom early to make certain that everything was ready. Although Jim had taught this particular class many times before, he thoroughly enjoyed it. It was specifically designed for "new hires" and gave a comprehensive overview of all company products. As such, it was considered a "must" course, to be taken within six months of joining the organization.

Looking up for a moment, Jim noticed Frank Jordan standing in the doorway, looking a bit hesitant. The following conversation ensued:

Jim: Hi Frank! Come on in. Class won't start for another 20 minutes, but it's nice that you came early.

Frank: Well, that's why I'm here. I wanted to catch you before the seminar begins. I seem to have a bit of a problem.

Jim: Sorry to hear that, Frank. Can I help?

Frank: Actually you can. I have to cancel your class this week, but I'll attend the next one given in about a month. Frankly, I'm just not up to attending today.

Jim: What's the problem?

Frank: The problem is *this company*! They expect trainees to do just about every job handed to them—meet all deadlines, and still attend classes and pass tests! It's just not fair.

Jim: Hey, slow down. As a starter, I have 18 trainees in my class, and they face the same pressures that you do. I don't think the answer is to be absent from this class. Besides, if you don't take it now, you will have double the classroom load next month.

Frank: That's just the point. I spoke to my manager last night and he said that I definitely should attend, unless you personally excused me. How about it?

Jim: Just curious, Frank. Have you done the three chapters of prereading plus the case study for the class today?

Frank: Well . . . not really. I was sure that you would excuse me so I didn't see any need to. Look Jim, I've really been under a lot of pressure lately, and my work has been suffering. If you force me to come to class, I could really "blow it"—maybe even lose my job. You wouldn't want that to happen, would you?

Jim: Well, I really don't know what to say. Besides, class starts in just a few minutes.

Frank: You still don't understand, do you? I'm in trouble, and I can't even get an answer from someone who supposedly knows all the answers.

CASE STUDY QUESTIONS

1. Would Jim be wrong if he refused to allow Frank to drop the class? What are the consequences of doing that?

2. Did Frank have a right to approach the instructor just a few moments prior to class with this problem?

3. Should Jim's decision be affected by the fact that Frank had not bothered to do the class prework? Why?

4. As the instructor (and assuming that time would allow), would Jim be justified in passing the decision back to Frank's manager?

THE NEXT STEP

More than any other skill, the art of effective communication remains essential for the instructor.

Regardless of product knowledge, good use of visual aids, and relevant class role plays, without top-quality communication between the instructor and participants, the class is doomed to various degrees of failure. That's a strong statement, but it's based on many years of experience and is a view shared by many platform experts both in the United States and around the world.

Because of its extreme importance in the teaching process, the entire next chapter will explore the subject in detail. It will be time well spent for both the novice and the experienced professional.

3

INSTRUCTIONAL
COMMUNICATION SKILLS

LEARNING OBJECTIVES

Upon completion of this chapter, you should have the necessary skills to:

Translate communication skills to the classroom environment.

Explain the importance of feedback in the communication process.

Describe the communication cycle and its various components.

Define the types of interpersonal communication.

Describe the frame of reference and its impact on interpersonal relations.

Integrate the principles of effective listening with the communication cycle, and explain how listening affects the dynamics of meaningful interchanges between individuals.

BACKGROUND

Many instructors have a basic misconception that communication is a relatively easy skill to master. It is not. Further, some people assume that when one person starts a conversation, the other party listens, then answers in a logical, well-thought-out way. Nothing could be simpler—or is it that simple? Consider the following situations:

An experienced instructor spent a full 30 minutes carefully explaining a relatively simple procedure to a new employee. He asked the trainee to do the task and was shocked to observe that it was not being done correctly. Obviously, the new employee had not understood the instructions given, yet had not bothered to ask even one question during the entire presentation.

You are traveling through Asia on vacation with a rented car. Although you speak only English, you have had no language problems since your short, daylight trips have been along the main roads. Somehow, you've lost your way this afternoon, and with darkness starting to fall, you begin to sense a deep feeling of uneasiness. As your car turns around a sharp bend in the road, you note a figure by the side of the highway. With a sigh of relief you pull up and ask for directions back to your hotel. It immediately becomes apparent that the man speaks only Japanese and does not understand you. Even the most simple hand gestures prove futile. Frustrated, the stranger walks away, and you are left completely alone. With darkness fast approaching, you feel the first signs of deep panic beginning to build. If only there were someone who could understand what you were trying to say!

Somehow or other, you've never had any trouble in communicating with other people. During most conversations, you instinctly seem to sense when to talk and when to listen. Most of all, it's obvious that you enjoy these interchanges and are considered by your peers to be an accomplished public speaker. Interestingly enough, this communication skill could not have been learned in college because you were a high school dropout.

The classroom instruction had gone very well. All participants were highly attentive, many questions were raised, and the students' interest level remained high during each of the four rather intensive days in class. It therefore came as a complete shock to the instructor, when marking the final exam papers, to learn that over 30 percent of the class failed to achieve the minimum passing grade.

Although everything appears to be going smoothly during a formal coaching session, the supervisor senses that something is definitely wrong. For whatever the reason, it is obvious that her subordinate is not absorbing the corrective techniques being presented. When asked about this, the subordinate's attitude dramatically changes from that of passiveness to outright defensiveness. The coaching session was clearly turning into a complete failure.

While all of the situations described vary in context, they all encompass a common element—a breakdown in effective communication is taking place. The word *effective* is important here since, in reality, we all constantly transmit various types of information from one to another. In a broad sense, we can communicate to one or more people in three different ways: (1) orally, via the spoken language; (2) in writing, through letter or memos; and (3) nonverbally, giving off "messages" or "clues" through facial expressions, gestures, or mannerisms. These are the three types of interpersonal communication.

No matter how the communication is sent, it will not be truly effective unless certain elements are present. While the importance of each can vary with the particular message being sent, they are all essential to the process. Briefly, the three levels can be described as follows:

1. *A Level of Trust.* We need to have some reasonable level of confidence in the person that we are listening to. Whether or not we care to admit it, when we distrust (or have a personal bias against) a speaker, it is very difficult to establish and maintain good communications. An important point here is that trust levels, while building slowly between two people, always remains a fragile intangible—and can rapidly disintegrate under unfavorable circumstances.

2. *A Nonthreatening Atmosphere.* When a listener, for whatever the reason feels uncomfortable or threatened by a speaker or conversation, the process of effective communication becomes highly unstable.

3. *Good Feedback.* Effective communication must always be a two-way process. Unless the other person truly listens and responds, the instructor literally has no idea whether or not the intended message has been prop-

erly received. For example, let's suppose that a supervisor has just received a lengthy and somewhat confusing memo from her manager. As the memo is being read, there is no chance for immediate feedback—unless of course the supervisor is able to contact the manager via telephone or in person at that moment to clarify it. A good lesson to be learned from this example is that since there is no automatic feedback in written communication, the sender should always write the letter or memo in the most clear and precise way possible.

Using this short overview as a background, the vital importance of effective communication should now come into a clearer focus. Unfortunately, most people tend to underestimate how difficult it is to communicate effectively. Since instructors rely mainly on interpersonal skills, it is vital that they understand how strongly proper communications can affect (either positively or negatively) the delicate balance in classrooms. It is important to bear in mind the very powerful catalytic effect that really good communication has on all parties concerned. To better understand this concept, let us focus on the word *catalyst*. A catalyst is any substance that causes a reaction (or change) in something else. In this regard, effective communication is one of the main catalysts in the overall process of classroom instruction.

Whether the teacher is conducting a program in management by objectives, team building, coaching, or problem solving, how successful the program will be depends directly on the way that it is communicated to the participants. Too often, a newly appointed instructor has been well trained in all the functional skills necessary to conduct a class, yet fails miserably because of a lack of effective communication techniques. Regardless of the curriculum, the type of product or service being taught, or the geographic location involved, the art of communicating effectively with others remains one of the most difficult skills to master, despite its seeming simplicity. This was true 100 years ago, it is still true today, and I venture to guess that the situation will not radically change in the foreseeable future.

For some, the entire area of communications must appear to be not only frustrating but an enigma as well. Why does the process of communicating appear to be so simple, yet in reality continually prove to be a complicated and difficult task? That is a fair question and one that deserves a comprehensive answer. Let us start by fully exploring the actual components of communication and how each is integrally related to the others.

THE COMMUNICATION CYCLE

The Process

To begin with, the overall process of effective communication should always be thought of as a complete cycle (see Figure 11). To look at it a bit differently, think of communication as a closed loop with each component of the loop interconnected with an adjoining segment. If at any time a segment of the loop (or cycle) becomes "short-circuited," communication *may* be taking place, but it will not be effective.

For example, compare the communication cycle to the common electrical circuit in a home. So long as there is a continuous flow of electricity, the household electric current runs smoothly with no interruptions in service. In a broad sense, the same holds true for the communication cycle—so long as there are no "breaks" in the cycle, an effective interchange takes place between two or more people.

While this is probably a very rudimentary example of the similarities between the two systems, the obvious difference comes into play when something occurs to short-circuit the cycle. To illustrate, assume that you are home enjoying your favorite television program when a sudden electrical storm sweeps into the area, disrupting power to your house. The effect will be immediate: You quickly sense the discomfort of having no lights, heat, or appliances, and you may even begin to experience the first feelings of apprehension. Regardless of how you react, it is obvious that something has gone wrong. Unfortunately, in face-to-face communication,

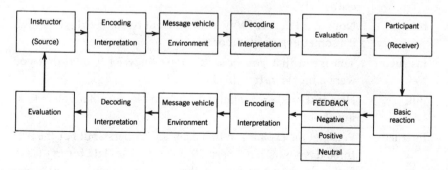

Figure 11. The communication cycle.

a short-circuit in the cycle is not as obvious. In many cases it may not even be noticed, and the conversation continues, despite the loss of effective communication.

Figure 11 displays a typical communication cycle as it relates to classroom instruction. Let's take a closer look at this process that at first appears quite simple, but in reality is not. To fully appreciate its complexity, consider a portion of a conversation between an instructor and participant, with no subsequent comment. Later, when the communication cycle has been fully reviewed, we will critique this conversation.

Scene:

A management trainee has just been called into the instructor's office. No reason for the meeting was given. He was told only to report at 8:30 A.M. sharp, a half-hour before the regularly scheduled class would begin.

Instructor: Good morning, Bob. Glad you arrived on time for *this* meeting. It's a refreshing change. We have a serious problem, but . . . wait a minute. Have to answer my telephone (a five-minute conversation ensues with the instructor arguing frequently with the person on the other end. The call finally ends with the instructor slamming the telephone down in apparent disgust).

Bill: Wow! That was some conversation! What was that all about?

Instructor: Oh, it was a consultant who is rewriting a section of one of our product knowledge programs. As usual, he is overcharging me. Guess he thinks I'm just stupid. Well, I straightened him out.

Bill: Now that I'm here, why did you want to see me? I gather that it's something very important.

Instructor: You mean that you honestly don't know? I figured that you were a bit slow, but this is absurd!

Bill: Hey, just hold on a minute! I still don't know what you're talking about!

Instructor: Well, let me explain, so that *even you* understand! For the past three days, you have been 10 to 15 minutes late for my class. Not only does this disrupt the other participants, but I personally don't like it. Remember, you're still just a trainee around here, and I'm a personal friend of your manager.

Bill: I can understand your concern, and I want to apologize for it. But there is a very good reason for it.

Instructor: (*sarcastically*) I've heard a lot of excuses from trainees. What's yours?

Bill: Well, for the past week, the customer service representative in the department I'm assigned to has been sick. My boss asked me to get to work every day at 8:00 A.M. to handle some of the overdue work. Sometimes it's difficult to hang up on a customer on a call placed to our section just a few minutes before 9:00. Sorry about that. I'll try to do better.

Instructor: Hey, speak up! Don't you realize how *noisy* it is in here? Okay, now I see! So it's my fault? You sound just like that consultant who just called me. Look, either get here tomorrow *on time*, or start looking for another job! Do you understand that?

Bill: But . . .

Instructor: There you go again, making more excuses!

Bill: Well . . .

Instructor: Well, what?

Bill: Nothing.

Instructor: That's better. Knew you would see it my way. Let's get moving. Class starts in five minutes.

Have you (or has anyone you know) ever experienced a conversation like this? Let's look at the communication cycle and later evaluate what really happened during that interchange. Many learning points are involved.

COMMUNICATION CYCLE COMPONENTS

Source

In the conversation example shown, the source (or original stimulus) starting the communication is the first-line supervisor. To bring this into sharper focus, let us assume that the communication is between the supervisor and the new employee who has just been assigned to the unit. It is the first day on the job for the new subordinate, and the supervisor is planning to spend the first few minutes with the new employee to outline the specific work tasks involved. This should be a simple, relatively easy procedure with no roadblocks to throw anyone off track. Do you agree? Well, read on and see for yourself just how multifaceted the process really is. (Refer to the diagram in Figure 11 as needed.)

Encoding-Interpretation

The message encounters the first step in the cycle, which is the encoding-interpretation stage, when the source (instructor) puts it into words. Basically, encoding should be thought of as the translation of messages that the source wishes to convey to the receiver into words. It is the way that the sender intends the message to be interpreted by the receiver. It is interesting to note that the process of encoding may in itself be affected consciously or unconsciously by the sender at this point. Furthermore, the process of encoding may be greatly influenced by both the physical and psychological state of the sender at that moment. Such physical factors as the degree of fatigue or energy level experienced at the time the message is sent can influence the sender's encoding. From a psychological viewpoint, the process can become much more complex. Here, encoding-interpretation can be influenced by such factors as (1) the sender's personal attitude toward the receiver, (2) the mood of the sender at that moment, (3) the positive or negative experiences the sender has had just prior to the communication, and finally, (4) the conduciveness of the setting where the actual conversation is taking place (whether the classroom is in a pleasant location or an irritating, noisy environment).

The combined impact of both the physical and psychological factors may help the sender to slant or highlight certain words to fit the situation. That is, many words can convey completely different meanings depending on how they are spoken. In each case, the same word may be used, but the connotations differ widely depending on the sender's tone, general body language, and specific facial expressions. Take the word *no* for example. It can be spoken pleasantly, in a soft voice and with mannerisms reflecting an atmosphere of refusal, but with no malice attached. At the other extreme, the same word can be shouted, with the sender's eyes narrowed and fists clenched toghtly. Obviously, in the latter example, the sender (source) is heavily emphasizing the negative connotation in the message. Finally, and as we shall discover shortly when investigating the communication cycle further, the situation can get even more complex when the sender believes that a certain connotation is getting across to the receiver, but in reality the reverse is occurring!

Message Vehicle-Environment

The next phase in the communication cycle takes into account both the type of vehicle used by the sender and the force of the environment impacting on the message. The message can take an oral form (such as face-to-face conversation), a written form (generally a memo or letter), or it can even be intentionally transmitted nonverbally. As a point of clarification, the environment includes those factors that are present during the actual transmission of the message. For example, if two people are talking in an office, the efficiency of the communication can be either negatively or positively affected by such factors as the room's temperature, relative humidity, seating arrangements, number and type of windows, and the level of noise within the area itself.

Here is an example of why many experts in the communication field stress the fact that truly effective interchanges are difficult to master and must always be handled with extreme care. A manager is chatting with a newly appointed product-knowledge teacher. It is now late in the day, and both men are tired. A faulty air conditioner has left the room hot and very humid. The manager is seated behind a rather formidable-looking desk; the teacher, in an uncomfortable chair positioned off to the side.

Manager: Well John, let's try to wrap this up in a hurry. I'm really busy these days, and haven't got all the time in the world.

Instructor: Sure.

Manager: Okay. Here are the facts. You need to do better on final exam class scores by at least 10 percent. Maybe you can improve the morale for each class also. Frankly, this whole classroom area is beginning to look like a morgue. I'm counting on you directly to shape things up during the next four weeks. Okay?

Instructor: I really don't understand. What's actually bothering you?

Manager: Nothing. Why do you say that?

Instructor: I'm not sure. I just get the feeling that you're mad at me for something. What's the story?

Manager: That's the craziest thing I've heard all day! Why, you are one of our best instructors!

Instructor: Wow! Now I'm really confused. Can we start this conversation over again?

In this situation an unfortunate combination of events transpired to make the communication ineffective. The vehicle consisted of both verbal messages (face-to-face conversation) and nonverbal messages (negative facial gestures and corresponding body language). Inadvertently, because fatigue and the poor environment within the room, the manager was frowning and sending negative clues without even realizing it! The instructor picked up these misleading (and certainly unfortunate) signals, which caused the short circuit in the conversation. As a result, the receiver's perception of the communication was quite different from that intended by the sender. This enigma in communication will be explained in greater detail as we probe deeper into the mysteries of the communication cycle.

Decoding-Interpretation

In its most basic form, decoding is the receiver's translation of the words just transmitted by the sender. In many cases, however, the meaning *intended* by the sender may be taken quite *differently* by the receiver, as we have just seen. The decoding process is quite fragile and can be affected by a wide variety of factors. Here are a few of them:

The "mood" of either party at the particular moment the message is sent

Fatigue levels

Conduciveness of the classroom

Room environment where the instruction is taking place

Events (either positive or negative) that happened to the sender or receiver just prior to the conversation

Noise levels or other distracting elements while either person was talking

If learning were to take place in an ideal framework for effective communication, both the instructor and each participant would *always* come to the classroom attentive, fresh, and completely relaxed. Further, the classroom setting would be ideal, with no outside distractions or interference. Unfortunately, in the very real world of instruction between teacher and student, the time and the location for training are rarely perfect. As a result any instructor who initiates the communication must be very much aware that negative conditions are common and must take every positive step to avoid or minimize their effects. It's not always possible to do this, but one should always try nevertheless.

Evaluation

The evaluation stage of the cycle is among the most critical stages of the total process. It is at this point that the receiver makes an initial judgment on what has been communicated and forms either a positive or negative attitude. Although the judgment could be the result of a slow, well-thought-out decision, more likely the receiver will take only a few seconds to make an evaluation. Those are a critical few seconds indeed, for what is taking place in the receiver's mind will usually have a significant impact on the conversation, the other participants, and even the learning efficiency.

Receiver

Once the receiver has evaluated the sender's message, the cycle is approximately half-completed. Students of interpersonal communications are usually amazed to learn that from the time that the source initiates the message until the moment that it is absorbed by the receiver, only a very few seconds will have actually elapsed. As shown in the communication cycle illustration, in those few seconds the following process took place:

1. The source initiated the message.
2. The communication was intended to be taken in a certain way.
3. The communication was sent via a selected message vehicle, through a contributing environment.
4. The communication was received and initially evaluated by the receiver, setting the stage for the next step.

We can delve a bit deeper into the cycle and note the variety of different factors that now come into play. At this point, the communication process is far from over.

Basic Reaction

It is at this juncture that the receiver forms a basic reaction to the message just received. An attitude (or mind set) has now been created that will shape the forthcoming response to the sender. This specific reaction is based primarily on the evaluation of the many factors (or influencers) that the receiver has perceived and is greatly affected by the steps in the communication cycle mentioned so far. At this point the die has been cast, and the stage is now set for the second half of the cycle to be completed. Remember, during this specific moment the sender (instructor) really has very few clues to the reaction of the receiver (participant) and to the events that will soon occur.

Feedback

As a point of clarification, note that the feedback segment of the communications loop is the only box with a dotted line in the circuit. This has been specifically drawn in this manner to reinforce the fact that in some face-to-face interchanges, there is really no verbal feedback at all; instead, there is an extension of a one-way conversation between two people. In other words, feedback may not really occur. This is a situation to be avoided at all costs; it represents the worst type of ineffective communication. In such instances information is merely conveyed to one or more persons with absolutely no check on how the message is being received; at best, this type relies on nonverbal body language (also a form of feedback) as the sole barometer of receptivity.

Let us assume, however, that some type of feedback has been encouraged. As noted in Figure 11, feedback can be classified as either positive, negative, or neutral. Ideally, when positive feedback occurs, the communication process becomes a free-flowing interchange between sender and receiver. Interestingly enough, even negative feedback (such as one person's disagreeing with the other's line of reasoning) can keep the flow of information both fluid and effective. Here's an example:

Instructor: So, as my slide shows, the blue form must be filled out immediately after the customer service contact.

John: Now I'm really confused. Would you mind repeating that?

Instructor: Sure, but what's the problem?

John: Well, use of the blue form was okay several months ago. Just last week we were told to reinstate the yellow form, which now has been modified.

Instructor: So why are you confused?

John: Use of the yellow form completely replaces the information listed on the blue copy. It just doesn't make any sense.

Instructor: Mmmmmm . . . .

The third type of feedback, neutral, can be quite misleading and, in certain cases, very dangerous. The sender (source) can never be quite certain what a noncommittal response from the receiver really means. Although neutral feedback can take a variety of forms, it is usually expressed as a short, impartial response of a few words such as "ugh," "Mmmm," and "I see." Is the receiver being affirmative, negative, or just plain indifferent? It's usually difficult to determine exactly, since there is a real possibility that a short circuit has occurred somewhere in the conversation. Unless the sender takes specific probing steps at this juncture to determine the receiver's attitude, the efficiency of the communication stands a good chance of being reduced. *Every instructor should be especially aware of this last type of feedback, since it could indicate a breakdown in effective one-to-one communication.*

Encoding-Interpretation

Similar to the encoding of words as originally done by the sender, the receiver (who now, in effect, h:.s switched roles and become the new sender), begins to initiate the process of transmitting words and meanings to the other party. As in the first transaction done by the original source, the new sender can either consciously or unconsciously twist the true significance of the message. This complete reversal of roles during the same conversation reinforces the true complexity of the entire process.

Message Vehicle-Environment

Another similarity arises in both the type of message vehicle used by the new sender, and the influence of the environment on the conversation. Naturally, during a typical one-on-one interchange, both the message vehicle (type of communication used, such as face-to-face conversation) and environment will most likely be the same—unless, of course, sudden distracting interruptions occur (for example, a third party noisily entering a room, or the incessant jangling of an unanswered telephone).

Decoding-Interpretation

In this stage, we see real evidence of role reversal, in that the new receiver must now decipher and interpret the words spoken by the other person. All of the factors mentioned earlier for this phase, such as the body language of the sender or the mood of the receiver at that point, come into play once again. As we have already seen, however, the roles of both participants are fully reversed at this point.

Evaluation

This represents the final phase of the communication cycle. Now the new receiver evaluates all of the new sender's messages, forms an opinion, and either terminates the conversation at that juncture or uses it as a platform for the next interchange. Whatever the outcome, it is important to remember that midway during each cycle the roles of both the sender and receiver are reversed and that the messages being transmitted can either be verbal, nonverbal, or a combination of both.

It should now be clear that the entire process of communication is by nature a complex and multifaceted set of transactions. Further, without a solid base of effective communications, the ability to supervise other people would rest on a rather unstable foundation.

It is now time to take the theory of the communication process and learn how it can be applied to an interchange between two or more people. Let's refer back to both Figure 11 (the communication cycle) and the conversation presented earlier between the supervisor and subordinate and see what really happened.

1. The instructor became the original source, since he initiated the conversation.

2. He consciously encoded his words to reflect both annoyance and impatience with Bill's lateness in coming to class. Unfortunately, it immediately put Bill on the defensive, which started to reduce the effec-

tiveness of the communication soon after the actual conversation had begun.

3. The message vehicle used was a face-to-face interchange; however, a distracting environment (the telephone interruption) reduced effectiveness to even a lower point than before.

4. The decoding process was an experience in frustration for Bill. While he correctly identified the instructor's anger, he had very little time to form an impartial evaluation in his mind as to what was really going on. Clearly, he was being placed on the defensive.

5. Bill's basic reaction was one of bewilderment and, of course, frustration. Apparently, he had a very valid reason for coming to class late, but in all fairness, he needed a chance to explain.

6. Bill attempted to explain via honest feedback and tried to encode his words in a sincere manner (even though the same poor environment was still operating). Unfortunately, the instructor decoded all of this in a negative manner, completely discouraging the feedback (explanation) being offered.

The obvious result was a perfect example of ineffective communication: What started out as a two-way exchange ended up as a biased, one-sided interchange that proved valueless to both parties. This is a sad but probably very common example of the numerous pitfalls that can be encountered when two or more people get together to exchange ideas, information, or viewpoints.

Although we have seen the many facets involved in the communication cycle, one vital element remains to be discussed: the frame of reference. While it is not shown in Figure 11, it impacts heavily on the efficiency of communication itself. How can something that operates outside of the cycle affect communication to such a large degree? Let's find out.

FRAME OF REFERENCE

If you are like most people, at least several times a month your reasoning and subsequent action in many situations will be directly affected by "something" that happened to you only a short time before. This phenomenon is called a *frame of reference*, and it can be roughly defined as those experiences, attitudes, ideas, and mind sets that have developed through past experiences, and that have an effect on your future behavior. We can put this in a clearer perspective by examining the experiences of Mary K. and Phyllis R., who have both worked for a medium-sized bank for the past seven years. Each of them are considered excellent supervisors in the check-processing department—a fast paced, "pressure-cooker" environment. It is a typical Friday morning as we look in on the following scene:

MARY K. Mornings were normally hectic anyway, since Mary always managed to have a fast breakfast with her husband and three children before driving to work.

On this particular morning, everything seemed to go wrong at once—from the eggs being overcooked to the children oversleeping and then rushing through their food in order to make the school bus on time. Mary wasn't sure how the silly argument over the recent telephone bill had started, but within minutes, it turned into a rather nasty disagreement with her husband. Both left the house without speaking to each other, something that rarely occurred.

Mary's morning at work went smoothly enough—in fact it turned out to be quite pleasant. By the afternoon, however, her mood began to sour rapidly. It was during this time, while observing a new clerk performing her duties, that Mary suddenly "exploded." Without even realizing it, she was at the new employee's side loudly criticizing the procedure being used. It was obvious that she overreacted to the situation, and she became quite embarrassed by her own outburst. What really bothered her was that she rarely lost her temper; in fact, she prided herself on her ability to remain calm.

PHYLLIS R. It had been a wonderful weekend for Phyllis. On Sunday, she had placed a deposit on a new condominium being built in Oyster Bay Cove. This was by far the nicest section of town, but it had always been a bit out of her price range. Suddenly, last month along with a new promotion at work came a hefty pay raise and, with it, she was finally able to have a "place of her own." She was quite proud.

Now, five days later, because of the hectic pace at the office, Phyllis had almost forgotten about her pleasant experience. As the day wore on, she was very shocked to notice that across the hall her friend Mary was reprimanding a new employee heavily for an apparently simple mistake.

After waiting a reasonable amount of time for the incident to pass, she approached Mary, and the following conversation took place.

Phyllis: Sorry to butt in. Mary, but weren't you a bit hard on her? After all, that woman only started in your section last week!

Mary: Guess you're right. But it sure makes me mad to see such stupidity. I wish that our personnel department would do a better job in selecting these people.

Phyllis: Stupidity? Is that what you call trying to learn a new job? What's the matter with you? Give her a fair chance!

Mary: Well, to tell the truth, I've been sort of "down in the dumps" for the last couple of weeks. The fight I had this morning with Bob didn't help matters any.

Phyllis: Hey, don't be too hard on yourself. We all have our off-days. You have a beautiful family, a great job, and a staff of loyal people who really like you—except when you yell at them for all the wrong things! Cheer up. The weekend is coming, and you'll probably feel 100 percent better!

Mary: My God, what put you in such a good mood?

Phyllis: I'm not really sure, but whatever it is, I love it!

These two examples, while perhaps somewhat oversimplified, nevertheless spotlight the strong effect that our frame of reference has on us during a typical work week. *It also applies to participants in any given learning situation.* Understanding how this phenomenon affects the average person can put the instructor in a strong leadership role in front of the class.

From a teaching standpoint it certainly would be ideal if each of us lived in an environment where our judgments, moods, and opinions would never be affected by outside events. As we all know, however, this simply does not happen. As instructors we may not always be able to remain calm and rational, but we can be aware of the frame of reference and how it can affect our behavior.

Figure 12 shows the complexity of this phenomenon. Note that there are three stages to an actual frame of reference: long-term, secondary, and immediate. The following examples will illustrate each stage and its possible effects on our personal and business lives.

Time Frame (or Stage)	Time Span	Event	Personal Behavior
Immediate (within past 72 hours)	Yesterday	My instructor informed me that I was failing the course— something that I never thought could happen to me.	Strong feelings of despair. Moody. Went home early that day. May look for another job. Yelled at my kids that night for no apparent reason. Wife upset.
Secondary (72 hours to 2 weeks later)	Two weeks later	(Same)	Still unhappy, but thinking of ways to improve my performance in class. In slightly better mood but still personally hurt. Home life returning to normal . . . almost.
Long term (From 2 weeks on)	One month	(Same)	Spoke to my boss—I just barely passed the course. Still a bit hurt, but can understand the company position. Determined not to let this happen to me again. Talked it over with my wife, and she understands how I feel. I will definitely do better next time!

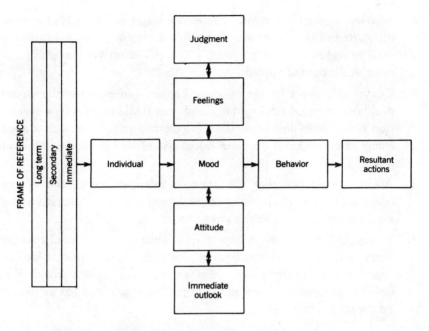

Figure 12. Frame-of-reference syndrome.

Note that the event (the danger of failing the course) had an immediate detrimental effect on the employee. With each succeeding week as the secondary frame-of-reference stage passed into the long-term one, however, the unpleasant event began to have less of a negative impact—in fact, it triggered a set of positive reactions to the situation at work. Explaining this in a slightly different way, our minds usually resort to "defense mechanisms" that, in time, enable us to repress unpleasant experiences while retaining positive ones.

With knowledge of these mechanisms as a base, both the effective instructor and class participants càn turn a negative frame of reference into a constructive one by using the following guidelines:

1. Never make an important decision (whether business or personal) when upset or angry. Let the negative feelings "blow over," and your decision will generally be more rational. This is especially important when teaching.

2. Be aware of the three frame-of-reference stages and be guided accordingly. Remember, however, that while a strong negative experience may be repressed as time passes, it can still affect your overall judgment, feelings, and attitude.

3. Conversely, never let the opposite happen—an exceptionally strong positive experience can begin to cloud your thinking. This type of reaction is especially insidious, since it generally puts us in such a good frame of mind that it becomes extremely difficult to distinguish clear thinking from pure impulse.

4. Always remember that the frame-of-reference experience is not restricted to yourself. It continually happens to both the people you are teaching and the people you report to.

5. Finally and perhaps most importantly, always keep in mind that the frame of reference operates both in your personal and business life (see Figure 13). In other words, these are not two distinct worlds that operate independently, but rather each acts, reacts, and has an impact on the other every day.

While it's certainly not the intention of this book to attempt to make each reader an "instant psychologist," it is vitally important for the classroom instructor to be aware that this phenomenon occurs with regularity. An understanding of it can put him or her well ahead on the road to good teaching skills.

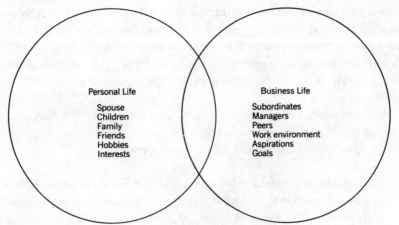

Figure 13. Total frame of reference.

EFFECTIVE LISTENING

No chapter on communication techniques can be considered complete without a full overview of listening skills and the vital impact that they have on the total communication process. A glance back at Figure 11 will serve as a reminder of the key role that feedback plays in the communication loop. Its significance lies in the fact that truly effective listening skills form the core of the feedback process. Put another way, once feedback is given, the original sender must listen effectively in order to properly respond and react. Without this response, the efficiency of the communication will be drastically reduced.

One of the problems encountered in discussing effective listening is the apparent natural apathy that some people have concerning listening skills. Although they may agree that these skills are important in the communication process, they assume that effective listening "comes naturally" from several years or so of supervisory management experience. Accordingly, the subject receives only a minimum of attention in some training programs. Yet, good listening is like any other type of management skill: It is rarely inherited but rather must be learned through study, hard work, and application. Like training in speedreading, which can easily double an average person's speed while maintaining an acceptable level of comprehension, proper training in effective listening skills can improve comprehension from 100 to 200 percent during a face-to-face conversation.

The consequences of these statistics can have a heavy impact on the real world of the classroom instructor. Although actual statistics may vary slightly with the nature of the individual job, the average person spends roughly 70 to 80 percent of each working day communicating—talking, writing, and listening. Of this time spent in communications, approximately 40 to 50 percent is spent in listening. To further compound the importance of listening, many experts in the field agree that during a typical 10-minute conversation the average individual (without benefit of specialized training) retains only 25 to 30 percent of what is spoken! Consider the possible ramifications of this point when the typical instructor:

Has to explain a difficult concept to the class when the majority of participants are experiencing heavy fatigue.

Is responsible for coaching marginal students who have no time to remain after class for special help.

Has to end each session promptly at 4:00 P.M., since management expects all participants to work until 7:00 P.M. to make up for "time lost" in class.

Must shorten a five-day program to three days, because people cannot spare more time for training.

Communication skills, including the art of effective listening, should always be a mandatory part of any formal supervisory training program. Fortunately, more and more companies are taking these skills into account and allowing them space in their programs.

LISTENING ROADBLOCKS

The road to truly good listening techniques is heavily strewn with a variety of obstacles. Understanding each one of them can place the supervisor in a much better position to avoid them in a typical conversation. Let's look at several of these blocks as highlighted in Figure 14. Try to be as introspective as possible, and see if any of these roadblocks have ever stood in the way of one of your conversations.

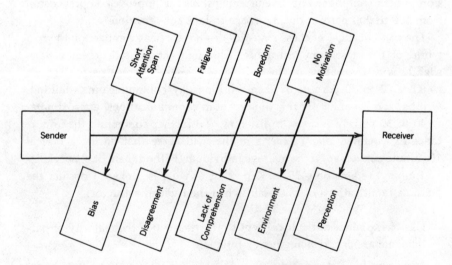

Figure 14. Effective listening barriers.

Short Attention Span

Most industrial psychologists agree that the average person's effective attention span lasts from a few seconds (under certain conditions) to several precious minutes at best. This key fact has obvious implications for the instructor, regardless of the industry or specific teaching responsibility involved. After a subordinate's attention span is reduced, that person will naturally begin to "tune out," letting his or her thoughts wander away from the subject being discussed. Accordingly, the instructor should, wherever possible, vary the pace and tone of the conversation and keep the participant actively engaged through the heavy use of probing techniques and feedback. A good rule to follow is to always encourage a two-way interchange so that the student is freely engaged in the exchange of thoughts and ideas. Remember that a reduction in the other person's attention span is not always clearly evident; constantly guard against engaging in a purely one-way interchange, which has always been a good breeding ground for losing the attention of the other party to the conversation.

Fatigue

The bottom-line results of either person to the communication being fatigued is usually the same—a conversation greatly diminished in effectiveness. Many people reach their most efficient energy levels from 10:00 A.M. to 12:00 noon, then from 1:00 to 3:00 P.M.; interest and attention levels rapidly diminish from late afternoon until quitting time. Naturally, peak attention levels will vary with individual participants and with the type of material being taught. As the experienced instructor knows, however, the task of teaching other people in the classroom can rarely be scheduled to match each person's peak energy level. But when possible, the prudent teacher avoids scheduling an important class very late in the afternoon if other, more conducive times are available.

Boredom

While we may think that the majority of our conversations are bright, stimulating, and to the point, other parties in the communication loop may not always share our opinion. They may start off being interested in the message, but for a variety of reasons soon become bored. Given the average individual's relatively short attention span, boredom can occur more frequently than we care to admit. As with most obstacles to effective listening, the constant use of good feedback techniques is essential to reveal to us occasional lack of attention on the part of the student. Although use of this strategy cannot guarantee the ultimate receptivity of the message, it can at least assure the receiver's involvement in the communication—which places the instructor well ahead in the total process.

No Motivation

On occasion, we are not motivated to listen at all. We see no need for the communication and naturally begin to drift away from it. When faced with that situation, an alert instructor listens very actively to the participants' responses (through good feedback techniques) and reacts in an appropriate, positive manner. When drawn into a conversation (instead of away from it), the average student will feel involved in the interchange instead of apart from it. In any case, the instructor must make every attempt to unearth the cause of a student's lack of motivation and deal directly with it—not always an easy task. But as we have already seen, effective communication is *not* an easy skill to master, especially in classroom learning environments.

Perception

As highlighted in Figure 11, the receiver's perception during a conversation is to a large degree based on the decoding-interpretation stage of the communication cycle. Faulty perceptions can be especially insidious roadblocks since, in many cases, a receiver's perceptions may remain hidden during the conversation. It may come as a rude shock to the sender that the message being received is entirely different from the one intended. Consider the following interchange:

Instructor: Look Mary, I believe that we are running into a very bad situation with your group on case-study assignments. As the group leader, you should be very concerned about it.

Mary: I don't see any problem. What's the matter?

Instructor: Well, I allow each participant a full hour before lunch to prepare their afternoon case-study presentation. While every other team spends at *least* the full time allotted, your team

	stays in the breakout room for about twenty minutes, then they start wandering all over the place.
Mary:	That's easy to explain. My particular group is much more experienced than the other teams, so we don't need as much time to prepare. What's wrong with that?
Instructor:	Look, I don't need any smart answers from you. How about coming to the point?
Mary:	Well, my point is this. If we can finish early, why should I penalize the team by making them stay in the breakout room? To me, that's ridiculous!
Instructor:	Because when your team leaves the room early, they walk around and usually wind up in another team's meeting! They don't seem to realize it, but they create serious disruptions and it's affecting the other participants.
Mary:	If it's that serious, why didn't you say so in the first place?
Instructor:	I tried to, but obviously you didn't get my message.
Mary:	Now I see your point. There's an easy way to fix this. As a starter . . .

This interchange shows how easily a conversation can be misinterpreted (as does the prior one between manager and supervisor) and the harmful results that can occur. Misperceptions are very dangerous at best, and the instructor must always be on guard against them.

Bias

Whether or not we care to admit it, all of us have a certain degree of bias. Bias can either be positive or negative, and it extends to many things that many of us take for granted. For example, whether consciously or unconsciously, we may have a definite bias against:

People with different backgrounds than ours

People with very short/long hair

People with mustaches or beards

People who don't look us "straight in the eye"

Very tall or very short people

Very skinny or very fat people

Those with foreign accents

Those who stutter when they get excited.

People who don't dress like us

We may not care for another person for any number of reasons, but it is imperative never to let that bias creep into the classroom. Among other things, it will definitely reduce effective listening. Striving toward an environment of mutual trust and respect is just one way to reduce bias, and it should be a goal for every platform instructor.

Disagreement

Whether verbal (where it's easy to notice) or nonverbal (which is far more difficult to discern), disagreement forms another rather formidable barrier to effective listening. During a typical 10 to 15 minute conversation between two people, there is a good possibility that some type of disagreement will take place. If the disagreement is minor, it can probably be easily resolved. On the other hand, a deep disagreement between sender and receiver can not only short-circuit the communication process, but drastically reduce the amount of listening that takes place. As with most of the roadblocks already mentioned, the ultimate responsibility to see that disagreement does not block effective listening rests with the sender, and again, the use of good feedback techniques is a definite aid.

Lack of Comprehension

If a person has difficulty understanding either the content of the message or the meaning of the actual words, comprehension will probably be reduced. When such a difficulty exists between instructor and student, the outcome can be problematic. One way to counteract lack of comprehension is to follow the message conveyed in the acronym PICK:

Plan for the communication, before you speak.

Inform your audience, never "lecture" to them.

Concise—always be as clear and precise as possible.

Keep the message simple.

PICK represents a very basic formula, but one well worth keeping in mind when attempting to communicate. At the very least, just being aware of it as an aid to communication can help to reduce comprehension difficulties—a plus in any management technique.

Environment

As noted earlier in the communication cycle, the environment surrounding the message is a definite factor in either the ultimate success or failure of the interchange itself. While we cannot always arrange for every communication to take place under ideal conditions, we should always strive for surroundings where distractions can be held to a minimum. Each of us has varying degrees of personal tolerance for distractions such as interruptions or loud noise; regardless of that degree of tolerance, it is always a safe bet to assume that when an environment is highly negative, a less than satisfactory conversation is taking place.

ACTIVE LISTENING

Our detailed analysis of roadblocks that impede effective listening plainly illustrates the numerous pitfalls that await those who assume that "anyone can listen effectively."

Throughout this book, the phrase *active listening* is used, and it is important to fully understand its meaning. An active listener can never sit back and relax, letting the other person do all the talking. The word *active* means that it is vital to become "part of the other person"—to see the other person's point of view. The active listener learns to analyze, grasp, and react to the message being conveyed, then uses the information gained to respond effectively. This skill may appear to be a bit formidable at first, but it is really quite easy to master. An abundance of commercial listening-skill courses are available today, and the majority of them are built around certain fundamental principles. We will consider these principles next, and see how they relate to the supervisor-subordinate relationship.

Maintaining Eye Contact

Although this technique would appear to be quite easy to master, it definitely requires a degree of practice. The key here is to keep a steady, fixed gaze on the speaker and to avoid distractions by not allowing your eyes to dart frequently around the room. Be aware, however, that there is a difference between a fixed gaze and a stare! The most effective method is to maintain eye contact with the speaker but occasionally glance at something else. Utilizing this simple technique assures the speaker that you are indeed paying attention to what is being said, thus strengthening the one-on-one relationship. Finally, maintaining eye contact has an interesting beneficial effect. If one person uses it effectively, then the other person is encouraged to do the same.

Keeping Ahead of the Speaker

Another aid to active listening is the attempt to stay ahead of the speaker mentally, anticipating what he or she will say next. Because the average person has the ability to listen and comprehend at speeds several times faster than the other person can speak, we naturally build up an excess retention capacity, allowing us additional time to anticipate the speaker's words. A further refinement of this technique is to listen selectively to the key words being spoken by the other person. The English language is made up of many extra "filler words" that supplement the main point of a sentence, but that are rather meaningless by themselves. Here is an example:

Original Sentence	Key Words (Filler Words Omitted)
The luscious, golden yellow pears stood glowingly on the dark brown branches, fully ripened to perfection and impatiently waiting to be picked.	Fully ripened pears ready for picking.

By using key-word selection, listeners can usually identify patterns of thought and ideas being presented by the speaker and, with this as a base, begin to anticipate what will be said next. This tool provides powerful reinforcement to listeners since it allows them to evaluate what was actually said and compare it to what they anticipated only a few moments before.

This device can strengthen the listening process, but it should be used with definite caution and moderation. Obviously, you should not spend the entire listening time during a conversation constantly attempting to anticipate what the speaker will say next! Instead, make a sustained effort to keep up with the topic being discussed and to use the conclusions drawn as a springboard for the next interchange. The ability to stay ahead of the speaker is a vital skill in active listening.

Mentally Summarizing Main Points

When used in conjunction with the skill of staying ahead of the speaker, the technique of summarizing main points further refines listening skill. Basically, it involves nothing more than analyzing the speaker's key words, then compiling the main points in your mind. The example that follows gives the key words stated by the departmental trainer in several related sentences, and the specific main points that should have been picked up by the worker on the assembly line.

Key Words	Main Point
Special care is needed for subassembly.	Critical factors in subassembly require special handling and quality control.
Pressure bolts can easily strip.	
Mechanism has many close tolerances.	
Torque wrench is essential for bolts.	
Highest quality control is essential.	
Use best assemblers on the line.	
If in doubt, reject part immediately.	

By carefully identifying the key words spoken, the participant should usually be able to make the transition from the main point to an appropriate reply in a matter of seconds. Once again, like many of the other effective listening aids, summarizing the main points will demonstrate to the speaker that the receiver was not only carefully listening to the conversation but actually highlighting the main points involved in the message.

Periodically Confirming That You Are Listening

Of all the aids to good listening, this is not only one of the easiest for the instructor to master but also one of the most effective. In general, it involves nothing more than a periodic verbal confirmation to the speaker that you are keeping up with the conversation and are actively involved with it. For example, an instructor, during appropriate moments in a conversation, responds with such phrases as "Yes, I understand," "Please go on," "I see," or "Mmmm . . . that's very interesting."

This skill, like all of the others mentioned, also enhances the communication. First, it helps the instructor's concentration, since he or she must actively listen to interject this type of comment. Second, it again confirms to the speaker that the listener is probably attending to every word spoken, which can only help to increase the rapport between the communicators. However, as with each of the skills mentioned, care must always be taken not to overdo it. Used too frequently, it could be interpreted by the speaker as a recurring interruption with annoying overtones. Done properly, it reaffirms your continued interest in the communication and adds a high level of personal effectiveness to your bank of management skills.

Paraphrasing Key Remarks

A final technique of active listening is to paraphrase (or partially paraphrase) the speaker's last point at appropriate pauses in the conversation. This is by far one of the simplest techniques to use, yet in the long run it can be one of the most powerful. Here is a typical example of it in use:

Participant: This particular management development class is really a turning point in my company career. I've really worked hard during the past three years and have met every goal assigned to me. Personally, I'm looking forward to being in your class today.

Instructor: Considering a management development seminar as a career milestone is quite natural. It's a tough course, but I know that you will do well. Nice to have you aboard!

Notice the heavy support that the instructor has given to the participant's main points through the simple use of partial paraphrasing. While the outcome of the management development program will stand on its own merits, the interface at least is off to a very good start. A special note of caution has to be introduced here. This is one skill that should never be employed too frequently. Here is what can happen if you do:

Instructor: As you probably have noticed, here in the training department we take a lot of pride in our work.

Trainee: I can see there's a lot of pride involved.

Instructor: Well, not only pride, but our section has the longest longevity of any department in the company.

Trainee: Mmmm . . . so your unit has the best attendance record. That's nice!

Instructor: Uh, that's what I just said. Finally, every one of our instructors has at least five years of prior line experience, which gives them a high degree of credibility.

Trainee: So, each instructor has five years plus of line experience.

Instructor: Young man, is there anything wrong with you?

Trainee: No. Why do you ask?

Instructor: You seem to be repeating everything I've just said! Are you trying to make a fool of me?

As with all of the platform skills taught in this book, a bit of old-fashioned common sense will go a long way toward increasing an individual's effectiveness, and good listening techniques are no exception to the rule.

SUMMARY

1. In order for communication to be effective, certain basic elements should always be present: a level of trust, a nonthreatening atmosphere, and good feedback.

2. The communication cycle should be thought of as a closed loop, with each component of the loop fully integrated with the next segment. If a segment of the loop is open at any time, a reduction in conversation effectiveness will result.

3. A *frame of reference* can be defined as those short- and long-term experiences that can affect an individual's current behavior.

4. Roadblocks to effective listening are: a short attention span, fatigue, boredom, lack of motivation, faulty perception, bias, disagreement, lack of comprehension, and distracting environment.

5. Several techniques for active listening include: maintaining eye contact, keeping ahead of the speaker, mentally summarizing main points, periodically confirming that you are listening, and paraphrasing key remarks.

CASE STUDY: THE PROBLEM WITH MARTIN

Martin's business profile matched the organization's executive trainee profile in every respect. Graduating from a large metropolitan university with a degree in management, Martin eagerly looked forward to his first full-time job. During his four years at school, he had constantly placed in the top 5 percent of all his classes, and he graduated with top honors. Although Martin was a bit outspoken at times, everyone at the university agreed that Martin would certainly go far in the business world.

Martin was hired during his first interview with the company recruiter. The stage appeared set for a wonderful career with the organization.

After the initial company orientation, Martin was assigned with the other 14 trainees to the 12-week executive-training rotational program that consisted of on-the-job learning coupled with four hours of classroom instruction each day. This experience proved to be an exciting time in Martin's life. Every day brought new challenges, which he always met with very high enthusiasm. As a highly motivated person, he naturally began to suggest new ideas and systems both to the departments he was assigned to and in the classroom. He spent his free time at night and on weekends carefully thinking out these ideas, but he never complained about his total involvement.

While many of his suggestions were encouraged during the on-the-job training, it was a far different story in the classroom. When he asked questions like "Why don't we try . . . ?" "Have we ever considered . . . ?" and "What if . . . ?" his line supervisors were supportive but Frank Lawry, the classroom instructor, definitely was not. "Perhaps it's my imagination," Martin thought, but he had an uneasy feeling at the end of the eighth week of training that resentment was starting to build in the classroom—and that it was being directed at him, mainly by the instructor. He decided to talk things over with Mr. Lawry, and made an appointment to see him the next day.

After a few minutes of pleasant conversation, the following conversation took place:

Frank: Hi, Martin. Come on in. What's the problem?

Martin: Well, I'm not sure if there is a problem. What I would like to discuss with you is the distinct feeling I'm getting that somehow you resent my presence in class.

Frank: *Resent?* What do you mean by that?

Martin: I may be wrong, but everytime that I ask a question, you seem to be annoyed. Am I correct or mistaken?

Frank: Look, I don't mind *appropriate* questions in my class, but it seems that you have a point to make every time I look up. Frankly, it gets to be a bit annoying—and makes us run late practically every day.

Martin: You mean I'm not supposed to raise my hand when there is a point to be made?

Frank: You just have to learn to be a little more patient around here. There are many others in the class who want to learn also. By asking all those questions, you're taking the time away from the other students. I'm sure that you can understand my position on this. Okay?

Martin: No, it's not okay. How am I supposed to learn if I can't ask questions?

Frank: Look, I never had the advantage that you are having. I came up the hard way—twenty years of service, and without any type of formal training. I'm trying to do my job, and you can't seem to understand that. All I ask is that you give everyone in class a chance to be heard, and stop dominating the questions. That seems fair enough.

Martin: Well, I hear you, but I still intend to ask questions when I'm not sure what's going on.

Frank: No need to get cute with me young man. Is that what you learned in college?

Martin was quite upset after the meeting and called in sick the next day. During the following two weeks, he remained very silent both in the on-the-job training sessions and especially in the classroom. It was clear that his efficiency had rapidly fallen off and his motivation had been diminished.

After several more days had gone by, one of the line managers approached Frank and asked, "What's the problem with Martin?"

The reply was brief and to the point. "Guess he finds it hard to take the pressure. That's the trouble with these fast 'rising stars'—they can rarely stand the pace."

CASE STUDY DISCUSSION POINTS

1.   Assume you are Frank, and Martin has just walked into your office. He is visibly angry and blames you for his recent weak performance. How would you handle the conversation with him?

2.   Do you believe that Frank was unfair in his original comments to Martin? If so, why?

3.   Was Martin correct in coming to Frank with this type of complaint? Or should it have been directed to someone else?

CHAPTER QUESTIONS

1.   In a typical conversation between an instructor and a student, whose responsibility is it to insure that effective feedback is indeed taking place?

2.   Can a reasonably effective conversation take place with only a minimum amount of feedback? If so, what guidelines should the sender be aware of?

3.   Are the guidelines involved for communicating in a business environment different from those for a personal setting? If so, why?

4.   If you plan on being a more effective communicator, to what technique or strategy would you give highest priority? How would you carry this out?

THE NEXT STEP

It's quite clear that truly effective communication is one of the basic skills of successful training. As such it will supply a common bond throughout all of the techniques outlined in this book.

While it is one thing for the instructor to communicate with a high degree of effectiveness, it is quite another to accomplish the essential task of developing course content *prior* to the program start. While a well-organized participant manual coupled with a comprehensive instructor's guide can never automatically insure the success of a given offering, it *can* place the overall process in a very good starting position.

Let's now turn to this highly crucial subject.

4

DEVELOPING THE INSTRUCTOR'S GUIDE

LEARNING OBJECTIVES

After completing this chapter, you should be able to:

Explain the importance of individual customization of the instructor's guide.

Describe the teaching advantages of a well-planned guide.

Develop an instructor's guide from a prepared set of participant materials.

Explain the common-sense rules governing proper use of the guide.

OVERVIEW

Participants arrive at the classroom with a broad array of expectations, mixed levels of motivation, varying degrees of apprehension, and perhaps

83

most crucial of all, assorted plateaus of *learning receptivity* to the instruction that will shortly begin.

As the class assembles for the start of the program, the instructor must rapidly bring the entire group to a cohesive, effective, learning-receptivity level that allows instruction to take place with maximum efficiency—in many cases, a task easier said than done.

With the benefit gained from our examination of *training's role in the organization*, our brief survey of *adult learning methodologies*, and an in-depth look at *instructional communication skills*, we are now prepared to spotlight the development and use of the *instructor's guide*. While the use of effective teaching techniques (such as keeping participants involved in the learning, securing constant class feedback, and the use of audio-visual aids) will enhance the overall learning process, *the proper use of a customized instructor's guide remains one of the most crucial tools for classroom success*. Viewed from a slightly different perspective, an effective instructor's guide offers the following classic teaching advantages:

Places the entire course in proper perspective regarding content, length, activities, and structure.

Benefits the instructor by providing a planned framework (or structure) of essential learning sequences.

Avoids the possibility of having the instructor inadvertently skip over a section of the program that should have been presented to the class.

Clearly aids the learning flow by indicating where specific teaching aids such as charts, films, or slides should be introduced.

Helps maintain the uniformity (or "evenness") of the instruction when several instructors are teaching the same program at different times and locations.

Provides a written sequential learning document that can—and should—be modified, expanded, or contracted for future offerings.

Facilitates the training of new instructors in the flow and structure of the program.

And last but certainly not least, provides instructors with a built-in "security blanket" as a defense against sudden losses of memory as to exactly what they should be teaching at any moment!

To position this chapter properly, one has to take into account the many variables facing the instructor prior to the start of the actual program. For example, consider the following variations that can occur in program development:

1. Both the participant manual and instructor's guide are developed by an outside consultant.

2. The outside consultant merely develops the participant material, relying on the internal training unit to customize its own instructor's manual.

3. The internal training department designs both the participant and instructor material.

4. Internal training merely creates the participant's manual, relying on each instructor to customize the guide to individual specifications.

In my opinion, instructors should *always* tailor an instructor's guide to suit their own teaching styles. That could mean either developing one (where none had been prepared) or modifying one that comes fully written and is handed to the teacher as part of the instructional package. Since teaching styles are never exactly alike, it would be a bit foolish to expect every instructor to follow a detailed course of instruction point by point throughout an entire program.

Accordingly, this chapter will acquaint the reader with the general components of the instructor's guide, then focus on specific areas of both flow and content where customization could be appropriate. To facilitate this experience, the following broad assumptions are being made:

The instructor receives a reasonably effective set of participant material that will be used in the classroom.

The material contains approximate time requirements for each of the learning activities involved.

A set of learning objectives has been identified both for the program and its individual components.

Use of audio-visual aids (such as flip charts, slides, and films) has been identified with the appropriate program components.

Various group activities, including role plays and case studies, have been positioned at appropriate junctures within the course.

Let's reinforce an important learning point here. Even if you received a thoroughly comprehensive teaching guide beforehand, I again stress the importance of *customizing* the instructional notes to suit your individual teaching style. It's precisely for this reason that the value of having the instructor cycle through *two* phases of learning, prior to teaching the class for the first time, becomes obvious.

PHASE 1: The fledgling teacher attends a comprehensive instructor-training program where both the flow and content of the course is presented from a teaching viewpoint.

PHASE 2: The instructor attends the first program in a *dual* role: (1) as a participant, experiencing the learning as a true *receiver* of the knowledge imparted; (2) as a future teacher of the program, viewing the instructional proceedings from an instructor's point of view and *annotating the instructor's guide accordingly.*

The advantages of proceeding through these two phases are significant. Specifically, after attending instructor training and then playing a participant role in an actual class, the instructor has a much better grasp of:

General flow of the course.

Which modules had greater learning impact than others—and why.

Which parts of the program were not effective and which were.

Significance and usefulness of the audio-visual aids used—and perhaps an insight into how they could be employed more effectively.

Where course timing was accurate and where it proved unrealistic.

The group dynamics of role plays, simulations, and small-group work.

The positive effect of constant class feedback as an aid to group learning.

The beneficial thrust that team synergism lends to learning motivation levels.

The positive effect that a good instructor can have on the learning process and specific situations where poor instruction can impede learning.

Using the foregoing as background material, let's now proceed to the instructor's guide itself and learn first-hand just how effective it can be in the hands of the class leader. While formats for this type of guide can vary widely, a number of sequential components have worked rather successfully over the years.

INSTRUCTOR GUIDE COMPONENTS

A glance at Figure 15, Elements of the Instructor's Guide, shows the main elements required for all guides. To make our discussion as realistic as possible, let's assume that an instructor's manual has been designed to support a one-day program on performance appraisal that will be taught to

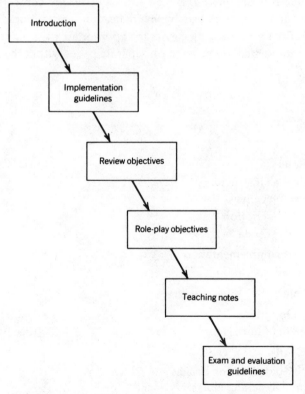

Figure 15.   Elements of the instructor's guide.

first-line supervisors. Further, we'll assume that a participant's workbook has already been prepared and will be used both as outside reading and in the classroom as a means of facilitating actual learning.

We're now ready to explore each of the components involved in sequential order. When segments are self-explanatory, very little comment will be made. Other segments will be presented in a somewhat longer format to enable the reader to grasp the *main content* being highlighted.

1. *Title Page.*   The title page simply identifies the title of the program and specific use of the material.

EXAMPLE: XYZ Corporation
              Performance Appraisal Program
              Instructor's Guide

2. *Table of Contents Page.*   To simplify use, the contents of the instructor's guide are displayed by main heading and subheadings where necessary. Each main heading carries the appropriate page number, and the segments represented are covered on separate pages within the instructor's binder.

EXAMPLE:

TABLE OF CONTENTS

PAGE

Introduction
    Your Role as Instructor
    Program Objectives
    Program Description
    Suggested Agenda
Guidelines for Implementation
    Precourse Preparation
Review Objectives
Role-Play Objectives
    Participant Materials for Role Play   (See Back Pocket)
Teaching Notes
    General Guidelines for Usage
    Sequential Teaching Notes
    Conducting the Role Play

Exam and Evaluation Guidelines
   Examination Objectives
   Evaluation Objectives
   Exam and Evaluation Activity Sequence

Note: Exams (including model and evaluation copies) are located in the back pocket of this three-ring binder.

3. *Introduction.* The four subheadings under the introduction are designed to give the instructor the required *overview* of the course structure. The examples that follow are typical. (Note that each subheading would start on a new page.)

YOUR ROLE AS INSTRUCTOR. Your responsibility as the instructor is to facilitate and enhance the learning process that will take place in the classroom. You should provide guidance and feedback to ensure that learning does take place. The programmed instruction (part of the required preliminary reading) will have provided each participant with a basic overview of the performance appraisal process. Your task will therefore be to reinforce and strengthen that learning. Since participants will also learn a great deal from class discussions, this should be heavily encouraged wherever possible.

Please familiarize yourself thoroughly with this entire manual and with all related course materials prior to conducting the actual training. You will usually be the "last word" in resolving questions in the participants' minds. Although you could refer participants to the course materials to answer questions, it will generally be simpler and faster for you to answer them yourself. You should permit longer discussions when appropriate since this is where much "incidental" learning will take place.

Remember, your primary role is to *provide guidance* and *resolve questions* throughout the entire program.

PROGRAM OBJECTIVES. At the conclusion of the program, each participant will have acquired the skills to:

Explain the function of performance appraisal in the performance loop.

Describe the steps required for a performance appraisal review.

Discuss both the pitfalls and the benefits associated with performance appraisal.

Integrate the basic principles of performance appraisal with those of human resource development.

Conduct an effective performance review with a subordinate.

PROGRAM DESCRIPTION. The program consists of:

Precourse reading and written exercises

Instructor/participant introduction

Outline of program objectives

Review of precourse material

Role-play exercise with group feedback and critique

Examination

Program evaluation

The Learning Sequence

Acquiring knowledge	Precourse reading, including written exercises
Reinforcing knowledge	Class review/discussion/feedback
Applying knowledge	Role-play exercises and small-group presentations
Testing knowledge	Examination

SUGGESTED AGENDA. The program is designed to take a total of eight hours (either one full-day session or two half-day sessions). While schedules can vary slightly with each program, the following timing is recommended:

Activity	Timing
Segment 1	
Welcome, introduction, and setting of objectives	15 minutes
Discussion of situational factors and performance loop correlations	60 minutes
Coffee break	15 minutes
Discussion of performance-appraisal benefits, problems in performance appraisal	2 hours and 15 minutes
Summary	15 minutes
	4 hours
Note: If a one-day program, add lunch here	1 hour

Segment 2

Review of Segment 1	15 minutes
Discussion of employee performance-evaluation forms, performance-appraisal action steps	1 hour and 15 minutes
Coffee break	15 minutes
Group role play	1 hour
Summary and wrap-up	30 minutes
Exam and course evaluation	45 minutes
	4 hours

4. *Guidelines for Implementation.* This section outlines activities that are required *prior* to the start of the actual program. Put another way, it provides a basic preprogram checklist for the instructor.

EXAMPLE: PRECOURSE PREPARATION

Activities Required:

Materials should be sent out at least two weeks in advance (note that the role plays are not included; they are distributed during the session).

A covering memo outlining objectives should be sent with the material.

Materials Required:

This instructor's guide

Copy of the program

Role-play material (for Dorothy Franklin case)

Supervisor's background

Subordinate's background

Observer checklist

Exams and evaluations

Flip chart, overhead transparencies, and markers

Name cards (one for each participant)

Pads and pencils

Walk-Through

Check out facilities and room arrangement where program will be conducted.

Review instructor's guide.

Review participant material.

Arrange handout materials for session.

5. *Review Objectives.*   The purpose of this section within the guide is to provide a realistic bench mark for the instructor at the conclusion of each topic within the program. This is accomplished through instructor-led probing and class feedback.

EXAMPLE: For each topic discussed in the classroom, participants should be able to:

Provide a working definition of the important terms used in performance appraisal.

Define the interrelationships of each performance-appraisal segment to the entire evaluation process.

Discuss common problems that participants might encounter during an actual appraisal session.

Bridge the elements learned to specific on-the-job applications.

Communicate knowledge gained through active class feedback and discussion.

6. *Role-Play Objectives.*   This section lists the desired parameters of new learning-skill levels (that is, exhibited participant behavior) that should have been obtained at the conclusion of the role-play exercise. A note of caution can be introduced here: The *degree* of success obtained in a role-play simulation usually has a direct correlation to such factors as prior skill of the instructor to conduct group role plays, the extent to which participants have done role plays prior to the program, and the age and experience level of the group as a whole.

EXAMPLE:

To give participants an opportunity to practice a true-to-life performance appraisal meeting with a subordinate.

To reinforce the correct steps required for a performance review.

To practice overcoming obstacles that can be encountered during a performance appraisal session and leading the meeting to a successful conclusion.

7. *Teaching Notes. Special note to the reader*: This section, by necessity, will be presented in an abbreviated format. The purpose here is to display (in sequential order) notes to the instructor regarding general guidelines for usage, followed by a step-by-step lead-in to both starting and conducting the program. Specific details on handling of the role-play sequence and the participant evaluation form will not be discussed here, but will be covered in subsequent chapters.

EXAMPLE: GENERAL GUIDELINES FOR USAGE. The instructor's guide has been designed to be inserted in a three-ring binder, for a simple step-by-step training sequence.

Note that its general format includes *sequential teaching notes on the left side of each page, with suggested flip-chart format on the right hand side*. A completed answer sheet for the final exam is provided and is located in the back packet.

Since this eight-hour program covers a great deal of material, your platform time will have to be used as efficiently as possible. Accordingly, it is recommended that *you prepare as many flip charts as possible in advance of the program*.

Prior to your first teaching assignment in this program, it is recommended that you spend several hours practicing the various segments of the course. As with all teaching, there is a direct relationship between the amount of preparation done beforehand and the degree of success obtained in the classroom. There are no specific guidelines involved, but a conservative rule-of-thumb formula is that *at least* two to three hours practice is required for every hours spent on the platform.

Sequential Teaching Notes

Good morning!

My name is _____.

I'll be spending today (or the next two half-days) with you as the instructor for this program.

I believe you'll find the program both very relevant and beneficial. We've got a lot of ground to cover to meet the objectives of this program.

The objectives are: _____➔

By the end of the program, we should have a good working knowledge of:

- Elements of the appraisal process.
- Skills required to conduct an effective evaluation.
- Barriers and opportunities involved in appraising a subordinate's performance.

Let's get started by participating in an exercise that will enable us to get to know each other.

Instructor:

- Divide class into teams of two participants each.
- Have them interview each other for about three to four minutes each.
- Then request them to introduce their teammate to the class.
- *Note*: If you have an odd number of participants, team up with the the last person involved.

Suggested items for the introduction are: _____➔

(Note to the reader: The last item suggested for the team introduction may bring a smile to some faces—but rest assured that the technique works! Even in classes where participants have never met before, most will volunteer *some* intriguing fact about themselves that generally raises the interest level of the entire group. I've personally seen 200-pound muscular athletes state that they are ac-

---

Program Objectives

- Explain the function of performance appraisal in the performance loop.
- Describe the steps required for a performance appraisal review.
- Discuss both the pitfalls and the benefits associated with performance appraisal.
- Integrate the basic principles of performance appraisal with those of human resource development.
- Conduct an effective performance review with a subordinate.

Name _____

Title/function _____

Work unit _____

Location _____

Number of years
with the company _____

Length of time in
current position _____

Primary job
responsibility _____

A little known fact
about this person! _____

_____

_____

complished violin players, and in one class what appeared to be a frail young woman turned out to be a black-belt karate expert! In any event, be prepared for some surprises, and make certain that you capitalize on this highly effective ice breaker!)

The program has been segmented into four parts: ————————→

Note that I've underlined participation! The more you contribute, the greater the benefit you will derive from the program. We call that "active learning" and you'll soon see how nicely it all works once we get underway.

We'll also work together in teams of three to give each of you an opportunity to practice a "real-world" performance appraisal from both the *supervisor's* and the subordinate's point of view.

Finally, we will end with a short written examination to measure your comprehension of the key terms and procedures used throughout the program.

1. The prework (which has already been done)
2. *Participation* in this eight-hour program
3. Simulations (role play)
4. Final examination

Basically, our class schedule will be ————————→

Segment 1
- Introduction/objectives
- Discussion:
  Situational factors
  Performance loop correlations
- Coffee break
- Discussion:
  Performance-appraisal benefits
  Problems in performance appraisal
- Summary
- Lunch
Segment 2
- Review of Segment 1
- Discussion:
  Employee performance-evaluation forms
  Performance-appraisal action steps
- Coffee break
- Role play
- Summary and wrap-up
- Exam and course evaluation

Now, to start, let's discuss a few of the "real-world" problems that were listed in Chapter 1 of the reading material (print the words REAL-WORLD PROBLEMS on the flip chart)

Solicit answers from the class and write them on the flip chart. The main points that should surface are:

- People do not like to be judged by others
- Low confidence level—where the supervisor does not have sufficient faith in his/her own ability to conduct the appraisal
- Fear of failure to produce a desired set of results
- Psychological factors—having a set of negative (or very positive) feelings about the person in general
- Lack of time to conduct the appraisal properly
- Strong bias from the "halo effect"

(Points are listed in pages 4–9 in participant's manual)

Real-World Problems
1.
2.
3.
4.
5.
6.

Note to the reader: As mentioned earlier, assume that the instructor has already completed the teaching notes (representing the balance of the course) through role play, summary, and wrap-up. We now pick up that final segment of the instructor's guide, focusing on the exam and evaluation guidelines.

8. *Exam and Evaluation Guidelines*

Examination Objectives

To determine participant's level of understanding of the performance appraisal process, including key terms and required procedures

To determine the individual's degree of need for review and/or additional training

Exam Format

Exam consists of 50 multiple-choice questions.

Each answer is worth 2 points.

Grade of 75 or higher is considered passing.

Exam takes approximately 35 minutes to complete.

Course Evaluation Objectives

To determine degree of participant satisfaction with program and instruction received.

To surface any suggestions made by participants to raise the overall effectiveness of the training.

Exam and Evaluation Activity Sequence

Ask if there are any questions before distributing the exam.

Discuss exam objectives.

Discuss exam format.

Distribute exam.

Also distribute evaluations at this point. Inform class they should complete the evaluation form *after* finishing the exam and *before* leaving the classroom.

Allow participants as much time as they need to complete exam and evaluation.

Be on hand to answer questions during the actual exam, but avoid having too much of "a presence" during the completion of the evaluations.

COMMON TRAPS

While careful use of the instructor's guide offers an array of teaching support tools, experienced instructors are always aware of the several potential traps (or pitfalls) that they can encounter—usually inadvertently.

Figure 16 displays these traps in graphic form. Let's spend a few moments reviewing these in more detail.

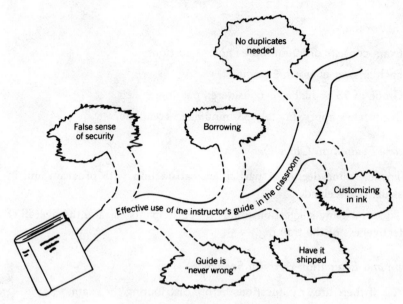

Figure 16.   Instructor guide traps.

Trap 1: A False Sense of Security

A well-planned instructor's guide can be compared to a detailed road map that plots (in detail) every significant landmark along given geographic points. A driver who may be unfamiliar with the terrain gains a false sense of security in having such a comprehensive travel guide in his automobile, only to realize hours later that he has become totally lost. The same problem awaits the instructor who does not bother to check progress along the way: the journey through the program stands a good chance of becoming a waste of time, money, and effort.

Unfortunately, the same false sense of security can lull the novice instructor into the meandering of disjointed learning sequences, uneven amounts of time devoted to various learning sequences, and worst of all, a falling-off of class interest and attention due to a disjointed learning experience. Such situations are most apt to occur when the platform instruction calls for a variety of activities in a relatively short time. On paper, it may appear perfectly reasonable to introduce a new topic at 9:00 A.M., reinforce it through class exercises at 10:00 A.M., conduct role plays until 11:30 A.M., then give an examination—all before lunch! Unless the instructor has actually run through the class beforehand (or observed it being taught by another teacher), the "timing" listed in the instructor's guide may turn out to be completely theoretical! *Never* be lulled into a false sense of security by what's written in the guide, especially if you are not certain who has actually done the writing.

Trap 2: The Guide Is "Never Wrong"

Another common trap is to assume that the views presented in a given instructor's guide are always the "final word" on the subject, leaving no room for class participants to doubt or even discuss alternatives to the views being presented. Many an instructor has inadvertently lost credibility early in the program due to a difference of opinion about a "fact" stated in the guide. As just one example, I would personally be suspicious of the accuracy of an instructor's guide that was prepared over a year ago, and one that was not subject to constant updating. It's only common sense to assume that a significant portion of the material in the guide can quickly become outdated. Changes in company policy, statistics, revenues, and product features and benefits can become dangerously outdated in a few months. The temptation (especially if one has a very demanding teaching schedule) is to use the guide "one more time," planning to make the necessary changes when more free time is available. In a word, *don't!* It's just one more potential pitfall that could cause you to lose vital credibility in front of a class—something an instructor must avoid at all times.

Trap 3: Borrowing

In some organizations (especially when the same program is given frequently and taught by a variety of instructors) one instructor may "borrow" a guide from another. If another instructor asks to borrow your guide, my advice is *not* to lend it, unless some emergency exists.

While this may seem a bit unfriendly, rest assured that it is not. An effective instructor's guide is one that has been *highly customized* over time by the instructor who uses it and as a result, is probably suitable only to the person who spent the time in modifying the material and notes to suit his or her own teaching style. Use by another instructor brings up two potential problems.

1. Unless the guide is carefully read in advance, many of the personal notes (usually written in the margins of the guide) will be either illegible, or worse yet, completely meaningless to the instructor who borrowed the guide.

2. Many instructors (especially in programs that run over several days) will have a natural tendency to write *their own* comments in *your* guide as the class progresses. Once the guide has been returned, you are now faced with the task of attempting to decipher someone else's handwriting in a guide that has already been customized. Even worse, this "discovery" is usually made during the early part of the *next* program taught by the lender—a situation to be avoided, to say the least!

Trap 4: Have It Shipped

This particular trap comes into play only when the program is to be conducted "off-site." In many cases, a great deal of material (such as participant manuals, conference supplies, and the like) must be shipped from the main office to the conference site. Since no one likes to travel like the proverbial pack mule, the temptation here is to include such essentials as the instructor's guide (together with the corresponding audio-visual aids such as films, overheads, or slides) in the material to be shipped. *Never* allow yourself to fall into this particular trap. You only have to experience the frustration of learning just minutes prior to the program start that the box with your guide is missing to know what I mean. The cardinal rule here is to forget whatever inconvenience is being caused by carrying these essentials with you at all times—the peace of mind alone more than makes up for it!

Trap 5: No Duplicates Needed

Experience has repeatedly shown that having just one copy of a customized instructor's guide is just not enough, two are usually needed.

The rule of common sense applies here. Why risk losing a highly customized guide and having to spend hours attempting to duplicate another, when (for a minimum of time) a second copy can always be maintained in a safe place? A related trap here is to create a duplicate (gaining a smug, warm sense of security), then neglect to update the second copy as changes gradually accumulate in the original! Over a prolonged period of time, the second copy becomes inadequate—and possibly even worse, gives you a false sense of security.

Trap 6: Customizing in Ink

Writing customizing notes in ink throughout the margins can be very reassuring, especially if you have a bold handwriting and use a dark ink in the pen! Unfortunately, that small bit of gratification is heavily outweighed by the probability that you will have to modify or completely change notes made from a prior program.

Instructor notes, like one's own teaching style, must remain flexible from one program to the next, and the only way to assure flexibility is to make all notes in a number 2 pencil with a very sharp point. It's simple, neat, easy to do, and best of all, it remains workable regardless of the number of changes required.

COMMON-SENSE GUIDELINES

As with all elements of effective classroom techniques, several common-sense rules also govern the proper use of the instructor's guide.

First and foremost is the continuing need for *flexibility*. Just as the participant's manual must be frequently updated to insure correctness of text, the guide also requires constant changes. It's rare indeed that a truly worthwhile program is presented year after year without significant changes being made to both structure and content. For the majority of changes made in the participant's manual, a corresponding change must be made in the instructor's notes. Flexibility is the key ingredient for success here, both in the teaching notes, and in the mind set of the instructor—especially when program changes occur frequently. Changing the instructor's guide can become a tedious business, especially when, by necessity, it has to be accomplished under heavy time pressures—but the responsibility (like the ultimate rewards of teaching) "comes with the turf."

The second common-sense guideline involves keeping a sharp watch for program deficiencies. The guide reflects the material being taught in class, and hence is directly related to the material in the participant's manual. Regardless of who is ultimately responsible for keeping the student material updated (such as the training department staff or an outside consultant), the main charge here will naturally fall to the instructor—and rightly so.

Since the instructor is constantly "on the firing line" in front of the class, no other individual is better qualified to pass judgment on the material being presented. Through the experience gained in "living" the material as it's presented to a group of participants, the instructor knows when the material needs rework, knows where the program seems to stray from its objectives. Timing errors during scheduled role plays and a host of other related instructional efforts become evident. The question, however, is once weaknesses are discovered, whose job is it to correct the newly found deficiencies? At the very least, the stand-up instructor should note problem areas for remedial action at a future date.

The last common-sense guideline addresses the fact that people learn at different rates of speed. By necessity, however, the instructor's guide is written for the norm (or average learner) and therefore should never be followed on a strict schedule.

For example, if a role-play sequence is scheduled for 20 minutes and the guide specifies three rounds of role play, the timing for the complete sequence will usually be listed as one hour. However, the guide seldom makes provision for *unusual* situations—say, a class of 15 trainees, none of whom have ever experienced a role play before. Because of heightened nervousness and anxiety, this group might need much more time than previous classes to complete the simulation, and the added time should surely be given. Or an instructor may have a class of extremely rapid learners and need only 60 percent of the time listed in the instructor's guide to complete each module in the program.

The instructor must strive for a reasonable balance between each class's effective learning rate and the time frames suggested in the guide. In the world of teaching, such balance can be quite elusive, and one is never absolutely certain that it has been reached completely. As with most things worth striving for, the proper balance is never easily achieved.

SUMMARY

1.   The proper use of a customized instructor's guide remains one of the most crucial tools for classroom success.

2.   The instructor's guide offers a wide array of advantages: It places the entire course in perspective; provides a planned sequence of learning events;

avoids the possibility of inadvertently skipping sections of the program; aids in maintaining uniformity of instruction; and facilitates the training of new instructors.

3.   An instructor should *always* tailor the guide to suit his or her own teaching style.

4.   Prior to teaching a new course, the instructor should first attend an instructor-training program, then attend a regular program in a dual role—first, as a participant (as a receiver of the learning), and second, as an instructor, annotating the guide accordingly.

5.   Elements of an instructor's guide include the introduction, implementation guidelines, review objectives, role-play objectives, teaching notes, and exam and evaluation guidelines.

6.   While an instructor's guide can be an extremely valuable tool, it does contain several potential traps for the novice teacher. The instructor should avoid developing a false sense of security, viewing the guide as "never wrong," allowing the guide to be borrowed by another instructor, having it shipped to a program site (instead of carrying it with you), assuming that a duplicate copy will never be required, and lastly, writing customizing guide notes in ink.

CASE STUDY: "TIME IS MONEY, OR HAVEN'T YOU HEARD?"

After only six months on the job, it was obvious to all that Julie was an excellent instructor. She came to the job with most of the ingredients for success: four years of varied line experience as both a supervisor and junior manager, plus a teaching degree from a local university (earned at night).

The training department gladly accepted her application for a permanent teaching slot with the understanding that she would specialize both in supervisory training and in management development. After four weeks of instructor training and observation in the classroom, Julie became a full-time instructor in the regular five-day scheduled management development program run twice a month. With each class she began strengthening her teaching skills further and within a short time became one of the top instructors in the department.

The problem began at 8:15 A.M. on a Monday morning. With no formal teaching assignment scheduled for the week, Julie had planned to spend the next few days in further customizing her instructor's guide for the management development class. She was looking forward to this activity as a much-needed break from the daily routine on the platform, which she found to be an exhilarating but exhausting experience.

Julie was reflecting on all this when suddenly her thoughts were interrupted. She looked up from her desk as Jack Fletcher bounded through the door in what appeared to be a mild state of panic. The following conversation ensued:

Julie: Hi, Jack. What's up? You look like you have the world's problems on your shoulders!

Jack: Something just as bad! I just found out that Bill has the flu and can't teach today's segment of the supervisory training class. It's going to start in the next half hour, and we have no one to teach it.

Julie: How about Marge? She's taught that class many times and is really good at it.

Jack: Unfortunately, she left for vacation last Friday and will be out all week. Look Julie, I hate to ask, but can you fill in for Bill today? I realize that you haven't taught this course before, but you are familiar with the instructor's guide, and I know that you can do it.

Julie: But Jack, I've never even been to instructor training for this course.

Jack: I realize that—but I'm sure that you can wing it where necessary. Besides, if you don't teach today, we have to cancel the course, and you know how *that* will look! How about it?

Julie: Well, okay, I'll give it my best shot, but I'm not too thrilled about it.

Jack: Great! I knew I could count on you. Thanks a million. I'll check back with you when the session breaks at noon.

The class started off well enough, and in fact proved easier to teach than Julie expected. The problem arose around 11:00 A.M., just prior to the start of the formal role plays. During the coffee break she realized the timing was off in each role-play sequence. There was simply not enough time to give each participant a chance to play the supervisor's role—an activity essential to the learning reinforcement.

She had to make a quick decision. If she stuck to the schedule in the instructor's guide, the class would end promptly at 12:00 noon—but she would have to abbreviate the role play. To conduct it properly, she would have to extend the session at least another 30 minutes beyond the regular closing time. Unfortunately, Jack was not available to consult. Julie decided that it was worthwhile to extend the session, since the reinforced learning would more than offset the extra time required.

She mentioned this to the class at the start of the role-play introduction, and no one seemed to mind. After viewing what appeared to be several successful rounds of role plays, she was convinced she had made the right decision. The class ended at 12:40 P.M. When Julie left the classroom, she found Jack waiting outside for her, his face clouded with anger. The dialogue that followed took Julie completely by surprise:

Jack: Well, how was the class?

Julie: Better than I expected. In fact, I was really surprised at the effectiveness of the role plays. They really added a lot to the class.

Jack: Well, *they should have!* Do you realize that you went *40 minutes over schedule?* I can understand running slightly over, but this is ridiculous. What happened?

Julie: Well, it was the *timing* of the role plays. The instructor's guide simply didn't allow enough time to conduct them properly. Whoever wrote them just didn't understand that.

Jack: That's interesting. For your information, *I* wrote them, and none of the other instructors ever had a problem with the timing.

Julie: Sorry about that! I still say, however, that more time is needed for that section.

Jack: Well, perhaps in your eagerness to teach, you didn't take into account that your students only had one hour for lunch today. After leaving your class, they had a grand total of 20 minutes for lunch. How do you feel about *that?*

Julie: Not very happy, but all things considered, I still think I made the right decision.

Jack: I'll chalk this one up to the fact that you are still an inexperienced instructor. But don't let it happen again.

Julie: But Jack . . .

Jack: No buts! Keep all future classes on schedule. Remember, time is money, or haven't you heard?

CASE STUDY DISCUSSION POINTS

1.   Under the circumstances, do you feel Julie was right to lengthen the class schedule by 40 minutes?

2.   Do you believe that Jack was completely unfair in his comments to Julie?

3.   What are the limits of authority an instructor should have in a classroom? In other words, what decisions can be made without consulting a higher authority?

CHAPTER QUESTIONS

1.   Should instructors ever take it upon themselves to change a unit of instruction without prior permission from the manager? If so, under what circumstances?

2.   Conversely, under what conditions do you believe that an instructor's teaching flow can be questioned? Are any specific guidelines involved?

THE NEXT STEP

With the role of the instructor's guide now well understood, the stage is set for a review of the advance preparation required *before* setting foot into the classroom.

Even the most experienced teacher, armed with the highest degree of instructional skills, cannot impart knowledge to a class that does not have the proper material in front of it. Nothing is more frustrating to both student and instructor than to arrive for a class only to discover that the material is not there! Even worse is learning during the session that the classroom (or site location) is not conducive to learning.

Although the next chapter focuses heavily on preclass logistics for an off-site program, many of the guidelines presented will be equally valid for in-house facilities. Either way, it should be mandatory reading for all instructors.

Are you ready for preclass planning? Let's go!

5

PRECLASS LOGISTICS

LEARNING OBJECTIVES

Upon completion of this chapter, you should be able to:

Complete a *meeting checklist* prior to a program start.
Implement key preclass logistics in a planned sequence.
Describe the most commonly used room arrangements.
Effectively use the *daily activity planner*.
Discuss common pitfalls of preclass logistics to avoid.

OVERVIEW

Practically everyone agrees that advance planning *prior* to conducting a program is essential. The problem, however, is that some instructors take precourse preparation a bit *for granted*. When this occurs, the effects can range from mild annoyance to a full-blown disaster in the classroom. However, with only a reasonable degree of effort expended *in a planned sequence*, most problems can either be avoided or, at the least, greatly minimized.

To put all this in context, consider the following three vignettes and reflect on whether you have ever found yourself in these situations or similar ones.

SITUATION 1: It took months of planning and tedious program development, but the five-day course on stress management is finally ready for a pilot presentation. You went over the budget on the program, but felt that no expense should be spared on so important a program. The instructor cadre, consisting of five top instructors from your staff, had carefully rehearsed every segment of the course and were looking forward to conducting it for senior management.

After careful consideration, it was agreed to hold the pilot not in corporate headquarters but in one of the main company branch offices, approximately 800 miles away. Since the branch had no training facilities, it was agreed to hold the program at a well-known hotel, a few blocks from the office.

Several days prior to the program, the material was shipped to the hotel, and a follow-up telephone call the next day confirmed that it was being held in storage, awaiting your arrival. Due to bad weather, you arrived at the hotel at 9:00 P.M. the evening before, and upon checking, you discovered that *all* of the program material was missing. The hotel staff was extremely cooperative but simply could not locate the shipment. The general manager mentioned that a tracer would be put on it "early the next morning." Then the sinking feeling hit you—the pilot was scheduled to begin at 8:30 A.M. *sharp* the next morning. Fifteen vice-presidents were planning to attend, including your own boss!

SITUATION 2: Fortunately, the class logistics were going to be easy—a blessing in view of your own busy schedule. Two separate classes were to be conducted in the main training facility just one floor below your office. Fred Simms would be conducting an interviewing skills class from 9:00 A.M. to 12:00 noon. Promptly at 1:00 P.M. you would teach basic policy and procedures to a group of 25 participants in the same room. Your session was scheduled to end at 4:00 P.M. sharp. Conveniently, you would be using exactly the same equipment (a 35mm projector, two flip charts, and an overhead projector) as Fred, so there seemed to be no need to get to the room early to set it up. The only significant difference between the two classes was that all of Fred's students came from within the building whereas many of your students would travel from the different branch offices around the city. At least four of them would be coming from out of state.

During that morning you were even busier than usual. Between the constant incoming telephone calls and endless interruptions, you hadn't realized how late it was until your secretary reminded you that the time was 12:55 P.M. Further, she had just been notified that approximately 20 of your students could not enter the training room since another class appeared to be in session.

You rushed to the room, attempting to ignore the angry stares of your soon-to-be students, and asked Fred what went wrong. Fred reluctantly explained that due to a sudden subway strike that morning, many of his participants inadvertently arrived late. As a result he had to start the class at 10:30 A.M. and therefore would not be finished until around 1:30 P.M. He apologized profusely and mentioned that he repeatedly tried to call you about this, but that your phone was constantly busy.

Then three of your participants, having overheard your conversation with Fred, asked to be excused from the forthcoming class since they were running on a very tight schedule and had other appointments at 4:00 P.M.

Unfortunately, there was no other available room for your class. It looked like the beginning of a real disaster, and nothing could be done about it.

SITUATION 3: It was time for division-wide presentations of proposed budgets for the coming year. On a given day, each department head reviewed accomplishments against the expense budget for the current year and gave a detailed analysis of proposed programs and allocations for the next 12 months.

Each presentation was extremely important since it was viewed by senior management, who then made decisions on the proposed allocations. This year's budget presentation would be especially important, since it was known that the company planned a 20 percent reduction in all but highly necessary expenditures, and the new vice-president of finance had already stated that he was deeply committed to this target.

Your entire presentation on training was scheduled to last for one hour, and you needed every minute of the allotted time. Full of illustrations, facts, and figures, the talk centered around 35 transparencies, all in full color.

With all of senior management attending, the first five minutes of the presentation appeared to be going well. Then the lamp blew on the overhead projector, and the entire screen went dark. After a hurried apology to the group, you requested a five-minute break to install the spare lamp. This met with little enthusiasm; the vice-president of finance, who was scheduled to attend another budget meeting in 30 minutes, seemed especially annoyed.

Then you discovered the spare lamp was missing from the projector. Apparently, someone had recently used the spare and not replaced it. Worse yet, you were then informed that your department had no spares in stock; the last ones were used several months ago and were never reordered.

You are standing in front of the now useless projector as the senior management group reenters the room to hear the balance of your interrupted presentation. Your mouth suddenly becomes very dry, and you begin to experience a sick feeling in the pit of your stomach as you notice the vice-president of finance staring at you very impatiently.

FACILITIES REVIEW

It's an enviable situation for the instructor when every class is held within the "in-house" training facility and all planning logistics can be easily controlled. As we all know, however, such ideal conditions are rare, and the knowledgeable instructor should be prepared for any contingency.

When a planned program is to be held away from the office, but only a "few blocks away," it is all too easy to assume that less attention to detail is needed since the location is just a short distance away. *Never* let yourself be lulled by this false assumption. It's tempting to believe that any last-minute details can be handled through the office, but all too often they can't. Recall the case of the replacement bulb for the overhead projector. Even assuming that the office did have another lamp, the fact that a presentation would have to be interrupted for 10 or 15 minutes is simply inexcusable—and certainly not very professional.

A second pitfall is to assume that when a bona fide conference facility is used for the program, no facility-related problems will arise. It's here that one finds a rather perplexing paradox. Since the average conference center has been specifically designed for meetings, one can mistakenly assume that there's no need to pay attention to details—that everything can be left to the support personnel at the center. Wrong! While these conference centers are usually fully equipped for all types of meeting needs, the ultimate success of the function rests heavily on the degree of *advance* planning done with the center. One must constantly have a healthy respect for *Murphy's law*: If anything can go wrong, it will! While it may seem terribly unfair for the meeting planner, the fact remains that if 20 details must be attended to, and 19 are done correctly, the twentieth is the one on which success depends. Participants will be annoyed and will remember that one detail long after the meeting has ended.

When planning for an off-site program, it's dangerous to trust major logistics to memory. On the other hand, a multitude of forms, reports, and assorted papers can become unduly cumbersome. The solution is to create *one* document, in checklist form, that contains the required information needed to plan properly.

Figure 17, Meeting Checklist, has been created specifically for this purpose and has proven itself in actual use. (As we review the checklist in detail, please bear in mind that it was designed primarily for my own operation, planning and conducting programs literally around the world from my headquarters located in New York City. With only slight modification, however, this form can be used for any type of meeting *regardless* of location, and I encourage you to do so.)

Prior to Meeting
    Conference site
    Meals
    Meeting room
    Audio-visual requirements
    Transportation
    Participant invitations
    Meeting management
    Recreational facilities
    Prizes and awards
    Daily activity planner
During Meeting
After Meeting

PRIOR TO MEETING

	Yes	No	N/A	Done	Not yet done	Assigned to	To be completed by (date)
Conference Site							
Site visited at least 2–3 weeks in advance							
Primary hotel contact							
Number of rooms required							
Number of singles/doubles/suites							
Check in/out time							
Parking facilities							
Number/meeting rooms required							
Number/breakout rooms needed							
Central or individual billing							
Accept Diners Club card							
Meet key conference people							
General Manager							
Maitre'd							
Reservation Manager							
Have duplicating services							
Xerox							
Transparencies							
Typing							
Other (that might be necessary)							
Need for day guests							
Who coordinates							

Meals						
Coffee/coke breaks						
Time dining room opens						
Time dining room closes						
Breakfast requirements						
Lunch requirements						
Dinner requirements						
Special diets						
Any food restrictions						
Wine service						
Flexibility of dining hours						
Individual or prepared menus						
Any meals eaten outside conference site						
If so, details arranged						
Transportation to/from restaurant						
Food service						
Billing						
Other						
Availability of room service						

Figure 17. Meeting checklist.

	Yes	No	N/A	Done	Not yet done	Assigned to	To be completed by (date)
Meeting Room							
How many required							
What size required							
Have windows							
Seating/table requirements							
Tent cards or name plates							
Who will print them?							
Name(s) on card(s)?							
Can speaker control:							
Lights							
Air conditioning							
Heat							
Screen							
Audio-visual equipment							
Height of lectern							
Room have dividing wall							
If so, is it noisy?							
Near elevators?							
Room within/adjacent to meeting site							
Audio-Visual Requirements							
By speaker/day							

Number of overhead
projectors needed   ———

Number of screens   ———

Number of pointers   ———

Number of 16mm projectors   ———

Number of 35mm slide
projectors   ———

Number of video monitors   ———

Video decks   ———

Video cameras   ———

Trained video operators   ———

Chalkboards   ———

Felt-tipped markers   ———

Cellophane tape   ———

Masking tape   ———

Pads   ———

Flip charts   ———

Easels   ———

Screens   ———

What equipment will be brought from office?

_____

_____

What equipment will be supplied by hotel?

_____

_____

What equipment will be supplied by audio-visual dealer? ***

_____

_____

***If so, at what charge, and who arranges?

_____

_____

Figure 17. (continued)

115

	Yes	No	N/A	Done	Not yet done	Assigned to	To be completed by (date)
Transportation							
Group transportation needed							
Cab							
Taxi							
Limo							
Cash or charge							
Parking facilities							
Bus service							
Valet service							
Near railroad stop							
Near airport							
Participant Invitations							
Sufficient notice given							
Memo to include:							
Name of meeting							
Date							
Time							
Location							
Meeting objectives/activities							
Schedule							
Arrival/departure time							

Meeting Management												
Person in charge of meeting												
Deputy												
Facilitators ⎱ sleep												
Administrators ⎰ over												
Recreational Facilities												
Availability of												
Pool												
Gym												
Tennis courts												
Handball courts												
Racquetball												
Sauna												
Time built in for this?												
Group/team sports planned?												
Who coordinates?												
Prizes/Awards												
Contests?												
Special prizes?												
Mementos?												
Photographer needed?												

Figure 17. (continued)

117

Activities Prior to the Meeting

Conference Site. While it possibly violates some principles of time management, I believe that all conference sites should be *personally visited* at least several weeks before the meeting, despite busy time schedules. It's difficult to state who should be sent to do this, since every meeting or seminar contains a different set of administrative logistics. For instance, if a full-time meeting administrator is assigned to the seminar, this person would probably be assigned the task. Otherwise, a facilitator assigned to the program would be a likely candidate. In small training organizations with little or no support staff, the job could be delegated to the instructor, who would be responsible not only for teaching but for all related administrative logistics.

Note that the entire checklist is segregated into appropriate columns, representing a series of action steps for each item. For example, the checklist shows that an item is either completed or it shows *to whom* the responsibility has been assigned, and *when* it will be done. Let's look at several items, with a short critique of each regarding its importance. Just keep remembering Murphy's law!

SITE VISITED AT LEAST TWO TO THREE WEEKS IN ADVANCE: Even if you have used the site before, check it out again. Facilities can undergo renovation, and the room you have always used may no longer be there. The same goes for their management staff. Your close working relationship with the general manager is useless if he or she has been replaced.

ROOM REQUIREMENTS: Generally a tricky situation to handle. Do you require all single rooms, or will two to a room be acceptable? How many male and female participants attending? Are spouses allowed to accompany the participants? Also, are certain rooms more desirable than others? If so, who gets them? Last, but not least, will any VIPs require a suite?

BILLING ARRANGEMENTS: Never take billing arrangements for granted. Will each participant be individually billed, or will the entire conference expense be charged to a master account? Regarding the latter, the conference site usually requires a guarantee of payment in advance, and it's always worthwhile to find out which major credit cards are accepted.

MEETING KEY CONFERENCE PEOPLE: One should always make it a point to meet all key personnel connected with your conference. There is simply no substitute for dealing with them on a first-name basis.

DUPLICATING SERVICES: This essential part of meeting support logistics is often overlooked. As just one example, are duplicating services available from the conference site only on a nine-to-five basis, or can arrangements be made to duplicate material at other times? Finally, what are the costs for both typing and duplicating services? Many an organization has learned the hard way that it would have been less expensive to send a company secretary to an off-site program than to pay a high daily fee for required support services.

Meals.   Although few training manuals mention meals, my own opinion is that the food service (especially over a lengthy program) can have a *significant impact* (either positive or negative) on the seminar. Placing participants in a room for an entire day (or days) and expecting them to both learn and retain significant amounts of material leads to varying degrees of stress on each person. As a result, the food service takes on added importance, providing not only the needed nourishment but a respite from the tedium of the classroom.

Careful attention should always be paid to those participants who require special diets, and conference sites must always be informed of this well in advance. In addition, it's always wise to check the hours that the dining room opens and closes, since one does not want to schedule a class promptly at 8:15 A.M., only to learn on the first day that breakfast service starts at 8:00 A.M.! To save time many meeting planners opt for preselected menus, especially for lunch and dinner. While this is generally acceptable, it's always prudent to make certain that an alternate choice is available for those who request it.

Over the years, I have found that the most effective meal arrangement for an all-day seminar consists of a light buffet at lunch, saving the main meal for dinner—*after* the classroom training has been completed. When one is conducting training overseas, especially in European countries, an interesting challenge arises. While it's dangerous to dabble in generalities, the participants will often object to this arrangement, since their daily routine usually consists of a large lunch, followed later on by a light dinner. Worse yet (for training purposes), the same group of participants may also expect wine or beer to be served at lunch, since these beverages are usually included in their daily mid-day meal. Such situations have to be handled with a great deal of tact. On one hand, it's far better for afternoon class synergism to have a light lunch with no alcoholic beverages served. On the other hand, "when in Rome . . ." As in all things, prudence and moderation dictate the best course to follow, but with overseas training, the instructor should *always* check and decide on the meal service before the actual start of the class.

Meeting Room.   Like the food service, a meeting room where the training will take place can either have a positive or negative impact on classroom learning efficiency. To illustrate, here are just a few selected factors that will definitely have some type of impact on the learning process:

Size of room (in relation to total number of participants)

Type of seating arrangements available within room

Whether or not the room has windows

Adequacy of lighting, venting, heating, and air-conditioning

The degree to which the instructor can control these functions

How the audio-visual equipment can be positioned within the classroom

The degree of comfort for participant's chairs

Number of "breakout" rooms available (called "syndicate" rooms overseas)

Efficiency of the acoustics within the main room

Closeness of the main room to meal service facilities

Noise level in the main teaching room (avoiding noise distractions from an adjacent area)

Efficiency of the sound system (such as a public address or microphone amplification system)

The foregoing factors may seem obvious, but if any one of them is not satisfactory, problems are likely to occur. For example, let's explore the various types of room arrangements and their relationship to group size and learning activities. Figure 18, Interactive Team Arrangement, displays an ideal arrangement for a class with a maximum of 18 participants. It is highly satisfactory for classroom instruction where the students will work mainly in teams throughout the course (such as supervisory training), and where the instructor and/or facilitators must have easy access to each team table. Note that the facilitator's table has been placed in the *rear* of the room, with

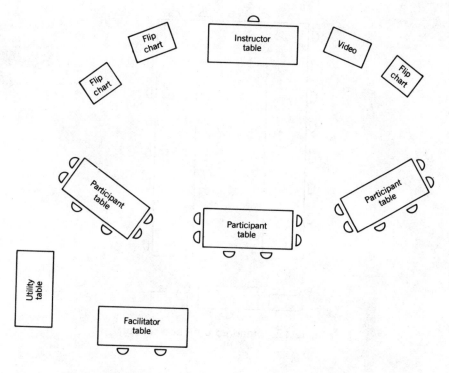

Figure 18.   Interactive team arrangement.

a utility table (for handouts and case-study material) located near the facilitator for ease in distributing materials.

This type of room arrangement gives the feeling of "togetherness" (less participant isolation) and also enables the instructor to move freely around the area with a minimum of distraction. Depending on room size, up to five participant tables can be used. However, no more than six people should be placed around any one table. Both the flip charts and video are placed strategically in the front of the room to allow easy viewing by participants regardless of where they are seated. Experience has shown that this type of room arrangement is particularly effective when small-group work is required.

One of the effective room arrangements for both participants *and* instructor is the standard U-shaped set-up shown on Figure 19.

While this arrangement still gives a feeling of togetherness, it allows the instructor to periodically move inside the U itself, establishing a much closer

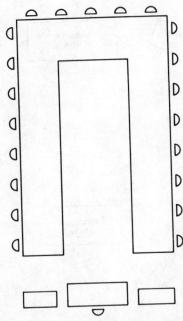

Figure 19. Standard U-shaped set-up.

presence to each student. Done properly, it greatly enhances learning effectiveness, since it allows a great degree of interaction between students and
teacher. However, the instructor must take care not to roam the U to excess,
since too much movement will cause distraction.

Depending upon physical room size, up to 25 participants can be accom-
modated with this seating arrangement. Probably the greatest disadvantage
with the U shape is that *unlike* the interactive team arrangement shown in
Figure 18, it's far more difficult to conduct small-group work inside the
main room. It can be argued that this could be offset by the use of breakout
rooms, but from personal experience, I've found that small-group work
often is more effective when done within the main teaching room.

One of the most common arrangements, the conference table, is shown
in Figure 20. Although the instructor does not have the built-in flexibility of
the U shape, the conference table set-up has proven quite effective for class
sizes of 12 or fewer. Avoid using a very large table that holds 20 to 25 participants. Although the participants may physically fit around the table, those

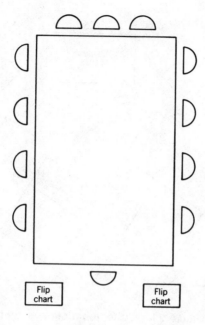

Figure 20. Conference table arrangement.

at the far end stand a good chance of feeling isolated, to say nothing of the difficulty they could experience in both hearing and seeing the instructor.

Every so often the instructor may want to use the interactive team arrangement but be restricted by room size. In certain cases the objective can be achieved by using the cluster arrangement shown in Figure 21. Here, the benefits of small-group learning can be achieved in less space. It could be a bit misleading to state *exactly* how many students can fit here (since every room configuration will be slightly different), but I have found that no more than 10 to 15 participants should be used.

Finally, we have the auditorium-style arrangement, as shown in Figure 22. This arrangement should only be used for large groups since the connotation is definitely one of a *lecture*. Each participant is usually supplied with some type of desk top (or support) for note taking. *Wherever possible, this type of seating arrangement should be avoided.* Since this format encourages a lecture approach to learning, the instructor must take great care to insure that, wherever possible, class feedback and interaction is taking place. Also, even before the session begins, participants must be encouraged

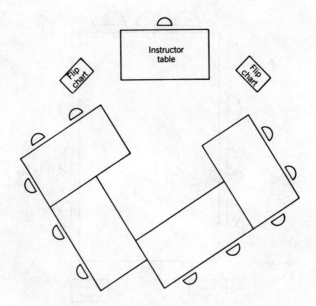

Figure 21.   Cluster team arrangement.

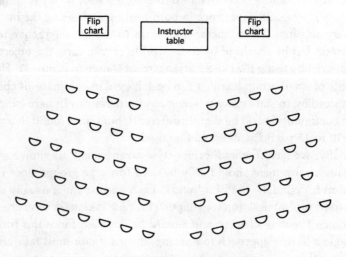

Figure 22.   Auditorium style set-up.

to sit in the front rows, rather than the back, which is a natural tendency with this arrangement. To make matters worse, those in the back rows will probably have a more difficult time in both seeing and hearing the instructor.

Naturally, other seating variations are possible. In essence, tables and chairs within the classroom should always be arranged to support the desired learning and the *way* learning will be carried out.

Audio-Visual Arrangements. The guiding rule for handling audio-visual arrangements is *threefold*. Check them out beforehand, inspect them again, then recheck them a third time!

Of all the things that can go wrong during a seminar, misfunctioning audio-visual equipment probably heads the list. The safest route in most instances is to use audio-visual equipment supplied by a conference center. As a rule, the equipment is kept in very good repair, and on-the-spot substitutes are generally available. Using one's own equipment in an in-house facility *should* be the least risky, but in some cases the hardware is not maintained properly, despite good intentions. Transporting equipment from the home office to a conference site can create problems; even with the most careful handling, there is usually a high risk that *something* will get damaged in transit. Wherever possible, back-up equipment should always be on hand, or at least nearby.

As a final thought, remember that when a hotel supplies audio-visual equipment, in most cases it has rented the equipment from a local audio-visual dealer. Here especially, a thorough check of the hardware is required *prior* to the start of the class, and one should *not* rely on the hotel staff for audio-visual expertise! Also, the experienced trainer *always* verifies the charges that will be incurred through these local dealers. In some cases, especially when the program runs over several days, the price is negotiable; in others, it is not.

Transportation. You may think you have found the "perfect" location for an off-site meeting—with excellent facilities, good food, superb recreational offerings, and all at a fabulous price—only to learn later on that it's practically impossible to get there!

When a seminar must be conducted within stringent budget guidelines, transportation costs can become a sizable factor. While it's one thing for participants to travel via rail or air to get to the location city, it is quite another to experience delays (or high travel costs) in *reaching* the program site from the rail terminal or airport. Whenever possible, it is prudent to use the limo service provided by the hotel or conference center. In the long run, it's usually less expensive and more reliable than public transportation.

Participant Invitations.   Issuing invitations is one of the easiest tasks in preliminary planning, yet it is often overlooked or done rather haphazardly.

Depending on where the forthcoming participants are based (whether in the home office, a distant office, or a combination of both), the participant must be given sufficient time for advance planning. If some participants have to fly in for the seminar, the program opening and closing has to be coordinated with flight schedules. If the majority of participants are coming from distant points, it's always wise to request their travel schedules in *advance* of the program start. The hotel (and limo service, if used) will need these schedules for their records, and of course, the program administrator will also need them for logistical purposes.

Although not specifically listed on the *Meeting Checklist*, any required preliminary reading for the program should also be included with the participant invitation letter and mentioned in it. Finally, in the same letter it is appropriate to solicit any special dietary needs or other requests.

Meeting Management.   For any given program (whether in-house or off-site), one individual must be clearly in charge—and should be so designated. A "deputy," or second-in-command, should also be selected *prior* to the program start. Regardless of who this person is, they must have the authority to make any on-the-spot decisions needed during the seminar. Such decisions could range from changing an unsatisfactory room to changing the food menu; it could even include revising the program's timing and content, where needed. When problems arise during a program, an immediate answer is usually necessary—there is *no time* to gather a committee together to find a solution!

Recreational Facilities.   Within this category, a perennial problem seems to occur when a resort (or conference site) is employed.

Any experienced instructor knows that intensive classroom work involves a great deal of individual concentration with its corresponding increase in fatigue levels. Ideally, when a program runs over several days, some time should be allotted for recreation. The problem is to place recreation into the schedule so it does not conflict with the learning. Let's examine

just a few of the scheduling possibilities for a typical five-day (9:00 A.M.–
5:00 P.M.) program:

1. *Starting the program at 8:00 A.M. and ending it at 4:00 P.M., allowing
recreation from 4:00 P.M. on:*

Pro:

>   Assuming dinner is scheduled at 7:00 P.M., a three-hour break would be
>   ideal.

Con:

>   Can the program start at 8:00 A.M.?
>
>   Is breakfast service available starting at 7:00 A.M.?
>
>   Will everyone be sufficiently alert at 8:00 A.M.? (especially if there is re-
>   quired reading the night before)?

2. *Start the program at 9:00 A.M., but give the participants two hours
for lunch (instead of one) and end at 6:00 P.M. instead of 5:00 P.M.*

Pro:

>   Two hours at lunchtime would give people a chance at a fast game of ten-
>   nis, a short walk, or a swim.
>
>   Participants would probably be more refreshed for the afternoon's work.

Con:

>   Participants could experience some frustration if a recreational activity
>   had to be curtailed to return to class; they could, for example, be in the
>   middle of the tennis game.
>
>   Will participants be unduly fatigued between 5:00 and 6:00 P.M.?

3. *Start the program at 8:00 A.M., give a three-hour lunch/recreational
break, and end at 6:00 P.M.*

Pro:

Three hours at lunchtime should be sufficient to satisfy the average participant.

Con:

Will they all return to the classroom on time?
Will they be unduly tired between 5:00 and 6:00 P.M.?

4. *Add one day for pure recreation to the schedule.*

Pro:

This is an excellent vehicle for "changing pace" and is especially opportune in a resort location.

Con:

One full day must be added to the five-day schedule.
Where does the day come from? Start on Sunday, or end on Saturday?
Additional hotel/seminar expense is involved.

Prizes/Awards.   While giving out prizes and awards seldom causes problems, simple (but significant) details can be easily overlooked. For example, if diplomas or certificates are to be awarded, they must be properly inscribed *before* the seminar takes place. If a group picture is desired, determine whether a professional photographer is available—and at what cost. Finally, if awards are to be given out, *who* will do it? Many a time, it's *presumed* that someone from senior management will give them out, only to discover too late that no one is available.

In summary, the *Meeting Checklist* provides a valuable tool for preliminary planning of the program, but its usefulness depends on how methodically one follows it. It should *never* be completed at the last minute; that will defeat its purpose—*analyzing* and *completing* all of the critical seminar functions *in advance of the program.* Like all of the other forms in this book, the *Meeting Checklist* has been both time- and field-tested and has proven workable in virtually every situation imaginable.

DAILY ACTIVITY PLANNER

As we have seen, careful use of the *Meeting Checklist* gives one a firm grasp of logistics *prior* to a seminar. The checklist provides a natural transition into the use of the *Daily Activity Planner*, as shown on Figure 23.

Usually, the meeting organizer completes a form for each day in the classroom, giving special emphasis to the *food service* area, which is most likely to change each day. If a course administrator is assigned to the program, he or she would probably be given responsibility for completion of the *Daily Activity Planner*. The administrator could then use this form to quickly review the logistics with the instructor prior to the start of the next day's work.

I've used this form for several years now and found it highly workable. However, as with any of the other forms presented here, it can be customized to meet the individual needs of any group. Of special importance are the two categories involving tasks *during meeting* and *after meeting*. All of the items listed should be self-explanatory. The important point is that each one should be reviewed *individually* and never taken for granted. As just one example, let's focus on checkout procedures, billing arrangements, and late checkouts necessary. Here are just a few of the logistics that may be involved:

Checkout Procedures

When is checkout time?

If it's earlier than the meeting time, can participants' luggage be stored? If so, where?

Can participants check out after breakfast? After coffee break?

When must the room key be turned in?

Is there a penalty for an unexpected late checkout?

Billing Arrangements

Will people be billed individually for all expenses, or just for "incidentals" (such as telephone, laundry, and bar bills)?

Does the hotel accept all major credit cards?

Does the master bill have to be paid by the administrator at checkout time, or can it be sent to the office?

Are any prior guarantees required by the facility?

Date: _____

Beginning Time _____ Ending Time _____

Meeting Room: _____

Coordinator: _____

Activity: _____

Speaker(s): _____

Intro to speaker(s) _____

Room Set-up

U Shape ___

Schoolroom ___

Auditorium ___

Other ___

Audio-Visual Requirements:

Overhead ___

Screen ___

16mm ___

Video ___

Video Operator ___

Easels ___

35mm ___

Pointer ___

Flip charts ___

Chalkboard ___

Pads/pencils ___

Nameplates ___

Handouts

Number and type ___

Supplied by ___

Distributed by ___

Special requirements ___

Food Service	Yes/No	Time required	Description of service
Breakfast			
A.M. coffee break			
Lunch			
P.M. coffee break			
Dinner			
Other			

Special instructions: _____

_____

Figure 23. Daily activity planner.

(continued)

During meeting

Administrator responsible _____

Audio-taping necessary _____

Video-taping necessary _____

Handling of messages _____

Speaker coordination _____

Note-taking requirements _____

Name/telephone number of hotel coordinator _____

Who closes meeting _____

Other _____

After meeting

Evaluations _____

Checkout procedures _____

Coordination of travel schedules _____

132

Billing arrangements

Late checkouts necessary

Follow-up required

Typing of notes

Typing of audio texts

Editing video

Equipment sent back to main office

Memo to participants

Figure 23. (continued)

Late Checkouts Necessary

Will the facility accept late checkouts?

How much time is allowed after regular checkout before a penalty occurs?

What is the procedure to be followed for unexpected late checkouts?

Use of the *Daily Activity Planner* provides the critical reinforcement necessary to run the program efficiently on a day-to-day basis. No one can be expected to remember all of the daily details required to keep a program running smoothly. As such, use of the *planner* makes good sense. It's simple, efficient, and easy to use—not a bad combination for someone charged with the total responsibility of running a program!

PITFALLS TO AVOID

Since this chapter focuses on preclass logistics from an *instructor's* viewpoint, it would be beneficial here to highlight several pitfalls to be avoided whenever possible. As we have noted, since the logistics of each classroom will differ, some generalizations are necessary as we examine some common traps.

Pitfall 1: "It's already been done by someone else, so why check it myself?"

This assumption usually lulls the instructor into a false sense of security—until it's too late. Even with the most capable staff available, one should never assume *anything* with regard to preprogram logistics. Here is a good example of the usefulness of both the *Meeting Checklist* and the *Daily Activity Planner*. When each form has been completed by an administrator, the instructor should take a few moments to review the form with the person who completed it. It will always be time well spent. A quick review of each document can immediately reveal any special factors that could have an adverse impact on the classroom activity, along with the remedial steps necessary. As an example, let's assume that over a five-day class, three breakout rooms are required on each afternoon. An examination of either form might reveal that only two breakouts were available in mid-week. The forms have provided a "red flag," giving the instructor or administrator sufficient time to take remedial action.

Pitfall 2: "Not much preclass planning is necessary since I plan to be in the classroom early on each day."

The assumption here is that if the instructor arrives sufficiently early for class, all problems can be rectified. While that may be a comforting thought in theory, it seldom works in actual practice. To illustrate, let's assume that three flip charts have to be drawn for the session beginning early tomorrow morning. All three shouldn't take more than 15 minutes, and since the instructor is tired at the end of the long teaching day, he decides *not* to draw them before leaving. Instead, he plans to arrive in class the next day at least 30 minutes prior to opening the session. Unfortunately, on the following day the instructor's train is inadvertently delayed, and he arrives, not 30 minutes early as planned, but 5 minutes after all participants have arrived and are impatiently waiting for the class to start. As a result, valuable class time is taken up while the instructor hurriedly draws the charts. Meanwhile, the participants have an opportunity to get bored, yawn, and stare at each other! A bit overstated perhaps, but not by much. In a word, *don't* put off till tomorrow what should be done today.

Pitfall 3: "I only teach; my staff handles everything else."

Classroom learning is a coordinated team effort not only between instructor and participants but just as importantly between instructor and others on staff. A case in point could involve a facilitator who administers and conducts all group role plays. Her duties would include explaining the role-play logistics (such as timing and role assignments) to the class, distributing the assignments, making certain that each group is in the proper breakout room, observing the activity, and concluding with group feedback as participants return to the main room for debriefing.

Some instructors might consider a few aspects of this task a bit "menial," especially those relating to role-play administration, and never bother to learn how to do them. The problem arises when one day the administrator cannot be there, for whatever reason, and no substitute is available. Five minutes before the start of role play is no time for the instructor to learn how it is done! The example speaks for itself: The instructor should always be capable of taking over *any* task required in the classroom. When it comes to conducting a class effectively, no task should be considered too difficult —or beneath one's dignity.

SUMMARY

1. Advanced planning in a logical sequence prior to conducting a program is an essential task, and one that should never be taken for granted.

2. The *Meeting Checklist* should be completed by the program planner at least several days prior to the start of the program. Its primary purpose is to provide a summary of all critical items required to support the classroom activity so that remedial action can be taken where necessary.

3. Various types of room arrangements are usually available to the instructor, with each configuration accomplishing a specific purpose. Some of these include the interactive team arrangement, standard U-shaped set-up, conference table arrangement, cluster team set-up, and auditorium style.

4. Combined with the use of the *Meeting Checklist* prior to the seminar, the *Daily Activity Planner* gives the meeting coordinator a high degree of control over the day-to-day logistics required to support the program.

5. Some common pitfalls for the instructor to avoid in preclass planning include failure to check all details, even when someone else has been given primary responsibility; leaving until tomorrow a task that could be done today; and failure to become familiar with *every* classroom activity required to support the learning progression.

CASE STUDY: "CAN I HELP IT IF I GET SICK?"

You are Jim Matthews, lead instructor and manager of the training and development department, and you are certain that tomorrow's program will be an important one. You have put in many weeks of work, including the successful conducting of a pilot session, and all is in readiness for the first official offering of the new sales management program for key managers of the organization. Since your own training facilities are too small to accommodate the large class of 20, the program will take place in a well-known hotel several blocks from the main company headquarters where you are based.

It's now 10:00 A.M. in the morning, and you are scheduled to teach all afternoon in your own training room. It's unfortunate that you couldn't get a replacement instructor, since your mind continually drifts back to tomorrow's big event and all of the ramifications involved with it.

Just to be on the safe side, you call in Don Gunther, who is responsible for all program details. Don is one of the best course administrators in the department, and you are quite certain that everything has been thoroughly reviewed. As Don enters your office, the following conversation ensues:

Jim: Hi, Don. Glad to see you. Just want to make certain that everything is okay for tomorrow. But knowing how you operate, I'm sure it is.

Don: Well, there's always a first time for everything. . . .

Jim: What are you talking about? Isn't everything all set?

Don: Not at the moment, but I'm hoping that the balance of details will get checked out by this afternoon—that is, unless I feel worse than I do now.

Jim: What's the matter? Are you getting sick?

Don: Well, I haven't been feeling up to par for the last couple of days. This morning I checked my temperature, and wasn't surprised to see it was over a hundred. Frankly, I was thinking of going home in a few minutes.

Jim: Tell you what. Let's have a quick look at the *Meeting Checklist*. I'm sure that most everything has been taken care of.

Don: I'm not sure you'll be pleased with this, but here you are.

[Don hands him the checklist, which is displayed on Figure 24. Jim starts to review it and quickly notes that many critical items remain to be done. Jim is about to speak when Don quickly resumes the conversation.]

Don: Look, I realize that many of the details are still incomplete, but I'm sure it will all work out.

Jim: You've got to be kidding! This whole form is a mess! Just a quick glance shows me that you haven't followed up yet on sleeping rooms, duplicating services, many of the meal requirements, and many of the details on the meeting room itself. I'm not sure if you even know the participants' plan to arrive at the hotel. And there's more! What a mess!

Don: Hey, wait a minute. I was planning to go over to the hotel in a few minutes and straighten everything out. Then, tomorrow morning, finish the balance of details before the program. There's just one problem.

Jim: What's that?

(continued on p. 144)

PRIOR TO MEETING

Conference Site

	Yes	No	N/A	Done	Not yet done	Assigned to	To be completed by (date)
Site visited at least 2-3 weeks in advance	✓						
Primary hotel contact	✓						
Number of rooms required	✓	X		OK	?	DON	Wed. 3/10
Number of singles/doubles/suites	✓			✓			
Check in/out time	✓			✓			
Parking facilities	✓			✓			
Number/meeting rooms required				OK			Wed. 3/10
Number/breakout rooms needed		X	?				
Central or individual billing	✓						
Accept Diners Club card	✓						
Meet key conference people	✓			✓			
General Manager	✓						
Maitre'd	✓						
Reservation Manager					X	DON	Wed. 3/10
Have duplicating services					X		wed. 3/10
Xerox					X		wed. 3/10
Transparencies					X		Wed. 3/10
Typing					?		NOT SURE
Other (that might be necessary)							
Need for day guests			✓				
Who coordinates			✓				

Meals

Item				
Coffee/coke breaks	✓			
Time dining room opens	✓			
Time dining room closes	✓			
Breakfast requirements				
Lunch requirements		X	DON	TUES. 3/9
Dinner requirements		X		TUES. 3/9
Special diets		?		
Any food restrictions		?		
Wine service			UNCERTAIN	
Flexibility of dining hours			"	
Individual or prepared menus			"	
Any meals eaten outside conference site	X			
If so, details arranged			DON	
Transportation to/from restaurant	X			
Food service	X			
Billing	X			
Other	X			
Availability of room service		NOT SURE	?	

Figure 24. Meeting checklist—case study.

	Yes	No	N/A	Done	Not yet done	Assigned to	To be completed by (date)
Meeting Room							
How many required	✓			✓			1 ROOM ALREADY DONE
What size required	✓				?		?
Have windows				✓			yes
Seating/table requirements					✓		
Tent cards or name plates					✓		
Who will print them?					✓		
Name(s) on card(s)?					✓		
Can speaker control:							
Lights					NOT SURE	DON	
Air conditioning					″		
Heat					″		
Screen					″		
Audio-visual equipment					″		
Height of lectern		X			″		
Room have dividing wall							
If so, is it noisy?							
Near elevators?					NOT SURE		
Room within/adjacent to meeting site							
Audio-Visual Requirements							
By speaker/day							

Number of overhead projectors needed	1	
Number of screens	? NOT SURE	
Number of pointers	1	
Number of 16mm projectors	N/A	
Number of 35mm slide projectors	?	
Number of video monitors	— ⎫ NOT	
Video decks	— ⎬ SURE	
Video cameras	— ⎭	
Trained video operators		?
Chalkboards		1
Felt-tipped markers		10
Cellophane tape		OK
Masking tape		OK
Pads		OK
Flip charts		3
Easels		3
Screens		1

What equipment will be brought from office?   NONE

What equipment will be supplied by hotel?   ALL A.V. EQUIPMENT

What equipment will be supplied by audio-visual dealer? ***
                                                    NOT SURE
   (BELIEVE HOTEL HAS EVERYTHING NEEDED)
                                          NEED TO CHECK ON THIS

***If so, at what charge, and who arranges?   ? NEED TO FOLLOW UP

Figure 24. (continued)

	Yes	No	N/A	Done	Not yet done	Assigned to	To be completed by (date)
Transportation							
Group transportation needed						DON	CHECK OUT ON TUES. 3/9
Cab							DON'T SEE
Taxi							A PROBLEM
Limo							HERE
Cash or charge							
Parking facilities							
Bus service							
Valet service							
Near railroad stop							
Near airport							
Participant Invitations							
Sufficient notice given	✓						MEMO SENT
Memo to include:							
Name of meeting	✓			✓			
Date	✓			✓			2 WEEKS AGO
Time	✓			✓			
Location	✓			✓			
Meeting objectives/activities	✓			✓			
Schedule	✓			✓			
Arrival/departure time	✓			✓			

Meeting Management

Item			Notes
Person in charge of meeting	✓	✓	OK ✓
Deputy	✓	✓	
Facilitators } sleep	✓	✓	
Administrators } over			
Recreational Facilities			
Availability of			
Pool			CHECK OUT ON TUES. 3/9
Gym			
Tennis courts			
Handball courts			DO WE NEED THIS?
Racquetball			
Sauna			
Time built in for this?			FOLLOW-UP
Group/team sports planned?			REQUIRED
Who coordinates?			
Prizes/Awards			
Contests?		NOT SURE	?
Special prizes?		X	?
Mementos?		X	?
Photographer needed?		X	NOT SURE

Figure 24. (continued)

143

Don: Well, in the last hour, my temperature has gone up and I don't feel well enough now to do it. If you don't mind, I'd like to go home now. I'm really sorry, but I'm starting to feel really lousy. I'll get Julie to go to the hotel for me.

Jim: That's not good at all! Julie has only been here for a few weeks and has *never* arranged a conference, much less a major one. That will never work out.

Don: Gee, I'm really sorry. I guess you either have to take a chance and send Julie, or . . .

Jim: Or, what?

Don: Or go yourself and try to be back in time for your class this afternoon. If worst comes to worst, you might have to cancel your class.

Jim: You don't leave me much choice. I'm not sure what to do, but I'm really upset that you waited until the last minute to arrange all these details.

Don: Well, I told you before, that if I hadn't become ill, everything would be fine today. Can I help it if I get sick?

CASE STUDY DISCUSSION POINTS

1. Was Don correct in waiting until the day before the meeting to arrange the balance of details? Before responding, consider the fact that the hotel is only a few blocks from the office and has an excellent reputation for efficiency in handling meetings.

2. Based on the facts given in the case study, would you send Julie to arrange the hotel details, or would you do it yourself, taking a chance that you might be late for your own class? Would you cancel the class?

3. Do you take any blame for the situation? As lead instructor for the forthcoming session and manager of the department, should you have waited until the day before the program to review the checklist with Don?

CHAPTER QUESTIONS

1. Who really has the ultimate authority in making the key decisions affecting a program—the lead instructor or the program administrator?

2. Assuming the responsibility falls to the program administrator, then who should be held accountable if the program proves only marginal, due in part to poor logistics that negatively affect the instructor's efficiency in the classroom?

THE NEXT STEP

With the overview of preclass logistics now behind us, we are ready to explore fully the first few critical minutes that an instructor spends in front of the class.

These early moments are indeed critical. Regardless of program content and the degree of preparation that went on beforehand, the average participant will form an opinion about the instructor—and correspondingly, the class itself—before the first 10 minutes have elapsed!

The next chapter will be solely devoted to those first few critical minutes that can truly make or break the entire program. In my opinion, it should be required reading for any instructor who stands in front of a class with reasonable expectations of success.

6

AND WHAT DO YOU SAY
AFTER YOU SAY HELLO?

LEARNING OBJECTIVES

After finishing this chapter, you should have the necessary skills to:

Describe a typical early sequential teaching flow.

Formulate a personalized preclass "ice-breaker" strategy.

Implement an effective participant cross-introduction procedure.

Explain the procedure for team assignments and implementation.

RATIONALE

To me, the first few minutes of a new class is in many ways similar to the proverbial tip of the iceberg. Figure 25, Advanced iceberg syndrome, displays this in graphic form, but let's spend a few minutes exploring it further.

As the reader may recall, in Chapter 1 we also used an iceberg illustration. In that case, it was meant to show how participant's expectations for

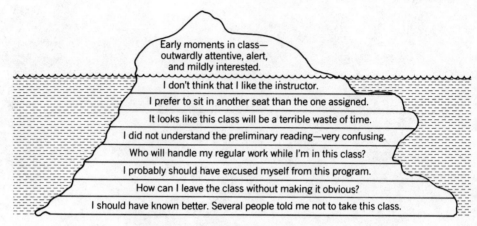

Early moments in class—
outwardly attentive, alert,
and mildly interested.

I don't think that I like the instructor.

I prefer to sit in another seat than the one assigned.

It looks like this class will be a terrible waste of time.

I did not understand the preliminary reading—very confusing.

Who will handle my regular work while I'm in this class?

I probably should have excused myself from this program.

How can I leave the class without making it obvious?

I should have known better. Several people told me not to take this class.

Figure 25.   Advanced iceberg syndrome.

the class could remain hidden from the instructor and how "obvious" motives for attending might be entirely different than the *real* reason for their presence. In other words, participants are in the expectation phase (Figure 1, Chapter 1) *up to the time they enter the classroom.* This chapter will illustrate how the instructor, through the *first crucial 15 to 20 minutes* of the program opening, can positively "bridge" both psychological icebergs (or mind-sets), getting the course off on a solid, positive footing.

Let's look at a typical scenario to see how all of this might operate. The setting is a standard in-house training facility, and the scheduled program, extending from 9:00 A.M. to 5:00 P.M. over a two-day period, will focus on problem solving and decision making. Participants have been informed that the program would begin promptly at 9:00 A.M., and that coffee and Danish pastry would be available in the room beginning at 8:30 A.M. Many of the participants have come from branch offices around the country, hence most of the class do not know each other. Following the traditional "herding instinct" (origin unknown), the students tend to cluster in small groups of known acquaintances, seldom introducing themselves to the others. A few participants make no effort to socialize; after getting coffee, they begin reading the morning newspaper at their assigned seat. Several other participants wander aimlessly around the room, obviously a bit uncomfortable for whatever reason.

The instructor arrives promptly at 9:00 A.M. (since her office is next door to the training room). She has been able to review all of the first day's notes for the class in the privacy of her office from 8:30 on. She even managed to review the incoming daily mail and sign several memos. As she entered the classroom, she was quite pleased with herself—at least from a time-efficiency standpoint. To increase her efficiency still further, she had even scheduled a staff meeting from 12 to 1 that day—the hour when the class would be having lunch and, at the same time, preparing for the afternoon role play. After all, she had taught this same subject at least 15 times, and through experience had learned a few teaching short cuts.

Following traditional format, a coffee break was scheduled for 10:15 A.M. At approximately 9:45 A.M. the instructor experienced the first feelings that the class was not going well. The exact cause of her apprehension was difficult to pin down, but it was becoming increasingly apparent that the class was not going well:

Very little class feedback was occurring.

At least 20 to 25 percent of the participants had lost interest.

Many of the other participants appeared restless.

A few students were making a valiant effort in looking interested but were plainly bored.

Perhaps she was imagining it, but the two participants in the back of the room actually looked hostile.

Small undercurrents of conversations could be heard from various parts of the room.

Perhaps the "last straw" was when one of the participants (closest to the instructor) inadvertently yawned, looked at his watch, and began absent-mindedly staring out of the window!

Any way viewed, here were the beginnings of a teaching disaster and the mere hint of it greatly alarmed the instructor. But what had gone wrong? She managed to continue with the session until the coffee break, then quickly returned to her office for a self-evaluation. This proved difficult, for as all instructors know from experience, it's extremely difficult to critique *oneself*, especially when on the platform. After several minutes of reflection, she could not pinpoint any one exact cause and had to assume that a combination of several factors had probably caused the session to deteriorate with alarming speed.

Upon returning to class, it struck her that perhaps one of the greatest mistakes she had made was in her overall *complacency* to both the subject and the audience. Perhaps, *just perhaps*, since she had taught this so many times before, she had not given many of the small but critical *early program logistics* the proper amount of focus. Silently, she vowed to herself that she would not allow that to happen again.

SEQUENTIAL TEACHING STEPS

If you have ever found yourself in a similar situation, then you will find this chapter especially helpful. We will concentrate on the sequence of steps that should be followed just prior to the program start, through all of the preliminaries, and concluding with the transition to the actual material to be taught. Figure 26 displays the sequence in graphic form and includes the following nine steps:

1. The "ice-breaker": meeting participants beforehand
2. Welcoming class
    Reinforcement of welcome
    Instructor introduction
    "Bridging" technique
3. Outlining program objectives
4. Participant introductions and expectations
5. Matching expectations to objectives
6. Introducing program content
    Related class logistics
    Examination/evaluation procedures
7. Reviewing assigned reading
8. Assigning individuals to teams (if appropriate)
9. Securing feedback and evaluating the learning climate

Let's explore each of these nine steps in detail, noting especially how one relates to the next, forming a time-tested learning bridge that can lead to a successful program start.

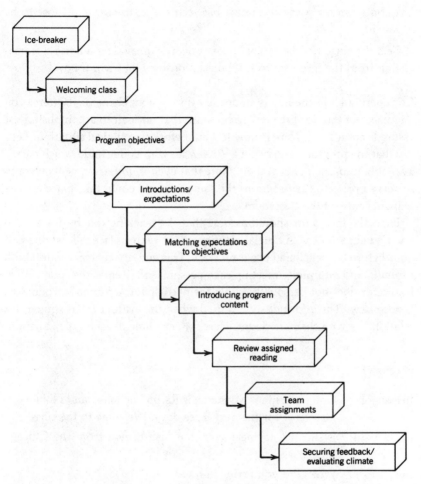

Figure 26. Early sequential teaching flow.

The "Ice-Breaker"

The "ice-breaker" is the one activity done *prior* to the actual starting of the program that is simple to do and offers the following important benefits:

Establishes a friendly, informal climate for the formal learning to follow.

Puts the participants at ease and in a more positive frame of mind.

Initiates an early social contact between the instructor and those to be taught.

Sets the stage for the official class welcome, providing a natural transition from the informal to formal relationships that will follow.

Considering all of the highly important instructional benefits it offers, you might expect the "ice-breaker" to be somewhat difficult to accomplish. Rest assured that it's not. Here is how it would work in a typical situation. Let's say that the program is to begin at 9:00 A.M., with coffee and Danish pastry available to participants at 8:30. Note that even if *no* refreshments were to be served prior to the program, the same scenario could take place as participants entered the classroom.

First, the instructor should assume that the teaching role begins at 8:30 A.M. and *not* 9:00 A.M. A crucial activity will be taking place at least one-half hour before the scheduled program start. This activity centers around both *formally* and *informally* meeting each person as they enter the room. If the instructor does not personally know the participant, a *formal* introduction is necessary. The *informal* style is used when the instructor has some prior relationship with the participant. Here's an example of each type in action:

FORMAL

Instructor:	Good morning. My name is Ralph Nicholas, and I'll be your instructor for the next three days. Welcome to the class!
Participant:	Well, nice to meet you. I'm Lisa Brown from the Chicago office.
Instructor:	When did you arrive in town, Lisa?
Participant:	Late last night. I had planned to arrive early yesterday afternoon, but we had terrible weather in Chicago, and all flights were delayed about three hours. The trip to New York was no bargain either—bumpy all the way in.
Instructor:	Wow! You must be a little beat. Why not get some coffee and relax a few minutes before the class starts.
Participant:	Thanks. I'd like that.
Instructor:	By the way, what's your job at the Chicago office?
Participant:	I'm chief supervisor in the order-entry section of customer service. I've been there almost five years now.

Instructor: Sounds impressive. It will be nice having someone with your experience in the class. Now, can I "buy" you that coffee?

Participant: Great idea! I'm beginning to perk up already.

Instructor: Incidentally, there's Lucy Lang, our course administrator standing by the coffee urn. Let me introduce you. I think both of you have a lot in common.

INFORMAL

Instructor: Hi, John! Good to see you again. How have you been?

Participant: Okay for the most part, but I've certainly had better days.

Instructor: Oh? What do you mean? Is anything wrong?

Participant: Well, sort of. For the last two weeks, I've been on the road. I must have visited at least six or seven branch offices, and each one had a different problem for me to solve. It got so bad that one night I woke up at 3:00 A.M. and for the life of me couldn't figure out what city I was in! Can you imagine that?

Instructor: I certainly can. The same thing happened to me a few years ago when *I* was on the road. One night, I was too embarrassed to call the front desk to find out where I was, so I rummaged around the night table next to my bed until I found some matches with the hotel's name on it!

Participant: Well, that makes me feel a little better! It's good to know that the guy teaching the class has had some real field experience and is not someone from the home office who just gives us a lot of theory.

Instructor: Well, I don't know all of the answers. That's why I count on people like you who can reinforce some of the points made in class.

Participant: Sounds good to me, but I think I'll help myself to some coffee first.

Instructor: Fair enough! By the way, on your recent trip, did you get a chance to visit the Chicago office?

Participant: No. That's one of the few branches that wasn't on my itinerary. I'll probably be there in a couple of weeks though.

Instructor: Good. Let me introduce you to Lisa Brown from that office. She's one of the participants in the class, and I think that you two might have a lot in common. As a matter of fact . . .

As the two examples have illustrated, the skillful instructor can easily blend both the formal and informal greetings during the all-important 30 minutes prior to the program start, paving the way for a natural transition to the official class opening. In addition to the several benefits already identified with the ice-breaker exercise, the instructor gains an additional *very strong* important benefit, especially if he or she is relatively inexperienced or a bit shy. By meeting and greeting participants *beforehand*, the instructor turns a group of strangers into an assemblage of friends, which can make the instructor much more comfortable as he or she leads the session. *Over the years, repeated experience with this technique has always been positive, and it remains a basic cornerstone of good teaching.*

Welcoming Class

Once the ice-breaker exercise has been successfully conducted, the stage is set for the first formal instructor role—that of officially welcoming the class to the session.

There are many ways to start the session with a class welcome, and one should never be so bold as to pronounce one particular method better than the next. What follows is a sequential flow that has worked for me over the years, not only in the United States but in most countries abroad. Let's start with the first segment of the three involved with this activity.

Reinforcement of Welcome.   Since the instructor has already met the majority of participants during the ice-breaker exercise, his or her very first activity on the platform should be a *sincere* reinforcement of the welcome extended to all those present. The word *sincere* is stressed here since it's very easy for participants to perceive that you are, perhaps inadvertently, slightly glib or even bored before the session even gets started. It's here that all instructors can take a lesson from the theatrical world; as all the seasoned entertainers know, *the show must go on*—regardless of how tired they are or how much stress they're under, regardless of whether or not they feel like giving a performance. While this may raise some eyebrows, I see instructors as very much like entertainers—for they both have an audience of people who have assembled before them for whatever the reason, have various expectations, have taken time away from something else to attend, and expect to gain *something* by being present.

As most experienced instructors already know, it's not always easy to stand up in front of a class and be bright, cheerful, and sincere when you don't feel like it! This is especially true when you carry a heavy teaching load and must constantly be on guard against *burn-out*—literally wearing yourself out through a continued, heavy teaching schedule. However, it's important to recognize that the average participant forms an opinion of the instructor (either positive or negative) *within the first five minutes of the program start*. The sincere reinforcement of welcome can play a key role in getting the program started on the right note.

Instructor Introduction.   Once the welcome has been reinforced, it's time for the instructor to formally introduce himself or herself to the class. This second introductory segment should not be neglected even if (a) the teacher has already met some of the participants, and (b) an instructor's biography has been included in the participant's materials. The duration of the introduction can vary, but it usually takes no more than three to four minutes and includes:

Instructor's educational background

Relevant work history

Some personal facts to "humanize" the introduction

Personal credibility factors, or why the instructor is qualified to teach the program

At this juncture, the reader may perhaps wonder at the frequent emphasis on instructor credibility. In my view a successful instructor *must* have two basic skills to teach a course:

1. *A reasonable degree of teaching skill on the platform.*
2. *Direct field experience in the subject matter being taught.*

It is the blending of these two experiences that separates the truly professional instructor from the marginal ones. Simply stated, even with the best of platform skills, it's unreasonable to presume that an instructor can teach others a new behavior when that person has never experienced it in real life! While many things can be learned from a textbook, *practical knowledge* has never been one of them. Here's a brief illustration of what might happen in a classroom. The setting is a five-day program in field coaching for regional sales managers. Of the 10 managers in the class, the great majority have from 5 to 12 years experience in the field. The instructor has never sold either the company's current product or anyone else's but obviously has excellent instructional skills. The instructor introduction has just concluded and a participant raises his hand. The following dialogue ensues:

Participant: [*Slightly sarcastic*] Forgive me for interrupting, but since we are going to be together for the next few days, I have a question that needs answering. I hope you don't mind.

Instructor: [*Confidently*] No, of course not. I'm here to answer all of your questions.

Participant: Good. Now, based on your introduction, I don't believe that you have ever actually sold before. Am I correct?

Instructor: Well, that's true. But, you will also recall that I received both my undergraduate and graduate degrees in marketing, so I'm quite familiar with the subject.

Participant: Sorry, I mean no disrespect, but do you think that your educational background *by itself*, qualifies you to teach *us*?

Instructor: [*Visibly annoyed*] Yes, certainly. I'm up on the latest techniques in the sales management area.

Participant: [*Very sarcastically*] That's wonderful. I know we all feel better about things now.

    [*Class laughter, then a dead silence fills the room.*]

This short example of what *could* happen speaks for itself. It is an unfortunate situation for all concerned and certainly lends nothing to the teaching experience.

Bridging Technique.   The third and final segment of activity under the banner of the class welcome is "bridging," or connecting, the instructor introduction with the listing of the program objectives. In effect, it reinforces the relevancy of the instructor to the participant's world, then transfers this positive image to what is to be learned. This can be accomplished in two ways. The first is used where the instructor has been introduced by another person. The instructor can then paraphrase a segment of the introduction, using it as a bridge to the program objectives. For example, let's assume that in introducing the instructor, the speaker refers to him as a "leading authority on time management." Later on, employing the bridging technique, the instructor could say something like, "By the way, I was really flattered when Tom referred to me as an authority on time management. Well, I'm not sure how much of an authority I really am, but I hope to show you over the next two days how to increase your efficiency by at least 30 percent *without* spending any more time at your desk. Fair enough?"

Note how this instructor also easily reinforced his credibility by bridging to his introduction, yet did so in a natural, free-flowing manner. It's an excellent vehicle that should be used by an instructor whenever the occasion arises.

The second technique comes into use when the instructor has *not* been introduced by another, yet needs to reinforce her presence on the platform. To accomplish this, the teacher need only select segments of her conversation with participants during the ice-breaker interface. Drawing from the two examples given earlier (formal and informal greetings), the instructor could say something like:

> I know that many of you have come a long way to get here, and I promise to do my best to make the time spent worthwhile. In any case, the classwork should proceed much more smoothly than Lisa's plane trip from Chicago last night!

or

> This three-day program will be intensive, but it will teach you the most advanced techniques of supervisory training. There are other benefits too. At least people like John will be able to stay in one place for the next few days, rather than hitting a new city every day of the week!

Here again a nice tie-in has been accomplished in a nonthreatening, easy way. If nothing else, the instructor is *guaranteed* to receive the close attention of the person referred to in the bridging! In summary, the class likes it, the individual mentioned in the bridging is flattered, and the instructor is more effective early in the program—not a bad combination in any classroom!

Program Objectives

With the conclusion of the bridging exercise, the listing of program objectives follows in natural sequence. There are several ways to accomplish this, but the most effective is to have these objectives both in the participant binders *and* listed on a flip chart.

This brings up an important instructional point that deserves special emphasis. Experience has shown that any visual aid (such as an overhead transparency, 35mm slide, or flip chart) is most effectively reinforced by giving participants a *duplicate* of it in their binders. This is especially important when conditions prevent some participants from clearly seeing the material being presented by the instructor—a situation that occurs even under the most favorable room environments. In addition, having the learning objectives included in their own binders not only gives students more "ownership" of the material but also allows them to add comments or special notations. As a final benefit, participants are freed from the tedious task of taking notes as the instructor reviews the course objectives. Nothing is more frustrating to students than to scribble notes furiously only to realize that as they are writing, they are missing some key points being made by the instructor! No instructor wants frustrated students so early in the class opening.

A preferred way to display program objectives is to have them *preprinted* on a flip chart. Let's review a typical chart for a time management program, displayed on Figure 27, and explore the rationale involved. As a starter, note that five objectives have been listed. While there are no hard-and-fast rules on this, in general, no more than eight to ten objectives should be used. If more are given, the overall purpose will begin to diffuse and the

---

Program Objectives

Upon completing the course, you should have the necessary skills to:
- Conduct a time-study analysis
- Identify both time-savers and time-wasters that impact on productivity
- Develop workable guidelines to improve time-management activities
- Allot priorities to future work to maximize personal productivity
- Develop a permanent time plan

Figure 27. Program objectives.

participants will be confused. Ideally, from three to six objectives should be posted. If a program is being conducted over several days, experience has shown that it's best to list the *overall* program objectives at the introductory stage of the program, then give specific unit learning objectives at the start of each day's activities.

While there are always exceptions to the rule, learning objectives should begin with a verb (for example, *conduct, identify, develop*) and, where possible, the performance criteria to be used should be stated. These objectives should never be written in vague or unclear language. Consider, for example, the objective, "To become more efficient in time management." The following questions immediately come to mind:

What is meant by "more efficient?"

How will this new efficiency be measured?

How does one define *efficiency*?

(I'm certain that the reader can add a few more!)

It was mentioned earlier that the program objectives should be preprinted, not drawn in class by the instructor. No matter how skilled the instructor might be, actually writing each objective in class will always prove somewhat distracting. While writing, the instructor must devote his or her attention to the flip chart, taking it away from the participants—something to be avoided wherever possible. Preparing the charts beforehand is far more efficient.

Finally, I prefer objectives on a flip chart since they can be later posted in a prominent spot within the classroom and referred to periodically by the instructor. Just prior to the session close, the instructor should again review the original program objectives, checking that the desired outcome has actually been obtained. This activity (periodic rechecking of stated objectives) should be announced to the participants during their first exposure to the objectives, which will immediately assure participants that they will be expected to achieve these objectives. Put another way, if you tell people that the course will do the following, then they'll expect their class performance to be periodically checked against it.

Introductions/Expectations

The stage is now set for participant introductions, and most importantly, the surfacing of individual expectations. Let's review both activities in sequential order.

Figure 28, Participant's Profile, can either be distributed in class or included in the student's binder. I prefer the latter, following the rule of the fewer handouts, the better. There are two approaches that can be followed here: (1) have each participant introduce himself or herself, or (2) pair off participants and have each introduce his or her partner.

Whatever alternative is employed, each person should be given at least three to four minutes to prepare. This is especially important if cross introductions (which I favor) are to be used. The big advantage to cross introductions is that it gets participants into an interactive mode early in the program and makes the introductions more fun for everyone. If there is an odd number of people in the class, the instructor or facilitator should act as a partner for the last person to be introduced.

A suggested scenario is recommended here, which will incorporate each participant's personal objectives for the course. Note that Figure 29, Personal Objectives, should be sent to all participants *in advance* of the program, along with any other preliminary reading assignments. The rationale here is that it only takes a moment or two to gather sufficient facts for an introduction. More time is usually required for stating one's personal objectives and special expectations from the course. In explaining this exercise to the class, I recommend the following instructions:

1. Have each participant interview his or her partner.

2. First one participant introduces the other, using the information obtained on the participant's profile.

3. At the conclusion of the introduction, the person who has just been introduced states his or her personal objectives for the program and the instructor posts them on a flip chart (using Figure 29).

4. Procedure is then reversed for the other partner.

You may ask, why not have the participant's partner (after the basic introduction) also state the partner's objectives for the program? Take a moment now and think about it. Can you guess why? The reasoning is quite simple.

CROSS-INTRODUCTIONS

Business
Profile

Name: _____

Division/Unit _____

Present job responsibility _____

_____

Number of years with company: _____

Previous job(s) held with company (if applicable): _____

_____

Other organizations worked for (if applicable): _____

_____

Most challenging part of current job: _____

_____

Personal
Profile

Name of spouse (if applicable): _____

Name(s) of children (if applicable): _____

_____

Hobbies: _____

_____

Little known fact about this person that most participants are

unaware of: _____

_____

_____

_____

Figure 28. Participant's profile.

OBJECTIVES

Please take a moment prior to the program to list your personal objectives for attending. Make certain to include any special expectations you may have for the forthcoming session. Your comments (along with those of the other participants) will be reviewed in class by the instructor.

1. _____

_____

_____

_____

2. _____

_____

_____

_____

3. _____

_____

_____

_____

4. _____

_____

_____

_____

Figure 29. Personal objectives.

Occasionally the response may be a bit vague, and since the instructor will post these personal objectives and expectations on the flip chart, clarification may be needed. When this does occur, it would be awkward for the instructor to have to ask the original partner to clarify what was intended. It's always far better to have the person's objectives stated *directly* by the participant who created them. It's a simple "reverse-procedure" technique, and well worth the extra few seconds required. Once the official program objectives have been reviewed, it is wise to flip the page over so as not to bias the participants when stating their own expectations.

Matching Expectations to Objectives

With this phase of the sequential teaching flow comes the first platform challenge to the instructor. By challenge, I mean *matching participant expectations to the previously discussed basic program objectives.* The instructor must take great care to insure that:

1. The class expectations (taken as a group) have been clearly defined and coded in a manner to show where duplications of objectives and expectations have occurred.

2. Each expectation is then cross-matched against the original program objectives, clearly showing:

    a. Where a definite match is present, and

    b. Where an expectation or objective that has been expressed by a participant is clearly *outside* the course scope.

Both steps appear to be simple, straightforward exercises for the instructor. But unless great care is taken, the process can become deceptive, leading to participant dissatisfaction and a growing sense of uneasiness. Unfortunately, even though this may originate with just one participant, it could be psychologically damaging to the rest of the class—a condition to be avoided wherever possible.

Posting of a participant's expectations is not as easy as one might think. In many cases, a person might inadvertently become vague when called on, and the instructor could, just as inadvertently, begin to lead the participant. Consider the following example:

Instructor: Now that Milt has told us of his objectives, we're ready for the next. Okay Dorothy, you're next.

Dorothy: Mmm . . . well, I'm not sure . . .

Instructor: What do you mean? Didn't you prepare a list of your objectives prior to coming to class?

Dorothy: To tell the truth, I tried but couldn't come up with anything specific.

Instructor: C'mon, Dorothy. You should be able to think of *something*!

Dorothy: Well, I guess I just want to be a better supervisor.

Instructor: That's better. So I'll post that you need more practice in coaching and helping subordinates in on-the-job training. Correct?

Dorothy: Sure. If you say so.

Instructor: Good. Now, let's move on to the next participant.

No one but Dorothy can say for sure whether or not she believed that increased proficiency in coaching and training was what she expected. With the approach used by this instructor, the posting would most likely go unchallenged, but it could also produce a *negative* experience. Let's continue the dialogue between Dorothy and the instructor one more step:

Dorothy: Forgive me for interrupting, but something is troubling me.

Instructor: What's that?

Dorothy: I'm not sure if you understand me correctly.

Instructor: Well, *just what did you mean*?

Dorothy: If you give me a moment, I could probably tell you, but you seem to be rushing me. Frankly, I find it upsetting.

When all of the participants' expectations have been listed on the flip chart, another challenge is posed: which class objectives will be covered in the formal program, and which *will not*. Here is where the cross-matching between the official program objectives and those voiced by the students comes into play. An effective way to do this is to record each of the two classifications of objectives (those that match up with course objectives and those that are beyond the course scope) on separate flip charts, then place the two in close proximity to each other for direct comparison.

At this juncture, the instructor should always be prepared to hear of related participant concerns. Participants may express anxiety about role playing or ask for a clarification regarding the final examination (if applicable). These concerns should never be taken lightly and should always be handled with a great deal of tact. The same holds true when participants request topics not covered in the program. It is *not* sufficient merely to state that the requested topic is not included in the course curriculum. The instructor is expected to explain *why* it is not covered and *where* the subject knowledge may be obtained.

Introducing Program Content

As the reader may recall, in Chapter 4, Developing the Instructor's Guide, attention was devoted to a typical sequence in the introduction of program content. Now it's time to amplify this, positioning it in the sequential teaching flow.

To understand the significance of this next step, let's take a moment and reflect on what has happened to the participants up to this point. So far, they have:

Met several other participants informally just prior to the session start.

Formed an early opinion of the instructor (either positive or negative).

Had the official program objectives explained to them (and some might be slightly confused or apprehensive about this).

Were introduced to each other and had the opportunity to express their own expectations and possible concerns to the instructor, and hence the class.

Saw the cross-match between the combined class expectations and official program objectives.

Taking all this into account, the next thing on the minds of the participants would probably be the need to get into *specifics*—just what will be done in class and in what time frame? To accomplish this, the instructor would rely on two additional flip charts. The first, shown in Figure 30, displays how the program is segmented into various main activities, giving each participant an overview of the type of work expected from them. The second, shown in Figure 31, specifically lists each activity, noting the time that will be spent on each. This method represents a time-tested approach for effec-

1. The assigned preliminary work (which has already been done)
2. Participation in this all-day program
3. Class exercises (via assigned teams)
4. Simulations (role play)
5. Final examination
6. Course evaluation

Figure 30. Progress segmentation chart.

tive class learning, and these charts, like the ones representing program objectives and class expectations, should be prominently posted in the classroom throughout the duration of the program.

Review Assigned Preliminary Reading

This step in the teaching flow would be applicable only if reading was assigned to the participants. While there are probably differing opinions on the value of assigning reading prior to class attendance, I've always found it highly beneficial.

The key to making a reading exercise successful is to make certain that whatever is assigned in advance (1) is highly *relevant* to the program, (2) is *motivational* in the sense that the reader will both identify with and benefit from the assignment, and (3) is bridged (connected) to the early phases of the main program.

Depending on the nature and complexity of the program, the reading assignment can significantly add to learning effectiveness in the classroom. Whether the assignment consists of a straight reading of text material, programmed learning, computer-assisted instruction, or any combination thereof, the knowledge gained by participants must now be expanded and reinforced in class. Depending on the course design, this can be accomplished in many ways. For example, reading topics can:

Provide an overview of material to be presented in class.

Act as a source of related supplementary material.

Morning	
• Introduction, objectives	9:00–9:30
• Discussion:	
Situational factors	9:30–10:30
Performance-loop correlations	
• Coffee break	10:30–10:45
• Discussion:	
Performance-appraisal benefits	10:45–12:00
Problems in performance appraisal	
• Summary	12:00–12:15
• Lunch	12:15–1:30
Afternoon	
• Review of performance-appraisal factors	1:30–2:30
• Discussion:	
Employee performance-evaluation forms	2:00–3:15
Performance-appraisal action steps	
• Coffee/coke break	3:15–3:30
• Role play	3:30–4:30
• Summary, wrap-up	4:30–4:45
• Exam and course evaluation	4:45–5:30

Figure 31.   Activity schedule.

Be organized into sections, with each segment covering a main block of learning.

Be used mainly as a reinforcement for material taught.

One of the most efficient and cost-effective methods used throughout the past few years is the programmed learning approach. Using this method, a student would read several paragraphs of material, then, as a check on retention, answer several questions about the material just read. The correct answers usually follow each group of questions, enabling the student to check proficiency quickly. If something proves unclear or confusing, it can immediately be reread.

When programmed instruction is employed, it's important that the instructor thoroughly review the material with the class, making certain that the main learning points have been thoroughly understood. Going a bit further, for a class held over several days it's not uncommon for an instructor to assign reading on each night, then merely reinforce and expand on the material during the next day. Done properly, it provides an effective learning vehicle for the participants and allows the instructor to be more creative on the platform. However, the instructor must make certain that all reading material is clearly covered in class. Otherwise, participants are apt to perceive the reading as a useless exercise, and one that can be ignored.

Team Assignments

In order to capitalize on synergism, participants should be assigned to teams wherever possible. By definition, *synergism* is the action of separate substances that, in combination, produce an effect greater than that of any component taken alone. Translated into teaching usage, it means that a group of participants will always produce more effectively as a team than as separate individuals.

Organized properly, the employment of teams throughout a program can provide a highly motivational learning force. To insure success, however, teams must be selected *in advance* of the course, so that each team has a proper "balance" (for example, the right mix of experienced and inexperienced people).

Using a team approach is simple, motivational, and certainly challenging. During this phase of the sequential teaching flow (usually occurring just prior to the first morning coffee break), the instructor:

Explains to the class the benefits of team synergism.

Describes how teams will operate throughout the course.

Displays names and groupings of teams that have been assigned in advance.

Challenges the newly formed teams to decide upon a name (animal, mineral, or vegetable) that will best describe how their team will operate throughout the course (to be done during the forthcoming coffee break).

Asks each team to appoint a spokesperson who, immediately upon returning to the classroom after coffee break, will announce to the other participants *both* the name of their team and its significance to them.

The results of this short exercise can be truly rewarding. It quickly transforms a group of individuals into a newly formed unit that will operate as a team throughout the remainder of the program. Naturally, the instructor must take special care with each team to make certain that no one person dominates the group, and see that each member gets a turn at presenting team findings during the various exercises that follow.

For those instructors who have never used this team approach to learning, I heartily recommend that they do so at the first opportunity.

Securing Feedback and Evaluating the Learning Climate

The final step in the sequential teaching flow (and just prior to initiating the main learning content of the program) is to promote two-way communication through active feedback from participants.

Through active feedback, that is, questions and comments from the class, the instructor is assured that each participant has fully grasped everything that has transpired to date and that no lingering concerns or questions remain. The instructor must take the lead through discreet probing since there are always a few participants who, for whatever reason, are reluctant to voice a concern or raise a question.

When full feedback has been secured, the instructor is in a good position to evaluate the learning climate of the group assembled before him. Active feedback indicates that in all likelihood a positive climate has been set for the learning that will now follow. When this magic moment occurs, the stage is set for the balance of the program.

The participants are ready.

The instructor is poised to start.

Let the effective learning begin.

SUMMARY

1. Participant's perception of events during the first 15 minutes of the program can either positively or negatively affect the balance of the entire course.

2.   The early sequential teaching flow of a typical program consists of the following steps: ice-breaker, welcoming class, outlining program objectives, introducing participants and learning of their expectations, matching expectations to objectives, introducing program content, reviewing assigned reading, forming teams, and securing feedback and evaluating the learning climate.

3.   Use of the preclass "ice-breaker" technique is a simple yet highly effective way to start a class on a positive note.

4.   Whenever possible, the instructor should make it a point to meet all participants as they arrive in the classroom just prior to the opening of the session.

5.   Two basic requirements for success as an instructor are: (1) a reasonable degree of teaching skill on the platform, and (2) direct field experience in the subject being taught.

6.   Program objectives should be clearly preprinted on a flip chart and a duplicate copy of them included in the participant's binder.

7.   When listing participant's objectives on a flip chart, the instructor must take great care not to misinterpret or incorrectly paraphrase what has been said.

CASE STUDY: "IN OUR OPINION, THIS WHOLE THING IS A WASTE OF TIME!"

From the start nothing seemed to go right in class. It was now 10:40 A.M., and since the participants had left the classroom for a coffee break, the instructor, Jeff Snyder, had a few moments alone with his thoughts—and they were troubling thoughts indeed. Jeff mentally reviewed the earlier class events in an attempt to pinpoint where the difficulty originated, but nothing specific came to mind.

Granted, several things about the program were not ideal. The five-day course in supervisory training seemed to have been scheduled at a bad time for everyone, and several participants had already expressed their dissatisfaction at having to attend a week-long program during a peak workload period. To make matters worse, Jeff was informed only yesterday that six out of the original class of fifteen had been cancelled out of the class by their managers, citing their heavy work schedule as an excuse. Apparently, their replacements were told only late yesterday afternoon that they had been selected to attend. Since preliminary reading would take at least four hours, Jeff was sure that many of the replacements had not had sufficient time to accomplish this. As if things weren't bad enough, the air-conditioning system in the main classroom had broken down last night, and the room temperature had already risen to 75 degrees, due in part to the unusually warm weather the region was experiencing.

Jeff was counting on the group's team synergism to get things rolling again and made a mental note to reinforce team efforts throughout the day. As he was mulling this over in his mind, the class slowly drifted back into the room. Perhaps it was his imagination, but Jeff sensed that the participants were unusually silent as they took their seats. In fact, a few even appeared sullen. Jeff thought he knew how to fix all that:

Jeff: Okay, now that everyone is back from the coffee break, we're ready for the team names. I'm looking forward to hearing some creative labels and learning why the team name was picked. Let's start with Team Number 1.

Participant: Uh, well, I hate to say this, but we weren't able to come up with a name.

Jeff: C'mon now! You must have arrived at some decision. After all, you will be working in teams for the next four days, and it's really important that you have a group identity.

Participant: Sorry, but we only got as far as electing *me* as team spokesperson. As a matter of fact, the entire class asked me to represent them.

Jeff: I'm confused. *Represent them* on what?

Participant: This has got nothing to do with you, but many of us resent the fact that we were *told* only yesterday afternoon that we had to attend this class. Do you realize what that means? Because this is our peak period, most of us will have to *return* to our desks when the class ends at five, and will probably have to work until at least eight or nine o'clock each night just to catch up. So much for good supervisory practices. Frankly, I think it's a joke.

Jeff: Hold on a minute! It's unfortunate that several of you were selected at the last minute, but I'm sure it could not be helped. Besides, the company strongly believes that this program is important for your careers and spends a lot of time, money, and effort providing it. Now, taking that into account, how do you feel about the course now?

Participant: Confidentially?

Jeff: Of course.

Participant: In our opinion, this whole thing is a waste of time!

CASE STUDY DISCUSSION POINTS

1.   Can Team 1's response to their assignment be considered unfair under the circumstances?

2.   If you were the lead instructor for this program, how would you handle the situation at this point?

3.   Would Jeff be within his limits of authority to terminate the program after the discussion with the Team 1 spokesperson?

CHAPTER QUESTIONS

1.   In a typical class offering, how much leeway does an instructor really have regarding program content and duration?

2.   If you were Jeff's manager and learned that he cancelled the program after the first morning's coffee break, what would you do?

THE NEXT STEP

Regardless of how knowledgeable instructors are in their subject areas, they also need a high degree of presentation skill to be successful on the platform.

Professional instructors may not think of themselves as entertainers or performers, but their roles in front of a class are similar to those of performers in many respects. While true learning is a demanding process for participants, the teacher has a prime responsibility to make certain that the required information is conveyed to the class in the most palatable way possible.

The next chapter will focus on effective presentation skills and the various techniques that help make the teaching day go a bit smoother.

Let's share the classroom spotlight together.

7

EFFECTIVE PRESENTATION SKILLS

LEARNING OBJECTIVES

After completing this chapter, you should be able to:

Identify cluster traits of truly successful speakers.

Describe the key elements of an effective presentation.

Develop a workable format for speaking notes.

Begin using the *Presentation Planner* for your next talk.

Understand the various types of audio-visual aids and their corresponding advantages and disadvantages.

Become a better speaker than you were before.

INTRODUCTION

An instructor is a presenter of knowledge and ideas to an assembled group of people. Too often in formal instructor training programs, the main emphasis appears to be on merely conveying pure product or skill knowledge.

Yet equal weight should be given to the techniques involved in successful public speaking, for one skill is simply lost without the other. Whether one stands in front of just a few people for a 10-minute presentation on company policy or spends two intensive weeks guiding a class of 30 in leadership training, a good grounding in effective presentation skills is required.

It's at this juncture that this book departs from the traditional instructor training mode and offers a comprehensive look at the elements of good public speaking. As head of a large international training group, I frequently find myself called upon to present ideas (or the rationale) for a proposed program in front of senior management. No matter how worthwhile the proposal might be, it would stand a good chance of being rejected if the presentation were not properly planned.

When you think about it, truly effective instructors are usually accomplished public speakers. Throughout the years that I've conducted classes in both instructor training and presentation skills, participant questions have always seemed to center around the following concerns:

How can a speaker present a complex subject and make it appear so easy?

Are the effective speakers born with a special talent or did they develop their skill through training?

How are they able to capture and hold the audience's attention so fast?

Good speakers often *enjoy* being on the platform! How can that be possible?

Can the special qualities of an effective speaker be readily identified?

How do they speak so well without constantly referring to notes?

Can I be trained to be just as good?

This chapter will respond to those queries. It will focus primarily on the basic skills an effective speaker needs. I should, however, add a note of caution here. No one book on effective presentation skills can fully substitute for actual participation in a class devoted to the subject. Unfortunately, many instructors simply do not have the time to attend such classes—hence, the need for this particular chapter.

Some instructors may never quite reach the highest presentation skill level, but they can learn, then reinforce, the same basic set of skills that truly effective instructors have developed in their climb to the top of their profession. A superb presenter is one who receives early audience attention, one who informs, persuades, inspires, motivates, leads, and initiates some type of action from the people listening. To become that accomplished is an interesting challenge. Let's see how it is done.

OBSERVABLE TECHNIQUES

A good way to gain proficiency in a new skill is to (1) understand the steps involved in doing it well, (2) observe someone with a high degree of proficiency demonstrate the skills, and (3) practice the new skill, seeking constructive feedback to further improve the new behavior.

When the skill is successful public speaking, a good way to start is to first observe the technique of really good speakers, then relate their performance to several basic steps involved in an effective platform procedure. To find a role model, take a moment and think about your favorite entertainers or public speakers. Most likely, whether or not you were conscious of it, they exhibited the following cluster of ten interrelated traits:

1. *A High Presence.*   It was obvious from the start that the speaker had a comfortable, very natural, high degree of presence. That not only made *you* comfortable, but it also heightened your interest.

2. *An Attention-Getting Opening.*   Within the first few moments, the speaker easily claimed the attention of all those present, making them want to hear more.

3. *Effective Eye Contact.*   Regardless of the size of the audience, each person seemed to feel the speaker was talking directly to her or him. Not only did this reinforce the audience's attention, but it seemed to make the talk highly personal.

4. *High Level of Sincerity.*   Whatever the topic being presented, it was apparent that the speaker was deeply committed to what he or she said. The high level of sincerity seemed to create a strong bond with the audience.

5. *A Natural Persuasiveness.*   You found yourself accepting the speaker's point of view without even realizing it. In no way did you perceive the speaker's persuasiveness as a high-pressure tactic. Instead, it seemed to emanate naturally as the talk progressed.

6. *Genuine Enthusiasm.*   The speaker generated a constantly high level

of personal enthusiasm—from start to finish. Without being conscious of it, your own enthusiasm level rose.

7. *No Visible Nervousness.* Not only did the speaker fail to exhibit any signs of nervousness, but at various times throughout the talk he or she actually appeared to enjoy being on stage.

8. *Controlled Voice Level.* From beginning to end, the speaker maintained a controlled rate of delivery, with a very pleasant voice quality. Both the modulation and pacing perfectly matched the intent of the message.

9. *Nonverbal Gestures.* The speaker's body language gave reinforcement to key elements of the talk. Use of hands, body movements, and facial expressions were all keyed to produce the most persuasive effect possible.

10. *A Forceful Close.* The presentation's close ended as smoothly as it began, and at closing you found yourself strongly committed to the speaker's point of view.

What actually happened to you during this presentation? If you carefully analyzed your feelings and emotions, you would probably find that:

You were quickly drawn into the talk.

You rapidly identified with the speaker.

Rarely did your attention/interest drift.

You never became bored, not even mildly so.

You found yourself "caught-up" in the presentation.

You even felt a bit disappointed that the talk had been completed.

Put a bit differently, as a participant you experienced the three stimuli produced by a successful presentation. You became *involved*, which rapidly led to *enjoyment* and culminated in *commitment*. These key personal feelings that good speakers convey to an audience are based on a time-tested structure of effective public speaking. Let's now examine this framework and discover how quickly you can adapt it to your next talk.

PRESENTATION FRAMEWORK

As an aid for an effective presentation, a four-cycle model, shown in Figure 32, has been prepared. The cycles are closely intertwined and should be thought of as a complete process.

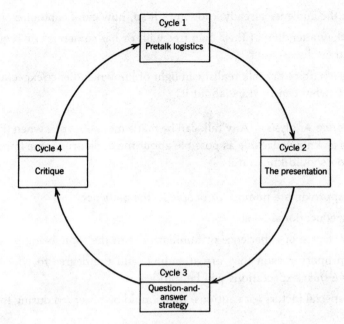

Figure 32. Four-cycle presentation model.

Cycle 1: Pretalk Logistics

All activities referred to in this cycle should be done *prior* to the presentation. A talk should never be attempted until the following points have been considered and appropriate action taken.

Customizing the Talk for the Audience. Any talk, regardless of its length or subject, should always be developed with the benefits to the audience in mind. As you prepare your talk, ask yourself:

What benefit will the audience receive from listening to me?

Specifically, "What's in it for them?"

To what degree can I customize my talk for this purpose?

Does the audience have any major concerns that can be interwoven into my presentation?

Does the audience already know me? If so, how can I capitalize on this?

Are they attending of their own free will, or has someone else requested that they do so?

Is the length of my talk realistic in light of known audience expectations? If not, what can be done about it?

Audience Analysis.   Any talk can be made more effective when the presenter is as knowledgeable as possible about the audience. Some important items you should know are:

The approximate number of people in the audience

Their educational level

Their degree of experience or familiarity with the topic being presented

The primary reason they are attending, and the degree to which they believe their expectations will be fulfilled

Any special factors (or cautions) that should be observed during the talk

Room Environment and Physical Layout.   Both the room layout and environment are critical factors that can either *positively* or *negatively* affect the presentation. You should always review the following points *in advance* of your talk:

Can heat, ventilation, and air-conditioning be easily controlled from within the room?

Will a podium be used? If not, what arrangement should be made?

Who should be contacted if something goes wrong?

Will the person be available during the entire presentation?

Are the room acoustics adequate without electronic amplification, or will a public address system and/or a lavaliere microphone be required?

Is the seating arrangement conductive to the planned talk? If not, can it be changed?

If audio-visual aids are to be used, can the room lighting be easily controlled from the platform? If not, who will do this?

Audio-Visual Logistics   Nothing can ruin an otherwise effective presentation more than a piece of malfunctioning audio-visual equipment. Any speaker planning to use audio-visual equipment would be wise to consider carefully the following:

Where will the equipment come from? (Will it be brought by the instructor, rented from an outside source, or supplied by an off-site facility?)

If brought by the instructor to an outside facility, is the location insured in case of theft? If not, will your own insurance cover it?

Who is preparing the audio-visual aids for the presentation? Can these be checked in advance of the talk?

Can the equipment be operated by the instructor, or is a trained technician required?

Has the proposed audio-visual aid been carefully selected to match the presentation requirements? Consider the following combinations:

Flip Chart

Informal meetings

Small groups (under 50 people)

Not for highly technical information

Flash Cards (poster boards, usually placed on an easel)

Formal or informal meetings

Small groups (under 25 people)

For key idea presentations

Overhead Projector Transparencies

Formal or informal meetings

Small to medium groups (under 75 people)

For detailed information

35mm Slides

Formal or informal meetings

Medium to large audiences

For highly detailed or technical information

Videotape

Generally, formal meetings

Small groups (fewer than 25 people)

Where movement and action are desired

For main-idea presentations

16mm Film

Usually, formal meetings

For both large and small groups

Where professional quality is mandatory

Where continuity of thought and ideas are essential

The Introduction "Kick-Off."   Although covered briefly in Chapter 6, planning for pretalk logistics deserves additional mention when a formal introduction of the speaker is planned.

If you are to be introduced, make sure that you know the content of the speaker's remarks *in advance.* Knowing what he will say allows you to start your talk on a smooth note with a high degree of continuity.

If at all possible, meet your introducer prior to your talk to help reduce your own nervousness and increase your confidence level.

Try to bridge your opening remarks into the introduction. This technique is always effective and gives your talk professional polish. It also ensures initial audience interest and continuity.

To enhance the presentation further, tie your closing remarks back to the original introduction.

Cycle 2: The Presentation

Use of the Ice-Breaker.   The ice-breaker is a good example of the similarity between techniques used by instructors in a formal class and speakers giving formal or informal talks.

The reader should be familiar with the ice-breaker technique from Chapter 6. One additional point should be emphasized here. Always remember to repeat each participant's name as you are introduced to them. It is pleasing to the person you are addressing, and it provides excellent memory reinforcement in case you want to speak with them after the talk is completed.

How to Avoid Anxieties and Relax!   A certain level of *pretalk tension* is quite normal; in fact it's productive since it keeps the speaker keyed-up and alert. There is a fine line, however, between having an acceptable level of tension and allowing anxiety to take over. High anxiety levels can produce stress and become counterproductive.

Seasoned speakers use a variety of relaxation methods. The method I recommend is the following. Just prior to speaking (a few moments before actually speaking):

Place your hands on table, palms down.

Uncross your legs under the table (if applicable).

Avoid focusing your eyes on any one object.

Let your body go completely limp.

Slowly inhale, and hold air in your lungs for several seconds.

Just prior to feeling uncomfortable, *slowly* exhale air.

Wait several seconds, keeping your body limp.

Repeat the procedure several times.

Just before speaking, repeat the procedure one more time.

Don't be discouraged if this procedure appears to be a bit awkward or does not work completely the first time you use it. Keep practicing. It could take at least several attempts, but it will work.

You've made it to the podium without fainting or stumbling over something on the way. You can now console yourself with the fact that the anxiety levels built up prior to the talk will quickly dissolve as you begin speaking. To launch into an effective start, here are a few guidelines to employ just *prior* to the moment of speaking:

Initially "sweep" the room with your eyes, taking in all parameters of the area. From a participant's viewpoint, this gives you a definite air of command, which will heighten audience interest.

Focus on one person in the audience who appears receptive. This immediately gives you a direct visual contact with an individual in the audience and also aids in furthering the group's attention.

Maintain eye contact until you have collected your initial thoughts. This pause should only take a few seconds, and will definitely boost audience interest in what you are about to say.

Begin talking in a measured pace to set the mood of the presentation. *Note*: Be aware that many speakers inadvertently begin talking at too rapid a pace (which is a sign of nervousness). Make every effort not to rush the first few minutes; use of a carefully measured pause during this period is highly effective.

Continue sweeping the parameters of the audience with your eyes, occasionally focusing on one person. Not only does this give you an added sense of presence on the platform but it also builds rapport with the entire audience.

The Introductory Remarks Booster.   During this early segment of the talk, the speaker (if introduced by another) now has the perfect opportunity to significantly boost the effectiveness of the talk. Recall that knowing *in advance* what the presenter will say about you gives you the opportunity to *bridge* our own remarks to that introduction, paving the way for heightened audience interest.

Here is an abbreviated example of an introduction followed by the tie-in comments of the main speaker, along with an example of bridging back to the introduction at the close of the talk.

Introduction: I know all of you had to take time out of your busy schedules to attend this program today. That is why I'm so pleased to introduce Maria Dominique—one of the foremost experts from B.M.I.—who will now demonstrate the latest in word-processing equipment and show how it can turn your secretary into two people—magically!

Maria: Thank you, Linda, for that very impressive introduction! But let me say right off, there's no "magic" about it. With the equipment that will now be demonstrated, an average secretary's productivity should increase by at least 50 to 75 percent.

[and later, when concluding . . .]

Maria: As all of you have now seen, with proper training of your staff, the new B.M.I. Model 700 Series will enable the office work flow to dramatically improve. No waving of a "magic wand" is needed—the increased productivity gains are yours, just for the asking.

Presentation Elements

An effective talk relies on a structure of supporting elements. Figure 33 displays this process in a sequential order, tying in each critical technique to the next. Let's take a closer look and discover how simple it is to develop an effective presentation on any topic of your choosing.

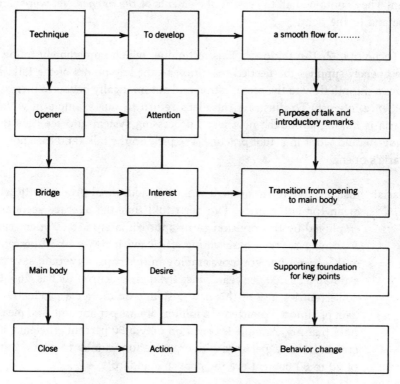

Figure 33.   Presentation elements.

Technique 1: The Opener.   To develop a good opener, a speaker merely develops several sentences designed to spotlight the purpose of the talk and to draw attention from the audience. Elements of the opener should:

Contain an attention-getting statement.

Reinforce and highlight the key point of the talk.

Help establish rapport with the audience.

State a benefit that the audience will readily appreciate.

Create anticipation for the balance of the talk.

Can you think of a good example of this? You are correct if you cited the opening remarks just illustrated—those Maria made after Linda's introduction! They contained all the essential elements of *the opener*, yet were concise and to the point.

Technique 2: The Bridge.   This technique, which immediately follows the opener, supplies the needed *transition* to the key points of the talk. It gives a smooth flow to the presentation and automatically begins to increase audience interest. To illustrate this, let's return to our example in which Maria is talking about the new word-processing system and see how the bridge would work in actual practice. We pick up the talk (and the end) of Maria's opener.

Maria: Just imagine for a moment what this additional productivity will mean for *your* office. I've been told that the average secretary employed by this division earns approximately $16,000 per year. Assuming a very *conservative* efficiency increase of 50 percent, each person that you now employ in this capacity would save an estimated $8,000 per year. Since the division currently has close to 30 secretaries, use of this new system would offer a productivity gain of almost a quarter of a million dollars per annum! And please note that my example is based on only a 50 percent efficiency increase. In our experience with organizations similar to yours, gains of 70 to 80 percent are the proven standard!

In this example, the speaker used the bridging technique to connect the early part of the talk (where attention was created by highlighting possible dollar savings) to the forthcoming main body of the planned presentation. The use of Technique 2 served to heighten audience interest by creating anticipation for the balance of the talk.

At this point, we might wonder if the bridge is needed. Why not go directly from the opener to the main body? Actually, an effective speaker could carefully include elements of the bridging portion of the talk (creating interest) into the final part of the opener. However, doing so saves little if any time; it simply combines two short steps into one longer one. To use a rough analogy, it would be similar to going from first gear directly into third gear on a manual-shift automobile. Certainly that can be done, but very few car manufacturers would recommend it. Moreover, as we shall see a bit later in this chapter, use of the bridge section will make it easier to create a smooth flow throughout the entire talk. That is a goal worth devoting some attention to!

Technique 3: Main Body.   Having completed the *opener* and *bridge*, you are now ready to proceed into the *main body*. Here is where the initial attention and interest developed by the audience is heightened with desire— or the need to know more about what is being said. The main body of the talk can be viewed as the supporting framework for the key points being presented by the speaker. As such, it provides:

A continuing vehicle to support the view being conveyed to the audience

A smooth transition into the "heart" of the talk, supported heavily by pertinent facts, figures, and examples

A clear rationale for the talk itself—by lending support and highlighting the key points being introduced.

Depending upon the particular talk, the *main body* can extend from just a few minutes to an hour or more. Let's go back once more to the presentation on word-processing equipment and "listen in" on an abbreviated segment of the main body.

Maria: In our experience with organizations similar to yours, gains of 70 or 80 percent are the proven standard!

Let's get quite specific now and show how this process would work in your own environment. Prior to this presentation, each department head received a fact sheet on unit cost and amortization numbers. Since this was distributed by your office manager, each sheet had customized cost figures based on requirements by area.

B.M.I.'s customer training headquarters is conveniently located four blocks south of here on Seventh Street. To become proficient in the use of the new word processor, approximately four hours of training is required. Since our facilities can train up to 10 people at one time (either in the morning or afternoon), you can expect to have all 30 secretaries brought up to speed as quickly as possible. The actual time needed, of course, would depend on your own office coverage requirements, but the training could be accomplished in three shifts over one and a half days.

By the time people have received their training at B.M.I., their new system will have been *installed*, *checked out*, and running *perfectly*. To insure maximum efficiency, a trained service representative from our company will be based in your locale for at least one week to handle any questions your people might have.

In case a technical problem should develop with any of our systems, a repair technician will be at your office within one hour of your call.

Technique 4: The Close.   Although it comes at the end of the talk, the close should be considered one of the most important elements of the entire presentation. For it is here that the speaker attempts to achieve commitment from the audience. Put another way, at the conclusion of the talk, depending on the speaker's objectives, the audience should either be:

Informed about a specific event(s)

Made aware of a new situation

Persuaded to do something

Reinforced in a current attitude

In this respect, the close of a talk is very similar to the close in a sales presentation. In both cases, the objective of the speaker is to achieve some type of commitment from the persons being addressed. To accomplish this objective, a simple three-step format is employed, as shown by Figure 34. Let us now look at this figure in closer detail, then relate it to specific examples.

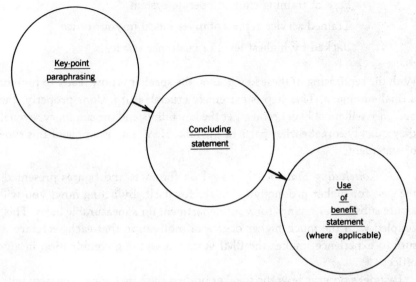

Figure 34. Closing technique.

1. *Key-Point Paraphrasing.*   As an aid to strengthening commitment and thereby gaining audience acceptance of the talk, the speaker should paraphrase, or partially paraphrase, the main elements of the presentation. The emphasis here should be on the *key points* the speaker wants the audience to remember after the talk has been concluded. Wherever possible, the speaker should use audio-visual reinforcement of these key points, such as displaying them on slides, overhead transparencies, or flip charts.

Let's look at an example of effective key point rephrasing. Assume that the speaker has just introduced a new overhead transparency and resumes talking:

> As you can see from the chart, many important benefits can be obtained in converting to the new BMI Model 700. These include:
>
> Measurable increase in work flow
>
> Minimum productivity increase of 50 percent
>
> $250,000 savings per year

Ease of training staff to operate system

Trained service representatives based in your office

Backed by highest level of customer service.

With the rephrasing of these key points, the speaker is now ready to present a final summary. This step is extremely crucial. If it is done properly, the audience will most likely remember the key points and the summary, even if they quickly forget earlier parts of the talk. Here is an example of this type of statement:

2.   *Concluding Statement.*   Based on the facts and figures presented, the case for higher productivity speaks for itself. By acting now, you will assure substantial savings for your department on a measurable basis. This, coupled with the much higher degree of motivation that each secretary is sure to experience, makes the BMI system a winning combination in any office!

Last, let's observe how the speaker bridges the concluding statement with a final benefit statement that smoothly incorporates the action request.

3.   *Benefit Statement.*   With the approval of the office manager, I have placed requisitions for the new system at the back of the room. I will be available at the conclusion of my talk to answer any additional questions you may have on the system. The completed requisition can be returned to your department head for immediate processing.

By taking action now, you can be assured of a minimum 50 percent productivity gain in your particular area. It's probably one of the wisest office investments you will ever make.

Cycle 3: Question-and-Answer Strategy

Every presentation is different from the next. In some, the audience may only ask a few questions. In others, the speaker may have to take a great deal of time to clarify points made during the talk. Every speaker must be prepared by anticipating questions *in advance* of the talk. In addition, the speaker should consider every question as an advantage. Let's examine some points that support this.

1.   Anticipating Questions in Advance

Preplanning involved:

a. List all possible questions that the audience can raise along with the answers.

b. As the talk is being prepared, write questions and answers on index cards or on a presentation planner (which will shortly be explained to you).

c. Thoroughly review each question and answer with an associate or peer prior to the talk.

d. Add additional questions and answers to your list, as required.

At conclusion of the talk:

a. Solicit questions from the audience.

b. If none are forthcoming, either ask a general question to "break the ice," then casually answer it yourself; or with firm eye contact, ask an active listener (as evidenced by their body language during your talk) a question.

Answering questions from the audience:

a. Always rephrase each question asked before answering. Doing so allows everyone in the audience to understand the question, and gives you time to plan your answer.

When you've forgotten what was asked or are not certain of the correct answer:

a. Ask person to "rephrase question" so that "it will be clear to everyone in the audience."

b. Or ask if anyone in the audience would care to answer before you respond.

Note: In either situation, you will gain a few moments to think about the answer. If, however, you simply do not know the answer, never try to fool the audience by avoiding the question. In the end, the effectiveness of your entire talk will surely diminish, and you will be the loser.

2. Considering Every Question

a. Always consider each question an opportunity to strengthen your own presentation.

b. Questions are direct evidence that the audience is involved with your talk.

c. Questions reinforce the speaker's role as a conveyor of information and one who is willing to accept honest feedback.

Cycle 4: Critique

Every talk, no matter how effective, can be used as a vehicle to make the next talk *even better*. A fundamental rule of public speaking is that "practice makes perfect." Everything considered, there is no substitute for repeated presentations in front of groups. The more you speak, the better you become! Ideally, in a formal training class in presentation skills each talk is videotaped, then played back to allow constructive feedback from both the instructor and the other participants. This technique is extremely valuable in that it allows the speakers to "see and hear" their presentations. They can then make plans to correct any deficiencies they observe.

When videotaping is not possible, I strongly recommend practicing in front of a mirror, using a timing device to warn when the planned duration of the talk is over. It is also advisable to tape the talk on a cassette recorder —but be aware that the average recorder will have a certain "drop-off" in voice quality. Finally, when you are satisfied that the planned talk is in reasonably good shape, repeat the talk in front of another person. This is important, since it is very difficult for us to judge ourselves in a completely unbiased manner; we need an independent observer.

When another person is asked to critique your talk, here are some vital areas that they should concentrate on.

Enthusiasm	Use of strong opening
Pacing	Effective closing
Voice projection	Handling questions from audience
Nervousness	Practice using flip chart
Use of visual aids	Positive body language
Distracting mannerisms	Timing of talk
Eye sweep	Paraphrasing of audience questions
Effective pauses	Introducing another speaker

All feedback from the other person—commonly referred to as "the coach"—should encompass both positive and negative aspects of the presentation. These comments then form the base for constructive criticism of the talk immediately after the practice talk has been concluded. When critiquing, the coach should be especially aware of the following areas:

Format

Did you follow the four keys to an effective presentation?

Was the opening really effective?

Did the bridge create interest in your talk?

Did the main body contain the essential points?

Was the closing appropriate?

Body Language

Relaxed posture on platform?

Appropriate facial expressions?

Smile?

Arms or legs folded?

Other?

Audio-Visual Aids

Were the audio-visual aids effective?

Were more needed? If so, what type?

Should they be in a different format?

Were they clearly visible?

Did they reinforce the talk?

Speech

Was the pause used correctly, and with the right timing?

Was the pacing satisfactory? Too fast? Too slow?

Were the tone and pitch appropriate? Enough variation? Proper mood created? Right emphasis on words?

Was the talk articulated properly? Any slurring of words? Each word spoken clearly?

Volume level: Can talk be heard by everyone in room? Any distortion present?

Nervous Gestures

Excessive use of "Umm . . ."?

Toying with pen, pencil, or other item?

Pulling at ear or rubbing face?

Hands jammed in pockets?

Talking constantly to flip chart instead of to audience?

Using the lectern as a crutch?

Having a constant "death grip" on podium?

Other?

PRESENTATION NOTES

A recurring problem for inexperienced speakers is the question of how to organize the format of the talk via a prepared set of notes to be used on the podium. Many speakers experience grave difficulty using notes. Some become "wedded" to their notes when speaking, which is very distracting to the audience. Over the years, I've encountered a wide variety of note-making methods, ranging from fully written out texts on 8½" x 11" paper to scribbling abbreviated notes on paper of every size to index-card summaries —not to mention an endless assortment of notes written on the most unlikely scraps and bits of paper!

One of the most time tested and consistently successful techniques for developing workable notes uses a simple three-step process:

1. Write out the main substance of the speech in paragraph form.

   Our new recruiting strategy will be to seek out and attract college graduates who wish to pursue a career in the banking and finance field. In many cases, these people are completely unaware of both the variety and scope of banking relationships that our company offers to the general public. Our revised strategy, therefore, should be directed into two specific channels. First, we should give all job candidates a clearer explanation of the expanded role that financial services play in today's economy. Second, we should emphasize the corresponding career opportunities that our organization can offer both on a short-range and long-range basis.

2. Next, mark up the paragraph into main points for emphasis and conversational phrases:

   Our new recruiting strategy/will be to seek out and attract college graduates who wish to pursue a career in the banking and finance field. / In many cases, these people are completely unaware / of both the variety and scope of banking relationships that our company offers to the general public./ Our revised strategy,/ therefore, should be directed into two specific channels./ First,/ we should give all job candidates a clearer explanation of the expanded role that financial services play in today's economy. Second,/ we should emphasize the corresponding career opportunities that our organization can offer both on a short-range and long-range basis.

3. As a final step, rewrite the main points into a tight outline. Use sub-headings where appropriate. Emphasize key words or phrases with a highlighter pen:

New Recruiting Strategy

1. Attract college grads interested in financial services
2. Create awareness of our total services
3. Direct revised strategy into two channels
    a. Clearer explanation of services offered
    b. Career opportunities—short and long term

Note the difference between Step 3 and the original draft in Step 1. This method has enabled the speaker to organize notes in a clear, concise manner. Most important, though in abbreviated form, the new format contains the main points and yet is far easier to refer to when speaking. How this new format is incorporated effectively into the talk itself is the subject of the next section.

PRESENTATION PLANNER

Throughout this chapter we have seen the need for a high degree of *pre-planning* prior to the talk. With the four-cycle presentation model behind us, we're now ready to employ a direct aid that will make *any talk* more effective.

To illustrate, let's look at Figure 35, the *Presentation Planner*, which has been specifically designed for this purpose. To facilitate learning, this form
(continued on p. 200)

SECTION ONE: Pretalk Checklist

Date: **Oct. 12, 1985**   Location: **Main conference room**

Title: **New sales management system**   Approximate Length **15-20 minutes**

Cospeakers (if applicable) **—None**

	Done	To Be Completed
Check Appropriate Box		
A. Customizing talk for intended audience		
Inclusion of applicable benefits	✓	
Major concerns/issues addressed	✓	
Audience expectations known in advance		NOT SURE
B. Audience analysis		
Number of people	✓	
Educational/experience level	✓	
Any special cautions to be observed		NOT SURE
C. Room environment and physical layout		
Adequacy of heating/lighting/air conditioning	✓	
Use of podium	✓	
Room acoustics/need for electronic aids	✓	
Conduciveness of seating arrangement	✓	
Lighting controlled by speaker	✓	
D. Audio-visual logistics		
Equipment source	✓	
Preparation of audio-visual aids		✓
Need for operator	✓	
Equipment type geared to requirements	✓	
E. Introduction kick-off		
Meeting beforehand (if possible)		WILL DO
Tying in to introducer's remarks	N/A	
Bridging opening to introduction	N/A	

Figure 35. Presentation planner.

SECTION TWO: Presentation outline

Title of Talk: NEW SALES MANAGEMENT SYSTEM

Key points	Visuals

1. Opener:

   NEED FOR REVISED SYSTEM

   • CURRENT PROCEDURES ANTIQUATED

   • AID TO SALES PRODUCTIVITY

   • WILL SUPPORT NEW STRATEGIC GOALS

   • CAN IMPLEMENT IN NEW FISCAL YEAR

   IMMEDIATE CHALLENGE

   • IMPLEMENT REVISIONS A.S.A.P.

   • HEAVY CUSTOMIZATION REQUIRED

FLIP CHART 1

> DIRECT BENEFITS
> OF A NEW SYSTEM

FLIP CHART 2

> SPECIFIC CHALLENGES
> TO BE FACED

2. Bridge:

   ARE WE UP TO THE TASK?

   • REQUIRE HEAVY INVOLVEMENT
    FROM REGIONAL MANAGERS

   • CURRENT TRAINING DEPARTMENT
    PRIORITIES MUST BE SHIFTED

FLIP CHART 3

> ACTION STEPS
> REQUIRED

Figure 35.   (continued)

195

Title of Talk: <u>NEW SALES MANAGEMENT SYSTEM</u>

Key points	Visuals

3. Main body:

SYSTEM DESIGN ELEMENTS

• MANAGENT STYLE ANALYSIS

• DIVISIONAL MARKETING PLAN

• REGIONAL MARKETING PLANS

• ANNUAL GOAL SETTING

• MONTHLY REVIEW ANALYSIS

• COACHING PROCEDURES

REQUIRES LINE RESOURCES

• APPROXIMATELY 10% OF WORKDAY

FOR 3-WEEK PERIOD

    - TWO REGIONAL MANAGERS

    - MARKET SUPPORT MANAGER

    - TWO FIELD SALESPEOPLE

TRAINING DEPARTMENT RESOURCES

• PROGRAM COORDINATOR TO BE

ASSIGNED FULL TIME

• 1 SPECIALIST IN NEEDS ANALYSIS

AND FORMS DESIGN (FULL TIME)

FLIP CHART 4

REVISED FORMS
TO BE DESIGNED

FLIP CHART 5

BENEFITS OF EACH

FLIP CHART 6

SPECIFIC HELP NEEDED
FROM THE LINE TO
INSURE REALITY

FLIP CHART 7

COMMITMENT FROM
TRAINING DEPARTMENT

Figure 35. (continued)

196

Title of Talk: __NEW SALES MANAGEMENT SYSTEM__

Key points	Visuals

4. Close:

ACTION STEPS REQUIRED

- SELECT LINE RESOURCES
- IDENTIFY TRAINING SUPPORT
- ESTABLISH PROGRAM MILESTONES
- DEVELOP PROJECT BUDGET
- SELECT PROJECT MANAGER

FLIP CHART 8

LISTING OF STEPS
TO GET STARTED

SUMMARY

- BENEFITS OF NEW SYSTEM
- NEED FOR CHANGE
- COMMITMENT TO PLAN
- CONSENSUS NOW REQUIRED

FLIP CHART 9

RECAP OF NEW SYSTEM
BENEFITS AND NEXT
STEP REQUIRED

Figure 35. (continued)

197

SECTION THREE: Question-and-Answer Strategy

Title of Talk: ___NEW SALES MANAGEMENT SYSTEM___

Anticipated Questions	Response (with primary benefit, if applicable)
1. WHY THE URGENCY?	ONCE APPROVED, NEW PROGRAM WILL TAKE 4-6 MONTHS TO DEVELOP/IMPLEMENT. NOT AN "OVERNIGHT" PROCESS.
2. LINE MANAGERS MAY NOT HAVE ENOUGH TIME TO DEVOTE TO PROJECT	SPECIAL SCHEDULES WILL BE ESTABLISHED TO WORK AROUND PEAK PERIODS — DONE AT THEIR CONVENIENCE
3. HOW ABOUT COST?	ENTIRE PROJECT TO BE DONE "IN HOUSE." WILL SAVE APROXIMATELY 50% OF NORMAL COST VIA THIS METHOD
4. WILL NEW SYSTEM BE "REAL-WORLD" OR JUST ANOTHER PROGRAM?	VERY "REAL-WORLD" THROUGH HEAVY CUSTOMIZATION OF FORMS/PROCEDURES AND CONTINUING INPUT FROM LINE MANAGEMENT
5.	

Figure 35.   (continued)

198

SECTION FOUR: Critique   Date: _10/12/85_

Title of Talk: _NEW SALES MANAGEMENT SYSTEM_

	Good	Needs Improvement
Format Effective opening		
Bridge		
Main body		
Strong close		
Dynamics Sincerity		
Presence		
Enthusiasm		
Persuasiveness		
Maintain audience interest		
Eyes Maintain contact		
Occasional sweep		
Periodic fixed gaze		
Mannerisms Distracting gestures		
Nervousness		
Voice modulation		
Pacing		
Tone		
Voice projection		
Suggestions:		

Figure 35. (continued)

has been completely filled out as a speaker would do in actual practice. Note that the *Presentation Planner* is divided into four sections:

Section 1: Pretalk Checklist

The standard heading on top of the form shows that the title of the talk was "The New Sales Management System," to be given on October 12. The presentation would last approximately 15 to 20 minutes and be held in the main conference room. No cospeakers would be present.

A quick glance also discloses the following:

The major concerns of the audience would be addressed in the talk, but their expectations were unclear; hence, further exploration is needed *prior* to the talk.

Audience analysis had been done, but it was uncertain what special cautions (if any) were to be observed—another area to look into.

The room environment and physical layout had been checked, and all was in order. At least the speaker could be guaranteed that there would be no "hidden surprises" here—a comforting thought, both *before* and *during* the talk!

Audio-visual logistics appear to be in order. However, the preparation of aids (slides, flip charts, and so on) remains to be done.

The speaker has mentally prepared himself to meet the participants beforehand during the introduction "kick-off." He knew that no formal introduction was planned and was able to develop an alternative strategy to open the talk.

Section 2: Presentation Outline

Note that this section facilitates organizing the talk into the *key points* with a corresponding *visuals* column. The key points column contains:

Separate headings for *opener*, *bridge*, *main body*, and *close*. (These techniques were already reviewed earlier in the chapter.)

Sufficient space under each heading to organize material in a tight outline (as described in the section on presentation notes earlier in the chapter.)

Under the visuals column, space is furnished to draw a rough sketch of desired visuals. In the case illustrated, the speaker was able to identify and visualize the supporting flip charts to accompany each of the separate headings involved.

A closer glance at Section 2 shows that the use of the form has enabled the speaker to place the entire talk into a well-designed framework, which will greatly enhance its effectiveness. It's a simple, easy-to-use section with proven results. Most important, once used, the results will speak for themselves.

Section 3: Question-and-Answer Strategy

Here we find a special section for writing in anticipated audience questions together with an appropriate response. Note, as illustrated, that the speaker has thought about four possible questions that could be raised and was able to develop appropriate responses *prior* to the talk. While this never guarantees a flawless question-and-answer session, it places the speaker in a very secure position and is well worth the few minutes of preparation required.

Section 4: Critique

Whether this section is used as a self-analysis tool by the speaker (immediately following the talk), or is completed by a "coach," it provides two important benefits. First, it will focus attention on vital components of the talk—where it was good and where improvement is needed. Second, it supplies an ideal basis for taking corrective action before the *next* talk, enabling the speaker to eliminate serious mistakes.

In summary, the use of the *Presentation Planner* offers a wide array of benefits to speakers. Just a few of its advantages are:

1. It takes into account all facets of the preplanning process.
2. It provides a uniform flow of thought through the four keys to an effective presentation—opener, bridge, main body, and close.
3. It facilitates all phases of pretalk planning in an organized, sequential manner.
4. It allows speakers to identify where each segment of audio-visual support will coincide with the text.

5. It provides sufficient space for a thoroughly planned question-and-answer strategy.

6. With its uniform size, it does away forever with "bits and scraps of paper" that contain unrelated assortments of presentation notes.

7. It prepares the speaker for questions that might be raised by the audience.

8. It provides a built-in critique system to increase the effectiveness of future talks.

AUDIO-VISUAL AIDS

No chapter on successful public speaking could be considered complete without some reference to the types of audio-visual aids available to speakers. While we touched on this in matching audio-visual aids to meeting requirements, it is appropriate now to address the subject in more specific terms. The following is an analysis of the most common types of audio-visual aids, with some pointers on their use.

Overhead Projector

One of the most readily available and worthwhile presentation tools, the overhead projector is used primarily with two types of transparencies:

1. Prepared transparencies, either drawn in advance by the presenter or prepared commercially

2. "Do-it-yourself" transparencies, prepared by writing either on a supplied acetate roll attached to the machine or on blank acetate sheets (done during presentation)

Advantages

Equipment is very simple to operate and usually highly reliable.

Speaker is freed from use of prepared notes.

Content can be easily changed or modified.

Room lights do not have to be dimmed.

Transparencies can be easily created.

Disadvantages

Projector can be bulky to carry.

Transparencies can be difficult to carry or store.

Slides

Like the overhead projector system, slides are generally inexpensive and allow a high degree of flexibility.

Advantages

Slides can be used with a variety of slide projectors.

Their small size makes slides easy to store.

Slides are easy to transport or mail.

Speaker does not need prepared notes.

Content can be easily changed or modified.

Slides can be converted to videotape if desired.

Disadvantages

Slides wear out with continued use.

There's a temptation to "cram" too much information on each slide.

Periodic cleaning is required.

Audio supplement may be needed to increase effectiveness.

16mm Film

One of the original "workhorses" in presentation techniques, film is used for a wide variety of visual effects.

Advantages

Film provides a high degree of realism.

Done properly, it offers both continuity and clear expression of thoughts and ideas.

Film generally creates high audience interest.

Films can be produced either "in house" or professionally.

If desired, 16mm films can be converted to videotape.

Disadvantages

It is often difficult to produce films "in house."

Customized outside productions can be expensive.

Films can become outdated quickly.

A 16mm projector must always be available.

Film can deteriorate rapidly (become brittle) when not stored properly.

Film is somewhat bulky to transport.

Audio Recordings

Available in either reel-to-reel or cassette format, audio recordings have remained a long-time favorite with presenters who require audio-visual support on a limited budget.

Advantages

Generally easy to operate

Usually trouble-free

Can be produced "in-house" or purchased commercially

Easily transported to different locations

Can be mailed inexpensively when necessary

Disadvantages

Usually require some reinforcement from speaker

Rely solely on auditory experience

Must be carefully positioned to avoid boredom

Videotape

This medium has become increasingly popular during the past few years—especially in view of the fact that many people have already become accustomed to videotapes at home.

Advantages

Very flexible

Easily transported

Combines visual and auditory experience

Can be produced "in-house"

Available in either black-and-white or color

Darkened room not necessary

Disadvantages

Requires video playback equipment

Expensive if not produced in-house

Can easily become outdated

Usually requires advance presentation

Since each of these audio-visual aids carry their own set of unique advantages and disadvantages, the prudent speaker carefully chooses the most appropriate. Never choose a medium because "everyone else uses it." Rather, select one that will satisfy your particular requirements at that moment. Finally, always be highly flexible when choosing a medium to supplement a presentation. What may have proven ideal for a talk last week could be grossly inappropriate for a talk planned two weeks from now!

VIDEO PRESENTATION GUIDELINES

Sooner or later, you may be asked to make a presentation in front of a video camera. While it's perhaps not as certain as "death and taxes," you should nevertheless be prepared for the eventuality.

When making a professional presentation in front of a "live" camera, you will gain confidence if you look and feel your best. Here are some general guidelines to follow before actually going on camera.

1. Always eat lightly and sensibly before the presentation; avoid heavy or fatty foods. Food and beverages are usually not allowed on the set. When sessions run over one or two hours, light refreshments are generally provided off the set. In any case, check these details beforehand.

2. Go through at least one dress rehearsal with your staff even if the set is not yet available. Remember to avoid the hot lights until the director is ready to place you on the set.

3. Try to get a good night's sleep the night before. If possible, get a reasonable degree of exercise the day before; it will leave you mentally and physically relaxed for your presentation.

4. While waiting to go before the camera, use the deep-breathing exercise. It's quite normal for people to be a bit anxious in the beginning, but these unsettling feelings will quickly dissipate within the first few minutes on camera.

5. For professional productions, special effects and makeup arrangements may be required; the producer will instruct you on this beforehand.

6. If you have a special situation that concerns you (for example, overweight, skin problems, or baldness), request the director's or producer's advice beforehand. Most of these conditions can be rectified by makeup, special lighting, and dress.

   a. For the men: Avoid light-colored clothing; wearing a medium-dark solid-color gray, blue, or brown suit. Generally, a blue shirt and conservative tie is a safe combination. If you will be on camera in the late afternoon or evening, bring your razor with you. You also may wish to bring a fresh shirt and tie.

   b. For the women: Avoid a very casual look on camera. Wear a medium-dark, solid-color fitted dress. An alternate could be a tailored suit with an appropriate light-colored blouse. Do not wear shoes with very high heels. Avoid very shiny or "flashy" jewelry in front of the camera. The director or producer will advise you on makeup requirements.

In closing this chapter, let's go back for a moment and consider some general guidelines that should be adhered to before any presentation. Carefully adhering to these simple rules will consistently aid in delivering a better presentation—any time, any place.

1. Always prepare your talk in advance, using the *Presentation Planner*.

2. Choose your visual support aids very carefully. Make certain that they are appropriate.

3. Prepare all flip charts in advance.

4. Check all equipment personally, prior to speaking.

5. Always rehearse your talk in advance.

6. Check the room facilities prior to your talk.

7. Use the relaxation technique outlined in this chapter.

8. Remember to talk in a conversational tone.

9. Always be prepared for questions following your talk.

10. Never forget that "practice makes perfect." Today's mistakes on the platform will be quickly forgotten when you make a better presentation tomorrow!

You are now well on your way to more effective presentations, whether in front of a group of two or two hundred.

SUMMARY

1. An effective platform instructor should also be a highly proficient public speaker. The two skills are closely related.

2. Successful public speakers generally exhibit the following observable traits: a high presence, use of an attention-getting opening, effective eye contact, a high level of sincerity, a natural persuasiveness, genuine enthusiasm, no visible nervousness, controlled voice level, effective use of nonverbal gestures, and a forceful close.

3. The four-cycle model supporting the presentation framework consists of: (1) pretalk logistics, (2) the presentation, (3) question-and-answer strategy, and (4) critique.

4. Within Cycle 2, the presentation, four key elements must be followed in sequential order: opener, bridge, main body, and close.

5. The close for an effective talk is usually very similar to the close for a sales presentation. In both cases, the objective of the presenter is to gain some type of commitment from the persons being addressed. An effective closing includes key-point paraphrasing, a concluding statement, and the use of a benefit statement (where applicable).

6. Use of the *Presentation Planner* helps the speaker plan an entire talk. It starts with a pretalk checklist and concludes with a formal critique of the presentation.

7.   Wherever possible, audio-visual aids should be used to heighten audience interest and provide a smoother flow of information from the speaker.

8.   An effective format for prepared notes centers upon a three-step procedure: (1) write out main substance of the speech in paragraph form; (2) mark up the paragraphs into main points for emphasis and conversational phrases, and (3) rewrite the main points into a tight outline, using subheadings where appropriate.

CHAPTER QUESTIONS

1.   The use of a *Presentation Planner* has been recommended as a direct aid to a more effective talk. Can you think of any situation where a speaker could follow its outline closely, yet deliver a mediocre talk?

2.   Can a speaker even be *overprepared* for a talk? List at least two of the potential pitfalls of overpreparation.

3.   If a male speaker were to give a talk to an all-female audience (or vice versa), what, if any, additional considerations should be given to the preparation?

4.   Finally, in your opinion, are there still a few people who will *never* be able to deliver a reasonably good talk, despite both training and continued practice?

CHAPTER EXERCISE

1.   Prior to your next talk, try to develop your skills to a higher level by using all of the effective presentation skills outlined in this chapter.

2.   Plan all phases of your forthcoming talk through the use of the *Presentation Planner*. A blank form (Figure 36) is included for this purpose.

3.   If at all possible, have an associate review the *Presentation Planner* beforehand, then assist you in the critique afterwards.

4.   If nothing else, remember the three "survival rules" behind every successful talk: *rehearse, rehearse,* then *rehearse* one more time.

THE NEXT STEP

A truly successful instructor is one who (among many other skills) is proficient at administering a variety of games in the classroom.

Games can be fun, support a learning principle, and at the same time,

(continued on p. 215)

SECTION ONE: Pretalk Checklist

Date: _____   Location: _____

Title: _____   Approximate Length _____

Cospeakers (if applicable) _____

Check Appropriate Box

	Done	To Be Completed
A. Customizing talk for intended audience		
Inclusion of applicable benefits		
Major concerns/issues addressed		
Audience expectations known in advance		
B. Audience analysis		
Number of people		
Educational/experience level		
Any special cautions to be observed		
C. Room environment and physical layout		
Adequacy of heating/lighting/air conditioning		
Use of podium		
Room acoustics/need for electronic aids		
Conduciveness of seating arrangement		
Lighting controlled by speaker		
D. Audio-visual logistics		
Equipment source		
Preparation of audio-visual aids		
Need for operator		
Equipment type geared to requirements		
E. Introduction kick-off		
Meeting beforehand (if possible)		
Tying in to introducer's remarks		
Bridging opening to introduction		

Figure 36.   Presentation planner (blank).

SECTION TWO: Presentation outline

Title of Talk: _____

Key points	Visuals

1. Opener:

_____

_____

_____

_____

_____

_____

_____

2. Bridge:

_____

_____

_____

_____

_____

Figure 36. (continued)

Title of Talk: _____

Key points	Visuals

3. Main body:

_____

_____

_____

_____

_____

_____

_____

_____

_____

_____

_____

_____

_____

Figure 36. (continued)

Title of Talk: _____

Key points	Visuals

4. Close:

_____

_____

_____

_____

_____

_____

_____

_____

_____

_____

_____

_____

_____

Figure 36. (continued)

212

SECTION THREE: Question-and-Answer Strategy

Title of Talk: _____

	Anticipated Questions	Response (with primary benefit, if applicable)
1.		
2.		
3.		
4.		
5.		

Figure 36.   (continued)

Date: _____

Title of Talk: _____

	Good	Needs Improvement
Format Effective opening		
Bridge		
Main body		
Strong close		
Dynamics Sincerity		
Presence		
Enthusiasm		
Persuasiveness		
Maintain audience interest		
Eyes Maintain contact		
Occasional sweep		
Periodic fixed gaze		
Mannerisms Distracting gestures		
Nervousness		
Voice modulation		
Pacing		
Tone		
Voice projection		

Suggestions:

_____

_____

Figure 36. (continued)

provide needed relief to an otherwise tedious classroom experience. Improperly used, however, games can inadvertently prove threatening, harmful to the participant, and a definite detriment to learning.

The next chapter will address this delicate, yet vital issue, and highlight four classroom games that have proved superior over the years.

Let's see how games, while fun, are really an extension of the serious business of learning.

8

CLASSROOM GAMES
THAT WORK

LEARNING OBJECTIVES

After finishing this chapter, you should have the necessary skills to:

Define a classroom game and its relationship to the learning process.

Distinguish between a game and experiential exercises.

Describe the basic characteristics of games and the corresponding cautions in their use.

Utilize the four games described in the chapter within a classroom setting.

BACKGROUND

It was fairly late in the afternoon and participant fatigue was beginning to appear throughout the class. Despite this early-warning signal, the instructor, Jan Larkin, continued to be pleased.

Certainly the day had been long and rather tedious, but much worthwhile learning had taken place. It was day 3 of the two-week basic management course, and all of the 15 participants were making excellent progress. She knew from experience that today's session on goal setting was the most difficult for most students to grasp, yet each person in the room appeared to be doing well.

It was 4:00 P.M., with an hour remaining until the class terminated for the day. All that remained on the teaching schedule was a goal-setting game, a reinforcement of basic principles, then a summary "wrap-up."

The game was simple enough, and Jan had successfully used it at least a dozen times over the past two years. Basically, its purpose was to illustrate that in goal-setting, one had to be specific, clear, and understandable when transmitting goals to another. To accomplish this, the instructor planned two scenarios.

Scenario 1. She would:

Call for a volunteer and have him or her leave room.

Place a wastepaper basket and three soft balls in front of room.

Place a chalk mark approximately five feet in front of basket.

Ask a class member to count the number of "baskets" the volunteer made within two minutes.

When the volunteer was called back into the room, he or she would be purposely given vague instructions as to what had to be accomplished. No time limits would be given, nor would any other guidelines be specified. The instructor, even when called on for clarification, was to remain silent and offer no guidance.

Scenario 2:

At the conclusion of the first scenario, a count would be tallied of the number of successful baskets made.

The instructor would then reinforce the principles of effective goal setting, and call for another volunteer.

This new volunteer would be carefully coached in all aspects of the game, and given heavy encouragement throughout the two-minute basket exercise.

The results, of course, would surely point to a more successful goal-setting exercise during the second scenario, which would reinforce the goal-setting principles in a very natural way to the participants.

Nothing could be simpler. It was a perfect way to dramatize goal-setting. Do you agree? Then read on.

After a brief introduction to the goal-setting game, Jan Larkin decided to change the rules slightly for Scenario 1. Instead of calling for a volunteer, she decided to call on Jim Gleason for the task. It seemed appropriate enough. After all, throughout the entire afternoon, Jim seemed to alternate between looking bored and noisily talking to the participant next to him.

Although he appeared a bit surprised to be selected for the "volunteer," Jim completely played out his part during Scenario 1. Jan didn't notice that he remained sullen and silent for the balance of the afternoon. When the class ended at 5:00 P.M., Jim lingered until he and Jan were the only ones left in the classroom. Within a few moments the following conversation took place:

Jim: Well, I hope you're satisfied. Just wanted to inform you that I am officially dropping out of this class tonight. I'll explain everything to my supervisor tomorrow morning.

Jan: Hey, wait a minute! Did you say "dropping out"? Why in heaven's name do you want to do that?

Jim: C'mon, be honest. Do you honestly think that I'm *so* stupid? You've made the point quite clear!

Jan: Look Jim, if this is supposed to be a game on your part, I don't think it's very funny.

Jim: This is no game now. You've already done the damage by the *earlier game* that you played with me. Personally, I'm surprised. I've always heard that you were a pretty good instructor. But to do this . . .

Jan: (*angrily*) Do what? Or do you like keeping people confused?

Jim: Oh no! I'll be specific, clear, and understandable, just as you taught us. The reason I'm quitting your class is that it was obvious you called on me since I *appeared* bored to you, and you didn't like it. You got your revenge by attempting to make a fool of me in front of my friends.

Jan: (*very angrily*) And you're not making a fool of yourself right now?

Jim: No, you are. Goodbye.

While this example may seem a bit harsh to some readers, rest assured that an outcome like this can *easily* happen if a game is not properly conducted by the instructor. This is not to suggest that games should *never* be attempted due to the inherent dangers involved. Far from it. Games have a definite place in class and should be used every time the setting is appropriate. Let's take a closer look at the entire subject of classroom games.

INTRODUCTION

By definition, a game is *a contest governed by a set of rules, entered for amusement, as a test of physical or mental prowess*. While this explanation is quite adequate from a broad viewpoint, it requires some refining when used in a learning situation.

To set the stage properly, it's important to place games in proper perspective for use in a classroom. Primarily, the *use* of a game should be centered on its value to enhance the learning process in a given situation, at a given time. Games should never be viewed as substitutes for program content, but rather as vehicles for *reinforcing* the principles of the skill being taught. Going a bit deeper, games should never be confused with other experiential exercises such as role plays, or small-group assignments. While a fine line of distinction is involved, a true experiential exercise is primarily designed to provide an opportunity for practice, thereby reinforcing the implementation of a skill or solution. A true simulation or experiential exercise will generally require more planning, be more complex, and call for greater care in implementation and follow-up than a game will.

A good example of the distinction involved could be made by comparing the *process* of behavior modeling via the role playing with the use of a game to support this process. Let's take the case of a five-day supervisory training program specifically designed around behavior modeling. For each of the modules presented in the program (such as communication, goal setting, and decision making/problem solving), the following six-step scenario would be implemented.

Step 1: Instructor discusses importance of the skill in relation to effective supervisory practice.

Step 2: Instructor then "bridges" or translates the principles and skill involved to the world of the participants, emphasizing its importance to their job.

STEP 3: Positive role model is then demonstrated, usually by videotape, film, or a sound-slide presentation, showing the correct steps for a supervisor to employ when faced with a certain situation.

STEP 4: Instructor encourages class feedback to insure understanding of the model and its relevance to the work environment.

STEP 5: Positive model just displayed is reinforced via a case study, usually followed by a role play in which participants would actually practice the skills.

STEP 6: Instructor the leads the class in a feedback session, exploring feelings, possible concerns, and use of the skill back on the job. The instructor would then give a summary, usually ending with a final reinforcement of the steps involved in carrying out the skill back on the job.

The above six steps in the behavior modeling *process* are designed as a self-contained system for increased skill proficiency in a given area. By contrast, a suitable game introduced into this six-step process would well provide an effective supporting vehicle to *reinforce* the skill being taught. This distinction may be viewed as a bit fine for some, but nevertheless it is quite important for every instructor to fully grasp.

With this distinction behind us, let's spend a few moments exploring games a bit further in detail.

GAME FEATURES

While every game employed in a classroom will be different from the next, each one generally contains certain basic characteristics that distinguish it from other, more intensive elements of the learning process.

A really effective game *involves the participants* either physically, mentally, or both. It appeals to their competitive instinct and brings people together in a highly synergistic manner.

Games can provide a needed *change of pace* from the tedium of a long classroom day—especially if the session is intensive or highly complex learning is involved.

Games are very *cost effective*. Generally, a game costs no more than a few cents to several dollars to create. It's a learning device that's truly inexpensive and highly effective in the classroom!

Games offer a high degree of *flexibility*. They can usually be modified or adapted to fit specific learning situations and provide a good reinforcer to the learning principle being transmitted.

Unlike a true experiential exercise, games are *easy to conduct*. They usually do not require a great deal of preparation and are relatively simple to introduce.

Participants *like* games. Probably the most important characteristic of all, in contrast to role plays or formal presentations by teams, games are generally viewed as nonthreatening, hence are well accepted by the class. The mere connotation of the word *game* will usually conjure up a mixture of excitement and fun to most students.

Games are an *excellent instructor aid*. Instructors, like participants, also need an occasional change of pace, and a properly placed game will do exactly that. Further, in many games the instructor plays a passive role throughout, merely summarizing at the end of the game the group insights and correlating them with the learning principles that surfaced.

GAME CAUTIONS

As with all other facets within the classroom learning experience, improper use of games can create both a threatening and dangerous *demotivating* situation for participants, as our earlier example illustrated. Let's spend a moment reviewing some important cautions to observe in the use of games.

1. Although games are usually easy to conduct, they must be guided by one who is experienced in their use. In other words, their sheer simplicity in implementation should *never* be interpreted as meaning that "anyone can conduct them." Even the most experienced instructors would want to observe a game being conducted by another before attempting to do it alone.

2. Games should *never* be used as a pleasant "time-killer" when there is looseness in the agenda for a given day. Every game has an intended purpose and should be introduced to a group within an appropriate

sequence of the learning cycle. To deviate from this cardinal rule is unprofessional and certainly unproductive, from both the instructor *and* student's point of view. *Never* fall into this trap!

3. Each game should have a specific learning objective and provide an easy transition from the game playing to a valid learning principle. In other words, they should provide a natural reinforcement to a broader simulation or experiential exercise being conducted.

4. Finally, an overriding caution of any game is that it should *never* be threatening to a participant, or even inadvertently prove a source of embarrassment to an individual. To demean a person in front of others can only lead to a total failure of the game's objectives. Worse yet, it could also undermine the overall program effectiveness—a condition to be avoided at all costs.

FOUR CLASSROOM GAMES THAT WORK

Every instructor with several years of platform experience has a personal collection of favorite games. These are usually ones that have proved effective over time, are generally trouble-free, and are well liked by participants. The balance of this chapter will highlight four of my own favorites, and I encourage other instructors to review them and implement them in their own programs where feasible.

A final note before proceeding: the four games being illustrated have been around for many years now, and I claim no original ownership of them. Each continues to serve a valid purpose in the classroom, and I wish to express gratitude to those who contributed to their development. As we shall now see, however, it's not only the mechanics of the game that makes it effective—but also the degree of "fine-tuning" woven in by the instructor.

The Communication Game: One-Way versus Two-Way Communication

Purpose. To have participants experience the difficulty—and corresponding frustration—in attempting to communicate on a *one-way* basis with no feedback, then experience a two-way communication and be able to compare the differences.

Background. This is an excellent game for several reasons. First, it generally provides a welcome change of pace during a classroom module on effective communication. Not only is it truly fun, but it also allows participants to experience the benefits of employing two-way communication wherever possible.

Materials Required:

Two flip charts
Communication Diagram 1 (Figure 37)
Communication Diagram 2 (Figure 38)
3½" X 11" pads (one per participant)

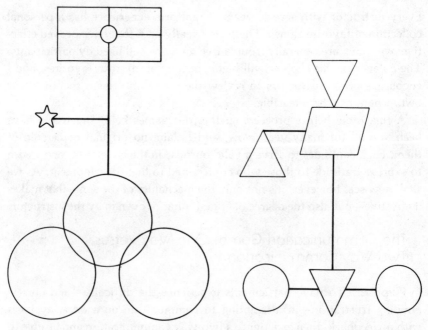

Figure 37. Communication diagram one.

Figure 38. Communication diagram two.

Time Required

Explanation of Game 1	3 minutes
Game 1 play	5 minutes
Class feedback	5 minutes
Explanation of Game 2	3 minutes
Game 2 play	7 minutes
Class feedback	5 minutes
Summary	5 minutes
Total time (approximate)	33 minutes

Procedure. This game should be positioned immediately after a review of the communication cycle. (Note: A detailed explanation of the cycle and its components is described in Figure 11, Chapter 3.)

STEP 1: Instructor checks for class understanding of one-way versus two-way communication. Participants are then challenged to experience both types of communication for themselves.

STEP 2: Each participant is told to place his or her chair back to back with the person sitting to the left (or right) of them. *Note:* If there is an odd number of participants in the room, the facilitator can team up with the last participant. Rules of the game are explained as follows:

1. You will be given five minutes for the exercise.
2. One person in the team will act as receiver of a message; the other, as sender.
3. Sender's task is to describe the drawing verbally to the receiver, who will draw it based on the sender's description.
4. However, the receivers are not allowed to ask any questions. They must try to reproduce the drawing as best they can, but they *cannot* ask for clarification.

STEP 3: Instructor circulates around room distributing Figure 37 to each designated sender. Once all senders have their copy of the drawing, class is told to begin.

STEP 4: Game is stopped after five minutes, and the senders are allowed to view drawings made by their partners.

BONUS STEP (optional): Have class take a vote on which drawing most faithfully recreates the original. A small prize can then be awarded to both the sender and receiver. (Note: The instructor should be prepared to arbitrate some fierce competition, but should always remain neutral, letting the class vote on the winning team.)

STEP 5: Using two side-by-side flip charts, post the following headings:

Chart 1: Receiver feelings

Chart 2: Sender feelings

Now, the instructor randomly asks participants to express how they felt during the game. Responses will naturally vary from class to class, but generally, feedback will be:

Receiver

Frustrating experience

Was "in the dark" most of the time

Very confusing

Didn't really feel in control of situation

Seemed like an impossible task

Was uneasy due to lack of direction

Sender

Wanted to help my partner more, but couldn't

Difficult to transmit information this way

High frustration level throughout the time allowed

Almost impossible to control the situation

High anxiety on my part

STEP 6: Instructor notes similarities in responses expressed by *both* senders and receivers. This paves the way nicely for a contrast between *one-* and *two-way* communication. It should be pointed out here that since one-way communication does not have the built-in advantage of *feedback*--which is what distinguishes it from two-way communication—the following guidelines must be carefully observed during the one-way process:

Plan for the communication.

Be as *clear* as possible.

Be *concise* at all times.

This leads into a natural teaching bridge to illustrate that in many cases one-way communication *must* be used. Probing the class for examples, the instructor should be able to bring out several illustrations such as sending a telex message, memo. or letter, or making an announcement over a public address system.

STEP 7: The stage is now set to have the class experience the direct contrast between one-way communication (as in the first game) and two-way communication. The procedure is exactly the same as in Game 1 with the following exceptions:

Receivers and senders switch roles. Those who were receivers during Game 1, now become senders, and vice versa.

Participants are now given seven minutes, two minutes for *planning* and five minutes to complete the game (using Figure 38).

Active feedback is now encouraged. Both senders and receivers can ask as many questions as they like—without, of course, looking at what is being drawn!

STEP 8: Game is stopped after seven minutes and participants are allowed to see the drawing made by their partner. (Note: the optional bonus step used in the first game may also be used here.)

STEP 9: Instructor again records feelings of both senders and receivers. In *most* (but not all) cases senders and receivers will have experienced a higher comfort level during the second game, and the drawings will usually be a closer replication of the original.

Class Discussion Questions

1. What were the main differences in feelings between Game 1 and Game 2? Why?

2. In some cases there was a lingering feeling of discomfort during Game 2, even though active feedback was taking place. Why?

3. During the second game how many teams used the first two minutes to effectively *plan* for the communication? How many merely used those extra two minutes to "jump right into the game"? (Instructors: Don't be surprised if the *majority* of the class did *not* use the extra time for planning!)

Cautions

1. During Game 1, watch for receivers who inadvertently begin asking questions of the sender. Remember, this is not allowed!

2. Be firm in calling time when each game is over. No exceptions should be made.

3. Some participants may experience very high frustration levels during either or both games. Never let the situation reach the point where the person stops the activity. Some discrete encouragement may be necessary at times.

4. Most important of all, you should realize that *some participants may feel better after Game 1 instead of Game 2*. This is a normal reaction for "high achievers" who do relatively well in the first scenario, then develop very high expectations for the second game.

The Listening Game

Purpose. To have participants experience the difficulty involved in effectively listening and responding to another person when emotions and feelings are involved.

Background. This game can provide a powerful learning experience in a classroom module devoted to effective communication or listening techniques. Its primary purpose is to display vividly how emotions, once stirred up, can thwart an individual's thought process, leading to increased frustration and bias rather than well-thought-out logic. Since the game will deal with participant emotions, which can turn rather volatile, it should be undertaken only by an *experienced* instructor, with participants being at least 18 years old.

Materials required:

One flip chart

8¹/₂″ × 11″ pads (one per participant)

Time Required	
Explanation of game	3 minutes
Team assignments/instructions	2 minutes
Team strategy planning	10 minutes
Round 1	10 minutes
Observer critique	3 minutes
Round 2	10 minutes
Observer critique	3 minutes
Round 3	10 minutes
Observer critique	3 minutes
Summary	6 minutes
Total time (approximate)	60 minutes

Procedure.   The game should immediately follow a teaching segment on effective listening techniques. The principles of good listening, such as maintaining eye contact, mentally staying ahead of the speaker, and occasionally paraphrasing or partially paraphrasing the other person's remarks, should have been heavily stressed during this segment.

STEP 1: Assuming there are at least 10 people in the class, the instructor probes the group for several *highly controversial* subjects of their choice and posts each one on the flip chart. Topics might include:

Should we have fought in Vietnam?

Does a woman have a right to abortion?

Should the death penalty be *mandatory* in certain cases?

Is premarital sex acceptable?

Is religion now becoming outdated?

Communism—pro or con?

Should we really get involved in South America?

Do police have the right to kill?

Should marijuana be legalized?

STEP 2: The instructor divides the class into three teams, assigning a topic to each team. The timing of each debate which has been predrawn on the flip chart, is reviewed. Each team is then given the following ground rules:

1. Within the 10 minutes allotted for each debate, the team leader (selected by the group) must make certain that everyone on the team has a chance to speak.

2. For each round, one team will debate the pros of the topic, the second team will take the opposite point of view, and the third team will act as observers for the other two teams.

3. At the conclusion of each round, the teams will rotate roles.

4. *The cardinal rule is that before responding, the debators must paraphrase or partially paraphrase the preceding person's remarks.*

5. The observer team will record how many violations each team has incurred during each debate. The winning team will be the one with the *least* number of violations during the two rounds in which they actively debate.

Note: After starting Round 1, the instructor does not play an active role, but merely acts as a facilitator—or arbitrator where necessary.

Class Discussion Questions

1. How easy (or difficult) was it to listen effectively to another person when emotions were involved? Why?

2. What were the advantages in employing the paraphrasing technique when communicating with another person?

3. What are the dangers involved in attempting to get a point across to another person when feelings are running very high?

4. What can we learn from this experience?

Cautions

1. This game should *never* be attempted by a novice instructor. Although it brings out many good learning points, the game could "backfire" if not handled properly, producing negative results with correspondingly high frustration levels.

2. When soliciting topics for the team debates, the instructor must remain highly sensitive to individual feelings on volatile topics. The game must be carefully positioned (and the learning principles strongly reinforced) so that participants are firmly aware that the purpose of the topics is merely to show how sensitive issues create a degree of emotional involvement that affects one's listening ability and *not* to judge the final merits of any one topic.

3. The final summary by the instructor (after the three debates have been completed) is a key element in the overall success achieved by the game. No one should leave the game with hurt or bruised feelings. Instead, the participants should have experienced an encounter with emotions and their impact on effective listening techniques.

The Motivational Self-Discovery Game

Purpose. To enable participants, through a series of self-discovery exercises, to recognize motivational factors within the job environment that can strengthen or inhibit individual performance at the workplace.

Background. As described in this section, motivational self-discovery is really a hybrid between a game and an exercise. I've classified it as a game, since its use (through a building-block series of exercises) will enhance the value of the learning process in a nonthreatenng, relaxed atmosphere. It is especially effective in seminars on motivation, which by necessity must be short yet direct, effective, and relevant. It will also fit into a comprehensive unit on motivation, which would be enhanced by giving participants "hands-on" experience with the principles involved.

Materials Required:

Three flip charts

$8^{1}/_{2}$" × 11" pads (one per participant)

Time Required

Instructor positioning	8 minutes
Team assignments	2 minutes
Small-group work	20 minutes
Team presentations	30 minutes (10 minutes per team)
Instructor summary	25 minutes
Total time (approximate)	85 minutes

Procedure. This game is most effective when positioned just after a general lecture on motivation but before the actual learning principles of motivation are introduced. The goal is for the participants to uncover, through self-discovery, those elements within the work environment that are motivating and, correspondingly, those that are demotivating.

STEP 1: Instructor informs the class that while many theories on motivation abound, they will now experience a self-discovery process that will most likely uncover the base elements of motivation—and they will do it *as a group*.

STEP 2: Prior to the game, the instructor sets up three flip charts side by side and places the following heading on each:

Flip Chart 1

(Left-hand side)	(Right-hand side)
Turn-Ons at Work	*Turn-Offs at Work*

Flip Chart 2

Best Manager	*Worst Manager*

Flip Chart 3

Motivators	*Demotivators*

Charts are now displayed to the class.

STEP 3: Instructor divides the class into three teams and gives each team its assignments:

Team 1 is asked a list of things that "turn on" the team members, not only within their current jobs, but in positions they have held throughout their business careers. "Turn-ons" are defined as everything that makes them feel good about the job itself and results in positive associations with the job. Once this list has been compiled, they are asked to list "turn-offs," which are those items that fall into the exact reverse category as the "turn-ons."

Following the same procedure as Team 1, Team 2 is asked to consider the attributes of both the *best* and *worst* managers that the members have ever worked for. The resulting lists should be a composite of *all* the managers that team members have ever reported to—those that they have truly enjoyed working for and those they resented.

Team 3 has the most difficult assignment of all. Without any coaching or prior knowledge of the subject, they are to attempt to develop a list of both *motivators* and *demotivators* common to most individuals in the workplace.

Teams will be allowed 20 minutes to develop their respective lists, then each team will be given 10 minutes to make a presentation to the entire class, with Team 1 presenting first, Team 2 second, and Team 3 last.

STEP 4: Responses by group can vary, but generally, Team 1's responses will be roughly as follows:

Turn-Ons at Work

My job provides lots of challenges.

Company always tries to promote from within.

I feel that I can "grow" with the company.

I always know where I stand with my boss.

My achievements are always recognized.

My boss backs me up when necessary.

I have a definite sense of identity on my job.

If I do something wrong, my boss will let me know right away.

I feel like an important part of a team at work.

The work is demanding, but my efforts are rewarded accordingly.

Turn-Offs at Work

Every good job that opens up within my division seems to go to an "outsider."

I have a job with no challenge—very boring.

It seems like I've stagnated in my job.

I'm never quite sure what my boss thinks of me—I get very little feedback.

My achievements are rarely recognized—sometimes my boss even takes the credit when I do something very well.

Everytime I need my boss to back me up, he's somehow never available or makes some excuse why he cannot help me.

I wonder if the company knows that I'm alive. I truly feel like "just another body" on the job.

I work in a cut-throat group—no teamwork and everyone out for themselves.

My current job is definitely below my capabilities, and my salary sure reflects it.

My boss never tells me when I'm doing something wrong but seems to "save it up" for just the right moment, then really "explodes" all at once.

Team 2's responses can also vary in content, but usually contain the following elements:

Best Manager

Is firm, but always fair with me.

Helps me grow on the job.

Backs me up when appropriate.

Is someone I can trust.

Makes me feel like a person—not a number.

Always lets me know where I stand.

Gives me a sense of importance.

Usually recognizes my achievements.

Gives me a clear sense of identity.

Helps me work as a member of the team.

Worst Manager

Never really lets me know what he thinks of me.

Never stands up for me when it really counts.

Can't really be trusted.

Doesn't care about my job advancement.

Never seems able to make a firm decision.

Makes me feel lost working for her.

Makes me feel like a small cog in the total machine.

Never encourages a group team effort.

Rarely recognizes my individual achievements.

Team 3's responses can vary widely, depending on the age and work experience of the group. Over the years, however, the following comments seemed to have surfaced with regular frequency:

Effective Motivators on the Job
(or, What Motivates People to Do Their Best Work)

Recognition as an individual

Sense of identity

Challenging assignments

Real opportunity for growth on the job

Good rapport with managers

Having a personal sense of importance at work

Open, nonthreatening work environment

Earning (and keeping) the esteem of others

Demotivators

A job perceived as dull and unimportant

A boss who doesn't care about me

No recognition for achievement

Feeling "lost in the crowd"

No challenge

Poor communication

Very little team spirit among group

Distrustful work atmosphere

STEP 5: Once all three teams have presented, have participants note the similarities among the various flip charts. Through "self-discovery," the participants should have learned:

1. There is a definite similarity between "turn-ons" and "best manager."
2. There is also a high correlation between "turn-offs" and "worst manager."
3. It follows, then, that the combined category of "turn-ons–best manager" will be closely correlated with "motivators" on the job. Conversely, the list of "turn-offs–worst manager" is tightly allied with "demotivators."
4. The real self-discovery should take place when the participants understand that those factors listed for their managers are, many times, the same type that their subordinates would use to describe them. The key learning point here is that *what you expect from your boss is exactly the same as your subordinates expect from you.*

Class Discussion Questions

1. Of the effective motivators developed in class, which are easily accomplished by a manager?
2. Conversely, which may be more difficult for a manager to accomplish in the work environment? Why?
3. Is it possible to list the single most important aspect of motivation? If not, what would be the most important cluster of traits involved?

Cautions

1. Never let a participant's personal dislike for his or her boss surface during team assignments. If names become involved, the entire exercise will suffer.
2. Avoid allowing a participant to draw you into a lengthy discussion of motivational *theory* during the game itself. The purpose of the game is truly a step-by-step self-discovery and should not be biased with preconceived notions.

The Nonverbal Communication Game

Purpose. To show the strong impact that nonverbal communication has in the total communication process between two or more persons.

Background. This is an excellent follow-up game to the one-way/
two-way communication game described earlier. The instructor can position this by probing the class for the *three* basic forms of communication
(spoken, written, and nonverbal). This game will strongly reinforce the
nonverbal aspect of communication.

Materials Required

Two flip charts per team of two people

Time Required

Explanation of game	4 minutes
Preparation	2 minutes
Nonverbal message (1)	5 minutes
Debriefing	3 minutes
Preparation	2 minutes
Nonverbal message (2)	5 minutes
Debriefing	3 minutes
Total time (approximate)	24 minutes

Procedure. The game is best employed during the teaching of communication and should generally follow (with a sufficient time interval) the
one-way versus two-way communication game.

STEP 1: Instructor should ask all participants to stand up and pair themselves with a partner whom they do *not* know well. One person is
designated as the sender of the nonverbal message, the other as the receiver.

STEP 2: The purpose of the game is for the senders to acquaint their partners
with pertinent details about their *personal life*, such as hobbies, life style,
and family. However, they must transmit the information *nonverbally*. The
sender, while not allowed to speak, may use pictures, photographs from a
wallet or handbag, gestures, or signs—in fact, anything of a nonverbal
nature. Before starting, senders must write on their flip charts several key
points that they wish to convey about themselves. During the transmission
of the nonverbal message, receivers will write the impressions received on
their flip charts (which should not be visible to the senders).

STEP 3: At the conclusion of the first cycle, both the senders' and receivers' notes on the flip chart are compared for similarities. The scenario is then reversed, with the senders becoming the receivers, and vice versa.

STEP 4 (optional): An award can be given to the team that has the greatest number of similarities between transmissions intended and actually received.

Class Discussion Questions

1. Why did some teams do better than others? Specifically, what techniques did the successful teams use?

2. What are some of the typical problems experienced by the teams? What effect would better preplanning have had on the transmission of the nonverbal messages?

3. Looking back on the exercises, to what degree did the sender's facial expressions affect the message transmission? (Note: This exercise can be greatly enhanced by videotaping each nonverbal interchange. Once the tape is replayed, it should become apparent that facial expressions can inadvertently convey important nonverbal information.

SUMMARY

1. By definition, a *game* is a contest governed by a set of rules, entered for amusement as a test of physical or mental prowess.

2. Games should never be employed as a substitute or "fill-in" for regular program content. They should be employed only as a vehicle for *reinforcing* the principles being taught.

3. While there is perhaps a fine line of distinction between a game and an experiential exercise, the latter has been primarily designed to provide an opportunity to practice and thereby reinforce the implementation of a skill.

4. Games generally contain certain basic characteristics that distinguish them from other, more intensive elements of the learning process. Games are highly participative, provide an effective change-of-pace, and are cost-effective, flexible, easy to conduct, and generally well-accepted by participants.

5. Unless properly conducted, games can induce a demotivating situation for participants. Some cautions should be observed: games should *never* be

implemented by an inexperienced instructor, *never* be viewed as threatening or a source of embarrassment to a participant, and *never* be used as a "time killer" when there is looseness in the day's teaching agenda.

CHAPTER QUESTIONS

1. Can you think of a particular learning skill where the introduction of a game would *not* be appropriate? Why?

2. How can you handle a situation where a student confided in you beforehand that he or she did not want to participate in a forthcoming game for fear of looking foolish in front of his or her peers?

3. Should instructors ever actively involve themselves in the playing of a game with the class? What are the pros and cons involved?

4. Can you imagine any situation where the instructor literally has to stop a game in progress? What guidelines might be involved here?

CHAPTER EXERCISE

My obvious request here is to encourage you to use the four games described in this chapter. In all good conscience, however, I suggest that unless you have considerable experience in instructional techniques, you do *not* attempt to conduct them without the guidance of an instructor well versed in implementing games.

Leading a class in a successful game exercise is truly a rewarding instructional experience. Conversely, conducting a game that demotivates students is something to be avoided at all costs.

THE NEXT STEP

On occasion, an instructor is responsible for *every* phase of the classroom training, from the sending of the invitational memo to participants through to the conclusion of the program.

Fortunately, in the majority of cases the trainer is part of an instructional team (however small it may be) that can give assistance in varying degrees to accomplish the task of learning and imparting knowledge to others.

The next chapter will focus on selected classroom strategies that will include not only how to work with a facilitator but also delve into related areas of responsibility in the total instructional process.

In my view it should be required reading for any trainer who will eventually assume the role of a lead instructor.

9

TEACHING STRATEGIES

LEARNING OBJECTIVES

After completing this chapter, you should have the necessary skills to:

Describe the role of a facilitator with its corresponding class support duties.

Formulate an effective scenario for a role play.

Explain both the advantages and disadvantages of role playing.

Discuss the most common types of classroom interruptions and guidelines for handling them.

Implement a personal strategy for handling class disruptions.

INTRODUCTION

If you were to analyze the trait clusters of an outstanding instructor, one characteristic sure to emerge would be that of a true team player. For the plain fact of the matter is that the imparting of knowledge from one person to a group usually is based on a collaborative effort of some type and to some degree.

Even where the instructor teaches "solo" (the only person on the platform during a program), the outcome of the session usually depends on the skill of *both* the instructor and the people who designed and created the material, from original idea to the final form of participant material. Going a bit further, instructors develop a personal set of teaching strategies built around those aids that will help transmit learning efficiently within the classroom environment.

This premise poses an interesting challenge. If you were to take a few moments, I'm sure you could produce a list of at least 10 basic strategies that an instructor could employ in the teaching effort. My own goal in writing this chapter was *not* to create a marathon list of strategies, since many related ones are interwoven throughout the text. Instead, I relied on my own experience and arrived at three basic teaching aids that consistently appeared to have a direct impact within the classroom. No doubt others could have been included, but I have found that with a comprehensive understanding of these three, instructors will accrue additional insights and become more effective as a result.

The three teaching strategies are diagrammed in Figure 39. They are the *use of a facilitator*, positioning and implementation of *role plays*, and finally, *handling class disruptions*, including participants who, often unintentionally, interrupt or engage in actions that reduce the learning effectiveness for the class.

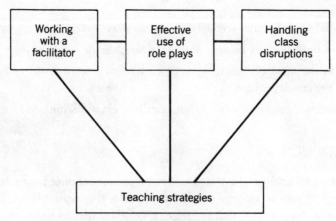

Figure 39. Teaching strategies.

USE OF A FACILITATOR

By definition, to facilitate is *to make easier or more convenient,* which is precisely the role of a facilitator as an integral part of the instructional team.

A few assumptions are made here. While duties and responsibilities of a facilitator can vary widely, this chapter will view the facilitator as having a *dual* function in support of the instructor. The first function will include the *administrative aspects* of the planned program; the second will embrace the pure *facilitation process* that occurs while the class is in session. While this dual role is certainly not as glamorous as that of the lead instructor, the facilitation (or support) task is a very essential ingredient for a successful program—especially when the class has more than 12 people and the program is conducted over several days. In a broad sense the relationship between an instructor and facilitator can be compared to that of a surgeon and the operating team. In both situations the leader of the team (whether surgical or instructional) *directly depends* on others for support and eventual success in the effort.

CHARACTERISTICS OF A SUCCESSFUL FACILITATOR

The requirements for an effective facilitator will vary widely depending on the program. However, in general, a facilitator should possess the following characteristics and skills to be proficient:

Personal Requirements

1. *Good Administrative Skills.* A facilitator should be proficient in attending to detail, able to delegate administrative tasks when necessary, and able to organize a series of related tasks in an orderly sequential flow. Simply put, people who cannot even organize themselves cannot be expected to organize others!

2. *Image of Self-Confidence.* A person with an air of self-confidence has a contagious way of radiating this image to others. In a classroom setting this becomes an essential ingredient for the success of the facilitator. The time-worn adage of "nothing succeeds like success" is quite appropriate here.

3. *Adequate Levels of Sympathy and Sensitivity.*   Facilitator must constantly empathize with participants going through the learning experience. Over a typical several day's worth of training, the *entire* instructional team must be highly sensitive to all those "on the other side of the platform." In no way does this imply a condescending approach to participants, but rather the *sharing* and *recognition* of the fact that students also have potentially high built-in levels of frustration, concerns, and apprehension.

4. *High Degree of Flexibility.*   As every experienced facilitator knows, Murphy's law (that if anything can go wrong, *it will*) abounds during a typical training program. Consequently, facilitators must have a high tolerance for change. What was once true in the class can change completely a few moments later. It can mean that a facilitator spends several hours after class drawing a complete set of flip charts, only to find out the next morning that most of them have to be redone.

5. *High Energy Level.*   All classroom instruction is fatiguing to varying degrees, and the facilitator's role is no exception. A typical workday for a facilitator can easily run to 10 or 12 hours, and at times, even more are required. However you view it, the role is both tiring and demanding—usually over several days duration.

6. *Initiative and Commitment to Assigned Tasks.*   No buzz words are intended here. An effective facilitator *must* be able to take the initiative throughout a program and carry out tasks with only a minimum degree of supervision. Usually, when an instructor and facilitator have worked together for some time, they develop a common team approach; the facilitator becomes highly effective—knowing *what* to do, *when* to do it, and *where* it should take place. That is a very nice arrangement for *both* people, and when that plateau is reached, the instructor has an able component of teaching strategy well in place.

7. *Voice Quality, Appearance, and Mannerisms.*   Although combined into one general category, all three personal characteristics are obviously important. Interestingly enough, the three are highly interrelated, for one trait usually depends on the next in order to give participants a total, positive image of the facilitator. For example, few things are more distracting than a teacher who is attractive but has a high-pitched whining voice. Or a person may have a wonderful voice quality but constantly revert to distracting mannerisms such as nose rubbing or pulling at one ear! Simply put, it detracts from learning in the classroom.

Our list would not be complete without a review of some skills that a facilitator can be trained in. Naturally, the list can never be considered all-inclusive, since facilitator requirements can vary depending upon the specific program.

Skills and Knowledge That Can Be Developed

1.   *Knowledge of the Organization, Its Mission, Organization Structure, and General Corporate Philosophy.*   Participants will view facilitators as not only teachers, but in a broad sense, company representatives. In a sense, they are like tourists who are told that, in addition to being tourists, they also represent their home country to all people that they meet abroad. Many a time a question about the organization will arise in class, and it's only reasonable to assume that the query will be answered to everyone's satisfaction.

2.   *"Hands-on" Expertise with All Types of Visual and Instructional Aids.*   Every facilitator should have a good working knowledge of all varieties of audio-visual support systems. The term *working knowledge*, however, means a knowledge not only of *how* something works but also of how to use it effectively. Here are just a few examples of what facilitators must know:

When using a flip chart, how to:
   Print legibly
   Tab pages with masking tape (where necessary)
   Use it effectively (for example, talk from it, not to it)
   Cover and uncover various headings on the chart at opportune times for maximum teaching effect
When working with video, how to:
   Operate the camera
   Use the monitor and video deck effectively
   Electrically connect all of the components
   Make minor repairs and adjustments, when necessary
When using 16mm or 35mm equipment, how to:
   Set-up and operate
   "Un-jam" the equipment

Replace bulbs and lamps

When working with an overhead transparency projector, how to:

Make transparencies

Make minor repairs

Replace bulb

3. *Group Facilitation Techniques.*   This is a rather broad category. The facilitator must be prepared to implement the following important learning activities:

Role plays

Positioning the group (acquainting them with the role-play guidelines)

Timing, roles, location

Debriefing techniques

Role of the facilitator

Team exercises

Positioning

Assignments by team

Time allotted

Team presentation

Critiquing techniques

Mentor group exercises

Explanation and positioning

Roles to be played by each mentor

Length of each exercise

Feedback procedures

Regardless of the learning activity employed, the role of the facilitator remains a core ingredient in its eventual success or failure. As one example, the effective *positioning* (a complete explanation) of a role play to a group of participants can go a long way to reduce apprehension and set the stage for a constructive interchange between role-play individuals. It's a skill not easily learned, but one that is definitely essential.

INSTRUCTIONAL ROLES

In using a facilitator as part of a basic teaching strategy, *the responsibility for the facilitator's performance rests solely on the instructor's shoulders.* The key to success lies in establishing a *partnership* in which the *roles* of both the instructor and facilitator are carefully defined *beforehand*, with full agreement on what is to be done individually and jointly.

While formats can vary, here is a sample of what the role assignment might look like in actual practice:

Role of Instructor

The instructor assumes full responsibility for the complete program. Duties include:

Preprogram

Meet formally with facilitator, to plan program logistics:

Date and location of program

Participants' names, work histories (if appropriate)

Location and number of breakout rooms

Meal functions, including all coffee breaks

Related administrative skills

Specific facilitator responsibilities

Responsibility for administrative details (such as room and equipment check prior to the program start)

During Program

Teach all selected modules.

Assist as cofacilitator or observer during role plays (as required).

Role of Facilitator

Preprogram

Insure that all program materials have been delivered to the classroom.

Set up and create flip charts (as required).

Set up classroom (pads, books, pencils, and so on).

Check all breakout rooms.

Review meal and coffee break details.

Check all audio-visual materials and equipment to be used during the program.

During Program

Introduce all role play and small group work:

Position

Give instructions

Set up teams

Observe or facilitate during role play.

Lead class discussion around role-play insights.

Lead selected small-group exercises.

Work with instructor to create a more effective learning environment.

Engage participants in informal discussion; provide information, advice, and structure for effective class and team synergism.

Participate daily in evaluation and critique of the day's session.

Assist instructor in program set-up for the next day.

Facilitator Overview

The responsibilities of a facilitator can be divided into three broad categories:

1. *Logistics.* As one who helps to create the environment where desired behavior change will occur, the facilitator is responsible for assisting participants, understanding roles, a thorough knowledge of timing (by class activity), and a full understanding of all role plays and selected group exercises.

2. *Observation.* The facilitator observes teams during role plays. He or she is responsible for making certain that observer's checklists are properly filled out, intervening with group if a problem should arise, and noticing behavior of participants. The facilitator also leads group discussions on insights and coordinates feedback on group exercises.

3. *Processing.*   The facilitator helps group members to generate their own observations about their behaviors, then assists them in an interpretative process to generate insights. He or she reinforces similarities in learning, both on role plays and class exercises.

Finally, to be fully integrated into an instructor's master teaching strategy, facilitators should always be guided by the following nine points:

1. Always make a point of introducing themselves to every participant *prior* to the start of the session.

2. Never take any participant for granted. Facilitators should realize that a student may know more about the subject than they do.

3. Always be aware that they are constantly being judged by participants. Within the first 10 to 20 minutes of the program, students will have made their primary evaluation of the facilitator.

4. Never forget the all-important feedback session with the instructor before leaving the classroom after the program. In essence, it's a brief summary of what was covered during the day, together with a review of the logistics for the next day.

5. Always get as much rest as possible during each evening. Facilitating is a tiring experience, and lack of sleep will definitely hurt effectiveness in the classroom.

6. Never become the group's "parental figure"; instead, become their learning resource. Facilitators should never let themselves become the final authority on any matter, but rather should habitually use the consultative approach.

7. Always spend as much time with participants as possible. Everyone will benefit from the experience, and the total environment will become more conducive to learning.

8. Never forget, that if they have promised to get back to a participant, they must do it!

9. Always *plan, plan,* then spend more time in program *planning.* When all of this has been thoroughly accomplished, *plan* some more.

ROLE PLAYING

As a traditional form of learning reinforcement, role playing within the classroom setting has consistently proved its value throughout the years.

Properly done, it is inexpensive, relatively easy to accomplish, and most important, allows participants to observe their increased skill proficiency. Moreover, it is an exercise that can be easily conducted by the facilitator. As such, it supplies the instructor with an integral part of the overall teaching strategy.

Before delving deeper into the subject, let's spend a few moments and review both the advantages and disadvantages of this type of learning reinforcement.

Advantages

1. Generally easy to administer.
2. Reinforces the skill being taught in an observable manner.
3. Allows for immediate coaching by an observer to improve a skill.
4. Gets participants involved in a real-world situation.
5. Reinforces communication skills (regardless of the role being played).
6. Provides an effective "bridge" between classroom theory and on-the-job application.

Disadvantages

1. Participants can view role playing as a threatening experience, especially if they are uncomfortable in the role or if the role play is being videotaped.
2. Many participants believe that role playing, however done, is artificial and adds nothing to the learning experience.
3. If a role play is poorly conducted and the proper guidance is lacking, the participants may leave the exercise feeling more frustrated than before.
4. In role playing, there is the ever present danger that egos can be painfully bruised. No one wants to look foolish in front of others.
5. If participants are not properly debriefed at the conclusion of the role play, much of the potential beneficial effect will be lost.

STRATEGY FOR ROLE PLAYING

Figure 40 displays an effective strategy for a typical role play. Note that it consists of four sequential steps: positioning, organizing, conducting, and debriefing. In most cases role playing should immediately follow the intro-

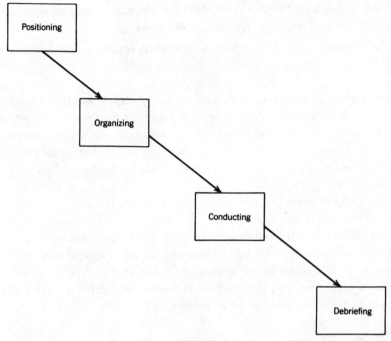

Figure 40.   Role-play strategy steps.

duction of a skill, thereby providing practice and reinforcement. Let's briefly look at each of the steps before delving deeper into the subject.

Positioning

For an example, let's assume a role play will be introduced to reinforce a communication module. The class has been introduced to the principles of effective communication, then to the guidelines for communicating effectively with another person. This activity was followed by an interactive videotape in which participants could easily observe effective communication strategies. The *positioning step* would have the facilitator explain to the class that they would now have the opportunity to practice what they just learned. It would be important here to stress the following points:

The role play will allow participants to practice the newly acquired skills and knowledge in a supportive environment.

It will enable them to "take risks"—experiment with new approaches and learn from any mistakes that they might make.

It will provide an opportunity to receive timely feedback, nonthreatening and constructive.

An important consideration in the positioning step is that the instructor probe the class for any concerns or apprehensions they may have before proceeding with the next step. Perhaps the most common concern encountered here is participant anxiety—a participant states that he or she has never role played before—and that anxiety *must* be dealt with before proceeding. A typical response here would be to ask for a show of hands of others who have never role played (usually there are several). The instructor must then reinforce the nonthreatening nature of the role play itself, and the fact that the activity will be done in *small groups with one's own peers*. (Note that in some cases I refer to the group leader as a *facilitator*, and in others, as an *instructor*. In my opinion, a well-trained facilitator can easily conduct a role play, and in doing so, *becomes the instructor during that moment in time*. It's a key point to remember.)

Organizing

The eventual success of the role play depends heavily on the *organization* of the forthcoming activity—how it is to be accomplished, in what time frames, and the basic logistics involved.

To illustrate, let's assume that our role play on communication will be done in groups of three (triads). The actual role play will be done three times (rounds), allowing each participant to play the part of a manager, subordinate, and observer. At this point very careful attention is needed, since any instructions to participants that appear confusing could adversely affect the simulation to follow. As a result, all of the detail that now follows should have been carefully *planned in advance*. That includes the selection of triads, assigned breakout rooms, and the timing and sequence of roles per participant.

In this case, each member of the triad (regardless of the number of triads in the class) is assigned a team letter; that is, the first person is *A*; the second, *B*; and the third, *C*. These letter designations remain the same for the three rounds. Here is the general sequence for the facilitator to follow:

1. Divide participants into groups of three (triads).

2. Inform them that material for the role play will be distributed to each team in the breakout room.

3. Assign each team a breakout room location.

4. Advise participants that the role-play material they will shortly receive is organized so that each "package" given to them represents the sequence of roles they will play in the three exercises.

5. The instructor then displays the following material organization on a predrawn flip chart.

Individual	Material Received	Round Assignment	Notation on Material
Team Member *A*	Langley	1	Round 1 (*A*)
	Moore	2	Round 2 (*A*)
	Observer	3	Round 3 (*A*)
Team Member *B*	Observer	1	Round 1 (*B*)
	Langley	2	Round 2 (*B*)
	Dominguez	3	Round 3 (*B*)
Team Member *C*	Savarese	1	Round 1 (*C*)
	Observer	2	Round 2 (*C*)
	Langley	3	Round 3 (*C*)

Note: To avoid any possible confusion, an illustration of roles during the three rounds should be given here. For example, Team Member *A* will play Langley (the supervisor) during Round 1, play Moore (the subordinate) during Round 2, and is the observer during Round 3.

6. Participants are then informed (also via a predrawn flip chart) that each round should take 25 minutes.

Preparation time	10 minutes
Interview (role play)	10 minutes
Observer's comments	5 minutes

7. When the three rounds of role plays are completed, each team should discuss the exercise and list three *key insights* gained from the experi-

ence. These insights will then be presented to the whole group when the teams reassemble in the main class room.

8. Total exercise will take 110 minutes, as follows:

Distribution of material and role assignments	10 minutes
Role plays (25 × 3)	75 minutes
Debriefing of insights	10 minutes
Coffee break	15 minutes
Total time	110 minutes

9. Facilitator reviews all details again, checking for team understanding of entire role-play sequence. Once accomplished, each team moves on to its assigned room for the start of the role-play sequence, accompanied by the facilitator(s) who ensure that the teams are properly organized for the activity.

Conducting

Prior to the start of Round 1, the facilitator distributes the appropriate role-play information. Let's review the material that each member of the team will receive for Round 1.

ROUND 1 (A), TEAM MEMBER A: MANAGER'S ROLE, J. LANGLEY. You have been with North Shore Manufacturing Company for seven years, the last three as General Manager. North Shore was your first job after graduation from Huntington College, and you take great pride in your fast rise achieved within the organization. You attribute your success to the fact that you are "action-oriented," move quickly, and make decisions without delay. What's more, you expect others to do the same.

To obtain maximum staff productivity, you have made it clear to everyone in your unit that you expect them to show initiative but you will be available to provide assistance and support whenever it is necessary. This should enable each person reporting to you to develop their skills to higher degrees and reach new levels of achievement.

You take pride in keeping your door open to your staff at all times. Glancing at your calendar, you notice that one of your supervisors, Nancy Savarese, has requested an appointment with you at 10:00 A.M. While her work is satisfactory in most respects, you are irked that sometimes she appears to rely on you for decisions that she could have made for herself.

Nancy has been with the company for a little over three years. She is currently in charge of the customer service department, but like most other supervisors, has a variety of other duties that you assign to her. Her latest assignment is to plan and coordinate all details for the forthcoming Christmas party, which is now approximately three weeks away. At a meeting two weeks ago, you had given her all the necessary guidelines, including the fact that over 200 people would be attending, and everything *had to go smoothly, from start to finish.*

You note that she has requested to speak with you on this subject. Since you have an extremely busy schedule today, you expect a very favorable progress report—given quickly and efficiently.

Concerns:

You hope everything has been handled properly.

You expect that Nancy has taken the lead and acted independently where possible.

You *do not* expect to have to make decisions for her.

Round 1 (*A*), Team Member *C*: Supervisor's Role, Nancy Savarese. You have been with North Shore Manufacturing Company for about three years, having joined the firm after graduation from Bunter College. After several assignments in the customer service department, you were promoted to supervisor about six months ago.

You enjoy this position very much, and the relationship with your manager (J. Langley) appears satisfactory. Your only complaint centers around the frequent assignments he gives to you that are *not* related to your current duties. While he appears to pride himself on being consultative with his staff, he can easily get very annoyed when he believes that a decision could be made *without* his help. You feel that's fine to a point but that sometimes he can be quite unfair.

For example, take the case of the forthcoming Christmas party. Langley called you in several weeks ago and announced that *you* would be in charge of all details—in spite of the fact you were already overloaded with your regular work! Actually, Langley did give you most of the major details needed for the party, but that still left you with a lot of follow-up telephone calls and several personal visits to the hotel. Unfortunately, time has slipped by, and you realized only yesterday that very little had been done.

Your purpose in seeing Langley today is to explain the reason for the delay and request his help in organizing a follow-up schedule to handle all logistics in time for the party. Considering all this, you are a bit apprehensive about the forthcoming meeting and hope Langley realizes that the delay is really not your fault.

Concerns:

You hope that Langley will carefully listen to your reasons for the delay.

You expect his help creating a follow-up action schedule.

You do not expect to have a confrontation over this.

To properly critique the role play, the observer is given *both* the manager's and supervisor's background information. In addition, the following observer's form is used:

ROUND 1 (*A*), TEAM MEMBER *B*: OBSERVER'S CHECKLIST: LANGLEY/SAVARESE MEETING. At the conclusion of the role play, you have the responsibility to critique how well the communication steps were followed. To aid you in this feedback, answer the following direct questions yes or no. Then in the comments section, describe techniques or methods used by the manager in the communication process.

A.   *Establish ease*

_____ Yes

_____ No

_____ Partially

Comments: _____

_____

B.   *Determine purpose of meeting*

_____ Yes

_____ No

_____ Partially

Comments: _____

_____

C. *Build on rapport/understanding*

_____ Yes

_____ No

_____ Partially

Comments: _____

_____

D. *Use of effective feedback*

_____ Yes

_____ No

_____ Partially

Comments: _____

_____

E. *Establishing common understanding*

_____ Yes

_____ No

_____ Partially

Comments: _____

_____

F. *Determining action steps/reaching agreement*

_____ Yes

_____ No

_____ Partially

Comments: _____

_____

Debriefing

After the conclusion and discussion of the three rounds, each team then reassembles into the main classroom for a full debriefing. It is here that a skillful facilitator, through the processing of insights, can lend significant value to the just-completed role play.

Usually with the aid of a flip chart, the facilitator probes each team to draw out ideas, feelings, and points learned. This should take the form of a free-flowing feedback session, with the facilitator taking special care to:

Always process observations, not personal interpretations.

Avoid assumptions when coding a participant's answer on the flip chart.

Never lead a participant into what you think is a correct response.

Never become too introspective with the feedback obtained.

Never get into a "lecture" mode when receiving insights; you are then to *process* responses only.

Remain as flexible as possible, both in gathering the feedback and interpreting it.

HANDLING CLASS DISRUPTIONS

Now that we have covered working with a facilitator and the effective use of role plays, the first two elements in a teaching strategy, the stage is set for the final element—handling class disruptions. Whether intentional, inadvertent, or even unintentional, disruptions are a common occurrence in the classroom. Left unchecked, they will surely decrease the learning rate for *all* participants.

It's been my experience that most participants who cause a class interruption do so unintentionally and certainly without realizing the problem that they are creating. Proper handling of this problem rests on two basic substrategies:

1. Never embarrass or "put down" the problem participant in front of the class.
2. Handle the situation early, before it becomes a serious matter.

Although it's sometimes tempting to react strongly to the individual causing the problem, don't do it. Your annoyance may certainly be justified, and expressing it may afford you a short moment of satisfaction, but doing so will create a still greater problem. The majority of the other participants will usually empathize with the embarrassment of the individual you just "put down," resulting in a downward spiral of class motivation. After all, participants expect the instructor, the true authority figure in the room, to use his or her power wisely—and certainly with discretion.

It's crucial for the instructor to understand that minor disruptions, if not handled early, stand a good chance of becoming major ones. Accordingly, the guideline here is to move *quickly* toward problem resolution but do so with liberal doses of *discretion*.

Even with the most careful planning, the planned flow of the learning is occasionally disrupted. Under the best of circumstances, this can prove taxing to the instructor. Usually, one or more minor interruptions can be tolerated by the instructor—and to some extent, by the participants themselves. If ignored, however, a minor annoyance can turn into a major disruptive factor. In other words, if a real problem begins to develop within the meeting room, simply ignoring the disruption will not automatically cause it to go away within a given time. Furthermore, if undetected, a small problem slowly and insidiously can grow; by the time it is recognized it may be out of control.

To complicate matters further, the disruptive behavior of one or more people can quickly become infectious. Other participants tend to "catch" the same kind of unsettled feelings. If this is allowed to occur, the class is in real danger of disintegrating into a fiasco—whether vividly apparent or, even worse, submerged in participant apathy. Unless the instructor takes quick action to squelch any prolonged disruption, the result usually is quite predictable—an unsatisfactory learning level.

Let's now list some general types of disruptive personalities by category, together with suggested ways to inhibit them. Experienced instructors generally agree that there is never an automatic set of rules for handling a disruptive situation. Put another way, do not fall into the trap of thinking, "If this occurs, I will immediately counter with that." Simply taking a moment to think instead of acting on impulse can go a long way in handling most problems that occur.

Although it's very difficult to categorize aspects of human behavior, the following groupings of *potential* problem personalities represent the six types of difficult participants that an instructor might encounter.

Type 1. "I'm too busy, but I'm here."	(Importance)
Type 2. "I know better than you."	(Superiority)
Type 3. "I'm in charge here."	(Authority)
Type 4. "I need your help."	(Dependency)
Type 5. "Everything is wrong, as usual."	(Complainer)
Type 6. The constant talker.	(Chatterbox)

Let's examine each type, reviewing their specific characteristics, then discuss some helpful strategies to employ when confronted by them. Keep in mind, however, that some of these types are heavily interrelated to others.

Type 1. "I'm Too Busy, but I'm Here"
Sub-Type: See How Important I Am

Characteristics. Whatever the hour, this person is generally late for class or, at best, the last one to arrive. He or she usually enters the room in a harried, frenzied manner, making certain that all other participants realize the "sacrifice" this person is making by attending. At the same time, this person will usually throw a mild glance of annoyance at the instructor to make certain that the message has clearly gotten across. In some instances this same individual will either be called out of the room on an "urgent" telephone call or will simply spend time in class writing down a huge variety of notes for apparent follow-up after the session has been concluded. On occasion, he or she will have to leave the meeting early and an apology will be made to the instructor. A favorite strategy here is, upon leaving the room (usually halfway out the door), to call out loudly to another participant to call him immediately at the conclusion of the meeting.

Counterstrategy. "I'm too busy, but I'm here" individuals seek constant reinforcement of their importance, coupled with liberal doses of positive ego strokes to feed their sense of self-worth. A workable strategy (as they arrive late) is to involve them immediately in a task that requires an important follow-up on their part.

EXAMPLE: "Hi John, glad you could make the class. Really pleased that you could attend, since we're about to discuss the matter of (name a subject), and I know that you have an expertise in this area. As a matter of fact, I'd like you to stay for a minute after we break to make certain that we've captured all of your thoughts on this. It will really help what we are trying to accomplish here."

Type 2. "I Know Better Than You"
Sub-Type: Superiority Syndrome

Characteristics. In most situations, these people will devote their main energy and attention to challenging the instructor in one way or another.

Whatever is said or done, these individuals will either contradict it or (at best) enter "clarifying" comment to what has just been said. While this rather cruel game can be played by those at any level of management, it can be accomplished most easily when the "I know better than you" person is of a higher rank than the person conducting the class. A very favorite strategy for making their presence strongly felt is to maneuver themselves into a position to give a final summary of what has transpired, then add their own opinions, which will rarely be the same as the instructor's. Cleverly done, this summary will almost appear to have come as an afterthought, but it will be presented with an air of authority.

Counterstrategy. A definite aid in this sort of situation is to first recognize the fact that these individuals strongly seek recognition and are continually building up their power base. While this *may* be a defense for their own strong feelings of insecurity, it is very important to them to always be noticed through their discreet interruptions, which give them a chance to impress others with their self-perceived importance. An effective strategy here would be twofold: First, call on them early in the class before they have had a chance to pick the "perfect moment." Second, immediately after they have expressed their opinion, tactfully mention that while it was a good point, there may be several alternate opinions on the subject, and quickly ask the other participants for their viewpoints. In many cases this strategy defuses the "I know better than you" type and may discourage their disruptive tactics.

EXAMPLE: "Well, Lynn, that was an interesting point of view and certainly deserves some additional thought. As a matter of fact, I'm sure that several people here can contribute even further on this subject. John, how about it? What are your thoughts on this?" (Note: Involving Types 1 and 2 here is an excellent strategy!)

Type 3. "I'm in Charge Here"
Sub-Type: Authority Figure

Characteristics. While closely allied with "I know better than you" types, Type 3 personalities concentrate their main energy on letting everyone know how important they are to the unit, group, or organization. This strategy naturally leads into the fact that they are responsible for the assembled group and should be accorded a special status. While they may occasionally challenge the instructor (if it suits their purpose), their primary objective during the class is both to heighten and to reinforce the fact that they hold a position of authority. As a result, each response made during the class is usually done in such a way as to convey a domineering viewpoint—in either a subtle or an obvious manner. Naturally, the situation can prove to be rather disconcerting (to say the least) to the instructor, since nothing worthwhile can be accomplished with even a faint hint of intimidation in the room—and the person conveying it may even be the instructor's boss!

Counterstrategy.   With this type, great care must be exercised at all times! Even though the instructor must walk a fine line here, objectives for a truly participative class can be reached. The technique is, first, to give the respect due the "I'm in charge here" types, since they have reached a high position of authority. Basically, this is common courtesy. Then, immediately following this deference, ask a carefully worded question that will encourage these persons to talk freely, based on their high status. In other words, you can turn their elevated rank (a definite disadvantage to have in the meeting) into an advantage by reason of their experience and background. Granted, people of a much higher rank than most of the other participants should generally not be in the classroom, where a nonthreatening, free-flowing environment is mandatory. As we all know, however, this situation cannot be avoided from time to time, and this suggestion offers one way to deal with it.

EXAMPLE: "As you can see Milt, we're faced with a really difficult situation here. The group has already come up with some worthwhile suggestions, but we could use the benefit of your own experience in matters like this. What are your thoughts, Milt? How would you handle it? Can you share some insights with us?"

Type 4. "I Need Your Help"
Sub-Type: Highly Dependent

Characteristics.   In contrast to the first three types described, the "I need your help" classification is a classic study in direct contrast. These types can be readily identified by their lack of self-confidence and strong dependency on others. They are generally plagued by feelings of insecurity and usually dread the thought of expressing an independent opinion and perhaps look-ing foolish in front of their peers. Left alone in a class, they will not partici-pate; if forced to, they will always agree with the majority opinion and never disagree with a point of view expressed by another participant. But these individuals usually do have some very good ideas; they must be gently drawn out by the instructor and always in a nonthreatening manner. (Caution: Pay special attention to this type during role plays and small-group exercises, which can be highly threatening to them.)

Counterstrategy.   Type 4 people can become productive participants through a series of nonthreatening questions that aid in building self-confidence, thereby paving the way for greater involvement. The instructor needs a high degree of skill to accomplish this, for the questioning must be done both discreetly and through carefully worded probes. Begin with a question they can easily respond to, one that has been designed to build their confidence levels. A bit later in the meeting, at an opportune time, pose a second question that is slightly more difficult. Once this second probe has been answered, the instructor is well on the way to having these individuals become productive members of the class. Again, however, extreme caution must be taken during this procedure to avoid having shy participants perceive themselves as being threatened in *any way*.

EXAMPLE (FIRST IN A SERIES OF PROBES): "Looks like we have a consensus on the decision to reduce departmental absences starting next week. It seems to be the most feasible course of action for us to follow at this time. Before we make it official, however, I want to make certain that we are in full agree-ment on this as a team. Let's see. There are still a few people we haven't heard from yet. How do you feel about this, Julie?"

Type 5. "Everything Is Wrong, as Usual"
Sub-Type: Complainer

Characteristics.   Nothing associated with the class is ever acceptable to Type 5 people. Furthermore, they appear to take a special delight in *point-ing out* what they feel is *unacceptable*. Complaints can run the gamut of possibilities—the class started a bit late, the coffee is too weak (or strong or hot or cold), the lighting, heating, seating, or air conditioning is not right, even the agenda is not to their liking. However they express their displeasure (verbally, nonverbally, or a combination of both), they appear to have a definite need to voice their displeasure about various facets of the class, the instructor, and whatever else that they can think of!

Counterstrategy. The key strategy here is to take the initiative *before it is taken from you!* In other words, respond to each "problem" as soon as it is voiced. Avoiding or deferring your response will only serve to strengthen the apparent unhappiness being generated. Conversely, by answering each complaint right away, the "everything is wrong, as usual" types will shortly become discouraged from further complaints. As with the handling of all problem types, a very liberal degree of tact, patience, and diplomacy must be used by the instructor. It's not easy to do so, but it's very necessary!

EXAMPLE: "I agree with you, Laura—it is a bit warm in the room. We knew about the problem in the air-conditioning system before the class started. The maintenance department has already been notified, and we hope to have it fixed within the next few minutes. Thanks for bringing it to my attention. We're all a bit uncomfortable."

Type 6. "The Constant Talker"
Sub-Type: Chatterbox

Characteristics. These individuals are perhaps the most disruptive of all, since they talk incessantly throughout the session. They appear to delight in carrying on side conversations with participants on either side of them, disrupting the flow of information for all concerned. On occasion, they even attempt to talk with a person across the table, completely ignoring what is being said by the instructor. Any way viewed, they present a serious situation for the instructor, and one that must be handled promptly.

Counterstrategy. The quickest way to terminate this type of disturbance is to draw "the constant talkers" back into the mainstream of the class. Without making it too obvious, thereby running the risk of being perceived as "heavy-handed" by the group, the instructor should periodically solicit the opinions of these individuals about what has just been said. Use of this strategy over several minutes will usually discourage the constant talkers from further interruptions. Finally, it is also an effective strategy to call on the people engaged in conversation with the "constant talkers." It is a subtle technique and generally works very well—but use it with caution.

EXAMPLE: "That's really an interesting comment, Jack. I'm sure, however, that everyone may not completely agree with you. Let's see how the others feel about this. Uh . . . Joe, what are your specific thoughts on this?"

When you reflect on the difficult people you encounter during a typical class, you soon realize that it is hard to fit these people into neat categories. Rather than exhibiting a single difficult characteristic, some individuals exude combinations of several problem clusters, making the situation even more difficult for the person conducting the class.

While there are never automatic rules for handling *every* type of problem situation, it's well to recall the two fundamental guidelines that were discussed earlier in the chapter. As you will recall, they are:

1.   Never embarrass a troublemaker.
2.   Always handle the problem early.

We can now add two more basic rules:

3.   Always use tact and diplomacy—even if it hurts!
4.   Never show annoyance or lose your temper.

Use of these four basic guidelines will not completely guarantee a trouble-free class, but they will go a long way in helping you accomplish your objectives smoothly. These four guidelines, coupled with a liberal sprinkling of common sense, become a combination that is hard to beat. After all, although the instructor is the one who has to react and deal with the problem, it is the participant causing the disruption who really has the problem.

SUMMARY

1.   The three supporting elements of an effective teaching strategy are use of a facilitator, role plays, and the proper handling of class disruptions.

2.   While the duties and responsibilities of a facilitator can vary widely, the facilitator's role can be categorized as having a dual function in support of the instructor: *administration* plus *facilitation*.

3.   Personal requirements of a facilitator include: being a good administrator; projecting an image of self-confidence; having high levels of empathy and sensitivity, flexibility, and energy; showing initiative and commitment to assigned tasks; and displaying an effective voice quality.

4.   The required skills and knowledge that a facilitator can develop are: knowledge of the organization, its mission, structure, and corporate philosophy; expertise with all types of visual and instructional aids; and group facilitation techniques.

5.   Properly done, role playing is inexpensive, relatively easy to accomplish, and most important, allows participants to demonstrate increased skill proficiency.

6.   The four role-play strategy steps are: positioning, organizing, conducting, and debriefing.

7.   In a typical class, several types of problem participants can be encountered by the instructor. These types can be roughly categorized as follows:

Type 1: "I'm too busy, but I'm here."

Type 2: "I know better than you."

Type 3: "I'm in charge here."

Type 4: "I need your help."

Type 5: "Everything is wrong, as usual."

Type 6: The constant talker.

8.   Guidelines for handling disruptions during a class consist of: (1) never embarrass a troublemaker in front of the group; (2) always handle the problem early; (3) always use tact and diplomacy; and (4) never display annoyance or lose your temper.

CASE STUDY: "TEACHERS AREN'T GOD, YOU KNOW."

It was just prior to the scheduled 10:15 A.M. coffee break on the first day of the sales planning seminar. Although everything was going smoothly, Bob Langley, the instructor, was becoming concerned. One of the key participants, Joe Bates, had not yet arrived, and his presence as national sales manager was definitely needed to reinforce the principles being taught.

The break took place exactly as scheduled, but as the participants returned to class at 10:30, Joe noisily entered the room, joining the others as they began taking their seats.

The next few minutes seemed to blur in Bob's mind. He was not certain when the interruption actually started nor of the events leading to the disastrous scenario that culminated in the class ending early—*without* accomplishing everything that was intended. Instead of holding class until the scheduled dismissal time of 1:00 P.M., Bob knew by 12:30 that it was useless to continue. Accordingly, he summarized the key points he had made earlier and ended the class a full 30 minutes ahead of schedule. Bob realized that several vital elements of the program had been omitted, but he could do nothing further at that point. By 12:30 the class had become restless, bored, and even worse, quite inattentive. But what had gone wrong?

Reflecting on this later in the day, some of the events were still blurred, but he did recall that the problem seemed to start when Joe Bates entered the class after coffee break. For some reason, Joe appeared intent on disrupting the session—perhaps inadvertently, but the *effect* was definitely there. At first, Joe only whispered loudly to the person sitting next to him. That was followed by a conspicuous rustling of papers as Joe searched for something he had brought into the room. When that noise died down (which had already distracted the class), he again started up a conversation, but this time with a participant several seats away. Bob ignored this as best he could, but decided to say something when Joe lit up a cigarette, despite the prominent NO SMOKING sign displayed in front of the room. At that point, the following dialogue took place:

Bob: Joe, I'm sorry, but you will have to put the cigarette out. We have a "No Smoking" rule in the classroom.

Joe: Sure. No sense wasting it though. I just lit it up. As soon as I'm done, I'll put it out.

Bob: [*A bit flustered*] But that will be a while. Please, would you put it out *now*?

Joe: What's the matter, Mac? You got something against *king-size* smokes? I notice that you smoke the same brand. [*Class laughter*]

Bob: Sure I do, but *not* in class!

Joe: [*Now carrying on a side conversation with another participant*] Look Mac, what's your problem? I had to rush here from a really important meeting—haven't even had a cup of coffee yet—and you're making a "big deal" out of nothing! *Why don't you get on with the class instead of worrying about little stupid things!*

[*Dead silence in class*]

Bob: [*Angrily*] All I'm asking is that you respect the rules. . . .

Joe: [*Interrupting and very angry*] Rules, you say? Whose rules? Yours? I came here to lend reinforcement to the class, and instead, get a ridiculous lecture on rules and regulations!

Bob: [*Very flushed and angry*] But . . .

Joe: Hold it! No more lectures from you—especially on rules. I've just decided to leave. I have many more *important* things to do with my time. But, I have a word of advice for *you!*

Bob: What's that?

Joe: Stop being impressed with your own role. Teachers aren't God, you know!

CASE STUDY DISCUSSION POINTS

1.   In your opinion, did Bob handle the situation correctly?

2.   If you believe he did not, how would *you* have handled it?

3.   Could Bob have used any of the points on handling disruptions outlined in this chapter?

4.   Is Joe Bates entirely at fault? Why?

CHAPTER QUESTIONS

1.   How much control should a lead instructor have over the facilitator's role?

2.   How would you handle a situation where a participant has absolutely refused to do a play because of shyness (and made a point of telling you this a day *before* the role play was scheduled)?

3.   Think about this *before* forming an opinion: Can you think of *any* situation where an instructor would be forced to request that a participant leave the room?

THE NEXT STEP

At this juncture, we have made the complete cycle of the instructor's role, beginning with preclass logistics and ending with the strategies for effective instruction.

However, one final task remains. All training must eventually be evaluated by the users—in this case, the participants who gave up an opportunity cost (that of doing something else with their time) to attend a particular session.

Accordingly, the next chapter will deal with the subject of evaluating training results. To paraphrase Ernest Hemingway, that is *"the moment of truth"* for the instructor.

10

EVALUATING TRAINING RESULTS

LEARNING OBJECTIVES

After completing this chapter, you should have the necessary skills to:

Design a relevant evaluation questionnaire for a given program.

Describe a variety of participant evaluation biases.

Implement appropriate categories within the design of an evaluation form.

Understand the cautions involved in interpreting questionnaire data.

BACKGROUND

After five intensive days in class, the seminar concludes at 4:45 P.M. on a Friday afternoon. As a final task, the participants are asked to complete an evaluation questionnaire. The instructor has allotted 15 minutes for this, and each student dutifully but hurriedly completes the form before leaving the classroom.

Later on, the instructor briefly glances through several of them, noting (with the usual mind set) that the majority of course components were, once again, rated satisfactory. What was *not* apparent on the evaluation, however, was the fact that most of the participants did not believe the program had real value, but (for whatever reason) did not want to "make waves." Another training program well done? Obviously not.

Does this scenario sound a bit far-fetched? Your answer may depend on your number of years as an instructor. However, written responses on the evaluation questionnaires are not necessarily a true reflection of the participants' attitudes.

EVALUATION BIASES

I believe that the great majority of participants truly want to give *honest feedback* to the instructor via the evaluation form. The problem arises when the participant either feels threatened in some way by the form or else truly believes that the whole procedure is a waste of time. Let's look at Figure 41, Evaluation Biases, and note why the sought-after honest feedback is not always forthcoming.

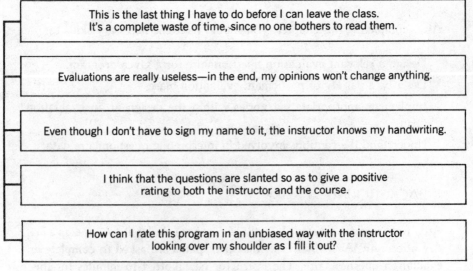

This is the last thing I have to do before I can leave the class.
It's a complete waste of time, since no one bothers to read them.

Evaluations are really useless—in the end, my opinions won't change anything.

Even though I don't have to sign my name to it, the instructor knows my handwriting.

I think that the questions are slanted so as to give a positive
rating to both the instructor and the course.

How can I rate this program in an unbiased way with the instructor
looking over my shoulder as I fill it out?

Figure 41. Evaluation biases.

1. *Students Feel Rushed, or Are Fatigued.*   This unfortunate situation occurs more frequently than instructors care to admit. When evaluations must be returned before participants leave the classroom, sufficient time must always be allowed for this task. For example, let's say that it takes a full 25 minutes to complete an evaluation. Let's further assume that earlier in the day the participants were informed that the class would end promptly at 5:00 P.M. Accordingly, many may have made plans to catch a certain train home, meet friends—and yes, even return to their desks to catch up on the work that had accumulated as a result of their attending the training session. Now, running a bit late, the instructor distributes the evaluations at 4:58 P.M., informing everyone that they cannot leave until the evaluation is completed. Honestly now, as a participant, how careful would you be in filling out every single line?

2. *Perception that the Evaluations Are Meaningless.*   If this unfortunate situation has been present for some time, it may also be time to change the training director! A good safeguard against this misperception is to make certain that participants *always* receive a summary of the completed evaluations, plus a comment on any significant problems that surfaced. For example, out of a class of 15 people, let's say that 10 noted that the room was stuffy and poorly ventilated. The instructor (or someone in the training department) should attach a note to the summary, at least *acknowledging* the poor ventilation, and mentioning, if possible, what will be done to remedy the situation.

3. *Doubts on Confidentiality of the Evaluation.*   This is perhaps one of the most puzzling "gray areas" in negative evaluation biases. Many training directors believe that they have fully protected the anonymity of the respondent by placing the word *optional* under the signature line of the evaluation form. The belief here is that if participants wish to identify themselves on the questionnaire, they can do so quite easily. Conversely, if they want to ensure their privacy, no signature is required.

Although that sounds perfectly logical, there is a problem. From a participant's point of view, the mere fact of not placing one's name on the form does not guarantee confidentiality. At the risk of sounding paranoid, every instructor, upon distributing the evaluations to the class, should take a few seconds and mentally play the "what if" game. Imagine yourself as a participant who is completing an evaluation but is concerned about confidentiality. Here are several perceptions that could occur:

What if the instructor recognizes my handwriting? After all, I have the sloppiest writing in class, and everyone knows it!

What if the instructor sees that I'm the only one in the class completing the evaluation with a *red pen*? Guess I better state that everything was wonderful with the class. No sense causing trouble for myself.

What if I write a negative report on certain parts of the program, and the instructor immediately knows it came from me? After all, I'm the only left-handed person in the class!

What if the instructor noticed that I just spilt some coffee on the evaluation form? Let's face it, mine will be the only one with a slight brown stain on the front page.

What if . . . (I'm sure you can easily come up with *many* more "what ifs" than I have.)

4.   *The Evaluation Questions Are Heavily Weighted to Produce a Positive Effect.*   Mark Twain described it aptly when he said there are three kinds of lies: lies, damn lies, and *statistics*. One does not have to be an expert in statistical analysis to know that a question can be worded to *slant* the results in a certain way. Consider the following two instructor evaluations:

EXAMPLE 1: Please rate your opinion of the course instructor(s)

Name _____   Name _____
1. Excellent _____   _____
2. Above Average _____   _____
3. Very Satisfactory _____   _____
4. Satisfactory _____   _____
5. Fair _____   _____

EXAMPLE 2: Please rate your opinion of the course instructor(s)

Name _____   Name _____
1. Excellent _____   _____
2. Very Good _____   _____
3. Satisfactory _____   _____
4. Fair _____   _____
5. Unsatisfactory _____   _____

Note: If you checked 4 or 5, please explain: _____
_____
_____
_____
_____

Obviously, Example 1 will force the participant to give the instructor(s) a more favorable rating in two ways: first, there is no *unsatisfactory* category to check, and second, there is no room under the question to write comments, if so desired.

5. *The Instructor Seems to Be Watching Me.* While this category might provoke some chuckles from some instructors, the situation can occur. Common sense dictates that the instructor should always leave the room while the evaluations are being completed, but remain nearby in case a participant has a question or clarification is needed.

Some instructors who remain in the room while evaluations are being completed offer the justification that much clean-up work remains to be done, such as taking down charts and ripping used flip chart paper off the easel. This creates two problems for participants. First, the mere presence of an instructor in the room during the completion of an evaluation is disturbing. Second, the clean-up activity is usually noisy and can easily distract participants—just when they should *not* be distracted.

EVALUATION TECHNIQUES

In selecting among the wide array of evaluation methods available to the instructor, the cardinal rule here is to always make certain that *the evaluation has been suitably matched to the learning objectives.*

Broadly speaking, most training falls within three categories:

1. *Product/Service Training.* Within this area would be programs to introduce basic company products or services to trainees or those employees being transferred from a different division or business group. For this category of training, it would be appropriate not only to evaluate the *training methods used* but also to test on *retention* of information about the product or service being introduced.

2. *Specialized Skill Training.* The term *specialized skill* covers those skill areas that are easily measurable. Examples of this would be training in word-processing equipment, computer equipment, or use of any type of office (or factory) machine where, through formal instruction, *a given level of proficiency is obtained.* Within this category, the use of both pretesting and posttesting is quite common, the objective being to evaluate specific performance upon completion of the training cycle.

3. *General Skill Training.*   The category of general skill training encompasses those areas that embrace skills that (while somewhat qualitatively measurable) rely more on the qualitative approach to skill building. It would include programs in selling skills, communication, problem solving, leadership techniques, and so on. Selective quantitative testing may be used here, but generally a more qualitative measurement, such as role plays and team assignments, is employed. Participant evaluation of general skills programs is very prevalent and in many cases quite detailed in both scope and content.

Since this book is written primarily for classroom instructors, this chapter will focus on creating a relevant evaluation questionnaire that can be used in a variety of learning situations. But first note that there is never an "ideal" form that can be used to evaluate all programs. What's important, therefore, is to review the essential categories that should be included, together with appropriate questions that can be used within each section.

SAMPLE CRITERIA

While evaluation forms can vary greatly in design, the following nine categories (and subsequent related questions) have proven to be both relevant and appropriate in questionnaire surveys.

1. General background information
2. Objectives
3. Relevance
4. Program format and instructional techniques
5. Course duration
6. Instructor/facilitator evaluation
7. Course design
8. Facilities evaluation
9. General comments

Let's review each category in greater detail, with specific comments on each section where appropriate.

General Background Information

The section on background information should be simple and easily answered in a concise manner. Its sole purpose is to identify the course, its location, and the actual dates attended. This information is particularly important when several similar programs are conducted frequently, and when the evaluations are to be filed for future reference. Here is an example:

> XYZ Corporation
> Metal Products Division
> *Confidential*

SUPERVISORY TRAINING PROGRAM EVALUATION QUESTIONNAIRE. Please complete this confidential questionnaire by checking your responses and (where appropriate) writing a brief answer. Your comments and specific opinions will be merged with those of others who participated in the class and will provide constructive feedback on any aspect of the course that might require modification. Please note that your signature is *not* required, but you may sign your name if desired.

Facility/location: _____

Course sponsor: _____

Dates attended: _____

Objectives

The aim of this section is to determine how well a participant's specific objectives prior to the program start were met at the conclusion of the learning experience. Although there is some latitude in designing this section of the questionnaire, I recommend the following combination of open responses with accompanying multiple choice selection:

OBJECTIVES

1. Please state your objectives in attending: _____

    _____

    _____

    _____

2. How well were your objectives met by attending the program?
    A. _____   Exceeded my objectives
    B. _____   Fully met my objectives
    C. _____   Met some of my objectives
    D. _____   Met very few (or none) of my objectives

    If you checked C or D, please explain: _____
    _____
    _____
    _____

Relevance

For any program to be truly successful, it *must* be highly relevant to the participant and be of direct value back on the job. The matter of relevance also extends to the use of the new skills back on the job and therefore naturally encompasses whether or not the program will be recommended to others, as we can see in this example:

RELEVANCE
3. How relevant was the program to your specific job responsibilities?
    A. _____   Highly relevant in all respects
    B. _____   Relevant to a satisfactory degree
    C. _____   Somewhat relevant
    D. _____   Not relevant

    If you checked C or D, please explain: _____
    _____
    _____
    _____

4. How do you intend to use the supervisory skills components taught in the program to increase effectiveness on the job?
    _____
    _____
    _____

5. Would you recommend this program to your peers?
   A. _____ Yes
   B. _____ No
   C. _____ Uncertain

   If you checked C, or wish to amplify further, please do so here.

   _____

   _____

   _____

Program Format and Instructional Techniques

The objective of this category is to rate the degree of effectiveness of all instructional techniques used in the program, thereby affording the instructor an unbiased view of the overall format. This is truly a key element in the total evaluation, since it will specifically pinpoint any weak structural component(s) in the overall course linkage. Here is how it might appear:

	Very Effective	Moderately Effective	Slightly Effective	Not At All Effective
Precourse reading assignments	_____	_____	_____	_____
Lectures	_____	_____	_____	_____
Instructor-led discussions	_____	_____	_____	_____
Small-group exercises	_____	_____	_____	_____
Videotape	_____	_____	_____	_____
Role plays	_____	_____	_____	_____
Team assignments	_____	_____	_____	_____
Evening assignments	_____	_____	_____	_____
Other_____	_____	_____	_____	_____

If you checked any category as either *slightly effective* or *not at all effective*, please explain: _____

_____

_____

Course Duration

This section can be filled in quickly by participants, and the information obtained is usually very relevant to course structure. This is especially true in both pilot programs, where the material is being presented for the first time, and courses that are more than three or four days in length. For example:

COURSE TIMING
6. In your opinion, was this timing:
   A. _____ Satisfactory
   B. _____ Would prefer more time
   C. _____ Would prefer less time

   If you checked B or C, please explain: _____
   _____
   _____

Instructor/Facilitator Evaluation

In all situations where only facilitators are used, they should be evaluated on the same basis as the instructor. To go a bit further, in my opinion, the rating categories for instructors and facilitators should be exactly the same. Note: If one were to presume from this statement that the skill traits required for both instructor and facilitator were the same, they would be entirely correct. For example:

INSTRUCTOR/FACILITATOR
7. Please rate the effectiveness of each resource leader:
   Name _____ Name _____
   A. Excellent _____ _____
   B. Very Good _____ _____
   C. Satisfactory _____ _____
   D. Fair _____ _____
   E. Unsatisfactory _____ _____

   If you checked D or E, please elaborate further: _____
   _____
   _____
   _____

Course Design

Although the questionnaire has already evaluated the duration of the program, more feedback is usually required on *specific course components*. Special attention should be given to the answers obtained in this section, since they can quickly isolate specific segments of course design that need work.

COURSE DESIGN

8. Please complete the following three categories, if applicable:

A. We should have spent more time on: _____

_____

B. We could have spent less time on: _____

_____

C. Areas that were not covered in program, but should have been:

_____

_____

Any additional thoughts or comments: _____

_____

_____

Facilities Evaluation

Here the facilities (and the entire training environment) come under review, as a reality check to those who were responsible for facilities planning. The questions should be brief and come directly to the point. For example:

GENERAL FACILITIES

9. Please rate each of the following concerning facilities:

	Excellent	Good	Satis-factory
Training facilities	_____	_____	_____
Food and service	_____	_____	_____
Other (please specify)	_____	_____	_____

Additional comments: _____

_____

General Comments

This final section of the evaluation is designed to encourage participants to write in any additional comments that they might care to make. Also, it provides an opportunity to thank participants for completing the evaluation, stressing the confidentiality that will be observed.

ADDITIONAL COMMENTS
10.   What further comments would you make for the benefit of others who might attend this program?

1. _____

_____

_____

2. _____

_____

_____

3. _____

_____

_____

Any information used from this form will be done so anonymously. Thank you very much for this information and your cooperation.

_____
Signature (optional)

Please print: _____
Name, Title (optional)

CAUTIONS

Some very definite cautions must be observed when evaluating training results via a questionnaire. As we have already seen, such factors as participant bias, design of the form, and even the room environment can slant results either negatively or positively. With this in mind, let's examine several other cautionary guidelines that should be observed.

1. *Never Let the Results of One Class Evaluation Heavily Influence the Course Design.* Several factors should be noted here. For one thing, the program itself could be quite satisfactory, but a poor instructor (or facilitator) could have brought down the rating of *the entire course.* In other words, even though the teacher received unsatisfactory marks, this negative influence extended to the material itself. The converse also holds true here. A really good instructor (via the halo effect) can enhance the evaluations of a mediocre program. Similarly, in the same manner, a poor room environment (or facility) can also cause participants to downgrade the entire program.

2. *Informal Class Feedback During the Course Is Just as Important as the Final Written Evaluation.* Every experienced instructor realizes the importance of feedback and is therefore not completely surprised by the results of the written evaluation. Taking this a bit further, by knowing *in advance* what is going well (and what's not going well) in the course, the instructor is able to institute "midcourse corrections," *before* the course is over. In short, securing and maintaining good class feedback throughout the program is the only sensible way to conduct a course in the first place.

3. *Minimize the "Negative Statistic."* In *every* class (especially when there are more than 15 participants) at least one participant is bound to dislike *everything* about the program. It's a fact of life that all instructors live with, and it will probably never change. For whatever reason, this person takes delight in supplying negative feedback, perhaps as a way of obtaining reverse gratification. While his or her comments should certainly never be ignored, they must be taken with a grain of salt. For example, if out of a class of 15 participants, 14 rated everything as *excellent*, the responses of the one who was negative on most points should perhaps be statistically minimized, but never totally ignored.

4. *Don't "Turn on the Charm" at the Last Minute.* Just prior to the evaluation, an instructor should never resort to such approaches as telling the class what a wonderful group they were, mentioning how hard he or she worked, and so on. In a word, *don't*. It's highly unprofessional and in most cases will not skew the evaluation upward.

5. *Leave the Room Gracefully.* Keep your exit simple and graceful; leave with as little fanfare as possible. Upon conclusion of the program,

thank the group for their participation, close with any other relevant remarks as necessary, distribute the questionnaire—and *leave* the room. The participants will appreciate the few moments of solitude necessary to complete their remarks, and you will be seen as more of a professional for your actions.

SUMMARY

1. Evaluation results can occasionally be distorted when participants feel rushed or fatigued, perceive the evaluations as meaningless, harbor doubts regarding the confidentiality of the process, believe that the evaluations have been heavily weighted to produce positive results, and have a feeling that the instructor is watching them while they fill out the questionnaire.

2. A broad array of effective evaluation techniques are available. The evaluation document selected must be appropriate to the program's learning objectives.

3. While evaluation forms can vary greatly in design, the following nine categories are generally included in the overall format:

1. General background information
2. Objectives
3. Relevance
4. Program format and instructional techniques
5. Course duration
6. Instructor/facilitator evaluation
7. Course design
8. Facilities evaluation
9. General comments

4. When evaluating the results of a questionnaire, the instructor should observe the following cautions: (1) never allow the results of just one class evaluation to unduly influence the overall course design; (2) realize that informal class feedback during the course is just as important as the final written evaluation; (3) minimize the "negative statistic"; (4) don't "turn on the charm" at the last minute; and (5) leave the room gracefully.

CHAPTER QUESTIONS

1. In your opinion, could participants view any specific categories in an evaluation questionnaire as threatening? If so, what are they?

2. As a general rule, do you believe that it's beneficial to send all participants a detailed summary of the evaluations from a program they have just attended? What are the pluses and minuses involved?

3. In your opinion, should the participant's signature on the evaluation *always* be made *optional*? Can you think of any situations where this would *not* be feasible? Why?

4. Considering the numerous categories to be evaluated in a typical questionnaire, is it really necessary to have participants rate the facilities? After all, isn't the adequacy of the facilities rather obvious to both the instructor and facilitator? Or is it?

THE NEXT STEP

With this review of evaluating training results now behind us, the stage is set for an overview of the critical partnership between the training function and the organization to which it supplies services.

As with any partnership, its eventual success is based on a foundation of clear purpose, specific objectives, and a good working relationship based on mutual trust and respect. In the world of high-powered competitive environments and ever-changing strategic planning, it's not an easy partnership to obtain, and once obtained, to hold and nurture.

With a strong partnership in place, the training department has a reasonable chance of organizational success. Without it, even with the best of efforts, it will undoubtedly be doomed to failure.

11

THE TRAINING/ORGANIZATION PARTNERSHIP

LEARNING OBJECTIVES

Upon completion of this chapter, you should have the necessary skills to:

Describe the required partnership between the training department and the organization.

Explain the five principles essential for the partnership's success.

Understand the STARS principle needed for an effective relationship with line management.

Implement an effective organizational strategy for a training department within a company structure.

OVERVIEW

For any training effort to be truly successful, a strong alliance must be forged with the parent organization and its corresponding line organization. To forge it properly requires a great deal of patience, insight, sharing of common objectives, and a mutual respect for entity and purpose. Any way viewed, it's much simpler said than done.

Being part of the training world, one frequently hears of the "inherent dangers" associated with the function. Comments such as "Training is a pure staff function, and as such, it's the first to go in a budget crunch," or "The training department represents a pure expense unit, and therefore should be looked upon differently than the line groups," are familar themes echoed by many. To these and other related comments I say, *nonsense*. The falseness of this argument lies not so much in intent, but rather in *perception*. In other words, these people also perceive training as a *secondary* function to other functions that generate revenue for the business.

In this sense, these same people would also state that in a downturn in business activity, all advertising expenditures should be drastically curtailed or altogether eliminated. Yet many leading business consultants, all other things being equal, would suggest that in an economic slump, expenditures for advertising and promotion be *increased* as a direct aid to the selling effort! Two points seem to surface in this illustration. The first is a lingering perception about the real value of staff functions; the second (closely allied) centers on value received for expenditures disbursed. Upon reflection—and a great deal of close examination—one usually finds a direct correlation between the perceived value of training and the vitality of the training-organizational partnership. Let's examine this in greater detail.

PARTNERSHIP FOUNDATIONS

As with all partnerships, certain guiding principles must be adhered to for the alliance to remain effective. While the following principles are not necessarily listed in order of importance, they represent the parameters that the training function must bring to the union.

Principle 1: The Organization's Commitment to Training Must Never Be Taken for Granted

Certain individuals consider themselves fortunate since they are associated with "training-oriented" companies. Such organizations are generally medium to large firms that consistently spend large amounts of money on training and continue to do so year after year. Individuals operating within this type of environment can be lulled into a false sense of security. After a time, they perhaps take a less disciplined approach to fulfilling training objectives and evaluating their continued relevancy to the business. Put in a slightly different perspective, once the training function is well established, it's all too easy to gradually throttle back into a state of complacency and even mediocrity. This sorry state of affairs usually does not happen overnight; like a cancer cell, it grows silently but insidiously, and unless detected early, can indeed be fatal. Accordingly, however successful a training function might be, one must never take the organization's commitment for granted. The commitment, which may have taken several years to build, can practically disappear overnight. That should *never* be allowed to happen.

Principle 2: Never Rely on a Successful Track Record

The second guiding principle to maintaining good partnership relations is to assume that the training department is judged *independently on every new program it presents* to the organization. Having a very successful track record of *previous* program offerings in no way insures that a less-than-satisfactory program will be tolerated. Assume, for example, that a training unit that has successfully presented three new programs a year for the past two years has just completed a new offering with less than favorable results. Too often trainers feel that because of all of their prior successes, the current fiasco will be quickly overlooked. They rely on the positive halo effect created by past events. It seldom works. The company will ask, "But, what have you done for me lately?" When you stop to consider the situation, the organization is well within its right with this line of thinking.

Principle 3: Do Not Use the Influence of a Training Mentor as a Shield to Protect an Image

Within every organization, you can usually find a high-placed individual who consistently supports every aspect of training. It's a fortunate training director indeed who can continue to nurture and cultivate this friendship, developing even stronger ties over the months and years.

However, you must never take advantage of this enviable alliance. In those times where perhaps the training department is *not* being run as efficiently as possible and starts being exposed to some adverse criticism, it is a natural temptation for the manager of training to place the mentor in a "buffer position" in an attempt to blunt or reduce the *level* of criticism being mounted. This may provide temporary relief in the short run, but it can never be a panacea for poor performance. Even worse, in the *long run*, the training function will stand a good chance of losing the mentor's influence. It is roughly similar to having a nagging toothache and relying on heavy doses of aspirin—you have to face up to a visit to the dentist's office, and by then the tooth will be in a lot worse condition!

Principle 4: Never Assume That Training Is Indispensable

The training function remains an integral part of most organizational structures and continues to fulfill a specific role in meeting defined business objectives. The inadvertent temptation here—usually brought on by a rewarding series of prominent training successes—is to assume an overwhelming sense of importance as the teachers (or knowledge bearers) of the company.

Symptoms of this sad malady include overspending on the assigned budget, showing less regard for fulfilling program objectives than for the fanfare accompanying the awarding of gifts or prizes to participants, and increasingly relying on the training mentor as an "invisible shield" to protect the department from criticism.

No one is indispensable—and the training department is certainly no exception to the rule.

Principle 5: Admit Failure When You Have Failed

To be successful, all partnerships must be based on mutual respect, an "open climate" and a sharing of experiences—both the successful and the not-so-successful. Failure to live up to this fundamental principle will certainly begin to sow the seeds of partnership failure and the consequent break-up of the union.

It's never easy to admit a training program failure, especially if it has involved a heavy expenditure of time, money, and effort. It is worse yet when ego is involved: the temptation is to downplay the failure by trumpeting the one or two good points that did come out of the program. If a program fails, *admit it*, then *learn from the mistake*. Following this one simple guideline distinguishes the true training professional from all the rest.

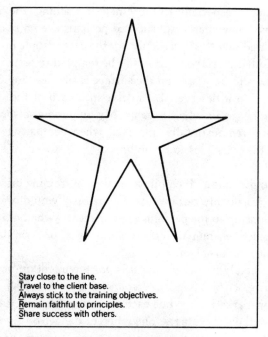

Stay close to the line.
Travel to the client base.
Always stick to the training objectives.
Remain faithful to principles.
Share success with others.

Figure 42. The STARS Principle.

BUILDING THE STARS TEAM

Although there is never a simple formula to insure a successful training partnership with the line, Figure 42, The STARS Principle, has proven itself successful over the years, standing the test of time in organizations both large and small. The principle revolves around the acronym STARS, and I heartily recommend it to everyone involved in the training function, from instructor to department manager.

Let's review this from a macro viewpoint, then look at each "tip of the star" in closer detail. There are five principles involved:

1. Stay close to the line.
2. Travel to the client base.
3. Always stick to the training objectives.
4. Remain faithful to principles.
5. Share success with others.

To some readers, especially to those new in training, the STARS principle might seem somewhat simplistic and perhaps even a play on the obvious. Rest assured that this is certainly *not* the case. People in training, like those in every other endeavor, can easily be tempted to assume that something that *appears* to be simple on the surface *is* simple—and therefore not give it the attention it deserves. Let's delve into each of the star points in detail, then *you* be the judge of its value. My only request is that those in a training function remain totally impartial when comparing their performance against the principles to be outlined.

Stay Close to the Line.   If a poll were taken of training directors around the world, I'm reasonably certain that the majority would disclose a direct reporting relationship to the personnel department—whether it be the vice-president of personnel, human resources manager, or a similar type function. Therein lies the problem.

Let me immediately point out that it is *not* the intention of this book to debate the merits of reporting to personnel rather than line management (such as sales or marketing). While each reporting structure has its own set of advantages and disadvantages, one inherent danger of reporting to personnel is that it puts the training department *one step removed from direct line involvement*, and that is a subtle obstacle that must be overcome.

Whomever the training function reports to, the cardinal rule involved is to *stay as close to the line as possible*. What is meant by that? Specifically:

1. *Have a Thorough Knowledge of the Organization's Products and Services.*   This does not simply mean having a general smattering of information regarding the company's products, obtained through occasional glances at product brochures and the year-end report to stockholders. Far from it! What is needed is a *thorough understanding* of all goods and services offered to the target markets.

You should learn every *feature* and *benefit* attached to products being marketed, and understand the benefits from the customer's point of view. Make time to meet the company's customers, even if you are not in the sales training part of the business. Stay closely involved with data-processing systems, spend time on the assembly line, and (where applicable) actually *get out into the field with the sales force*. The important point here is to acquire and constantly maintain an in-depth understanding of the company's offerings to the client base. It's not only appreciated by the line, but it integrates the training person much more fully into the income-producing segment of the business, which is an essential ingredient for success.

2. *Understand the Mission, Business Objectives, and Strategies of the Business.* Trainers cannot function without a clear understanding of company aims and philosophy, together with an appreciation of overall objectives and the strategies needed to achieve stated goals.

In staying close to the line, one must always be aware of the special situations they face both on a short- and long-term basis. This is not meant to imply that a training manager becomes a confidant to line management. Far from it. On the other hand, trainers who have and share an appreciation of line challenges are in a good position to *assist* whenever the need for specialized training arises. The Manager of Training can then take a *proactive* rather than a *reactive* stance, which puts training in constant good standing with the revenue-producing segments of the organization.

Travel to the Client Base. The second STARS principle revolves around bringing training to wherever the client base may reside. In its broadest sense, this means always getting to "where the action is," or, to put it a bit differently, taking the training *to the participants* instead of continually conducting it in the home office, where logistics are usually easier and controlled to a greater degree.

Naturally, this is not always possible. The extent to which it can be done depends to a large degree on the size of the organization and whether or not it has branch offices or overseas locations. However, the important point here is that when training is conducted for employees away from the home office, two important benefits usually ensue: (1) it's generally more cost effective to run a training program with the "home team" rather than an outside consultant, and (2) conducting programs at field locations can greatly enhance the overall training effect and its corresponding image throughout the organization.

At this juncture, you may ask how you can capitalize on this type of enhancement if the organization has a single location, without far-flung satellite offices. The answer here is two-fold. First, the training manager should always make it a point to visit periodically with all department heads, making certain that each is aware of training's capabilities and constantly probing for areas where training can be of some added value. Second, in addition to personal visits the training manager should have periodic written updates on training activity sent to key managers, thus powerfully reinforcing training's achievements and capabilities. A bit of public relations conveyed in this manner can go a long way in helping to build a winning training team.

Always Stick to the Training Objectives. In most organizations, training function objectives usually fall into two major classifications: *long-term*, with a time span of over one year, and *short-range*, usually over a 12-month period.

Training's long-term objectives are those that support and are closely tailored to the long-range goals of the parent organization. Training objectives that can be considered as continuous and long term include:

To provide relevant training programs in support of organizational objectives and the strategic business plan.

To insure maximum cost efficiency for each program offered to the business.

To keep all ongoing programs in the master training plan updated and revised to meet changing product/service requirements.

To retain a high degree of adaptability in both program design and duration, instituting quick and relevant modifications where required.

To maintain a *proactive* training approach to the changing needs of the business, building high levels of flexibility into both training staff and services offered.

In contrast to long-term objectives, the short-range objectives of the training department are closely matched to the *annual goals* set by the business. While these annual organizational goals can vary widely depending on company size and type of product/service being offered, the responsibility of training usually falls into two categories:

1. *Maintain* and update where necessary the current program offerings.

2. *Create* new programs in direct support of new business requirements.

Regardless of work pressures, possible staff shortages, or budget constraints, the training manager is expected to *deliver continuously* on both the short- and long-range objectives established for the department. As with all partnerships, a delicate balance of trust and commitment must be established and continuously reinforced in order to keep the union strong and viable. As the business progresses, senior management will be preoccupied with its own daily challenges and unexpected roadblocks, but will be counting on training to hold up its end of the partnership, regardless of difficulties that might be encountered. In the end, business objectives *must* be reached, or there might be no business at all. Close adherence to established training objectives, in spite of varying business requirements, goes a long way towards the STARS principle for the training group.

Remain Faithful to Principles. The training manager's *personal* principles should be reflected in the conduct of day-to-day relationships within the organization. These principles should act as a guiding force regardless of the interface level, whether the contact is with senior management, peers, subordinates, or participants in a given program. Shakespeare said it well: "To thine own self be true." Of all the guiding thoughts in the STARS principle, this one certainly ranks on or very near to the top. Staying true to yourself in both deeds and personal conduct reflects an extension of one's personal values and ethics, which can never be diminished by others regardless of stresses and strains of the everyday business environment.

The organizational partnership with training demands personal honor and integrity from the Training Manager, even though no words are spoken. They are the two built-in ingredients that an individual must *bring to the job* from earlier experience and environment. In my opinion, these two vital ingredients *cannot* be learned in a classroom or rapidly assimilated on the job. By setting examples for others through personal high standards, the training manager truly reflects an enviable yardstick of effective management and is a copartner in the successful relationship between line and staff entities within the company. To achieve any less is a personal failure—to the individual, coworkers, and the organization itself.

Share Success with Others. I have yet to meet an individual who has achieved something of significance without the slightest help from someone else. Most of us readily admit to this; a few unfortunates still cling to the false notion that personal success can be obtained in a vacuum. The training function is no exception to this rule.

The success achieved by training within the organization should *always* be shared with those who contributed in some way toward the total program development or implementation. This can include such a diverse population as:

Consultants, either internal or external

Specialists from within the training department such as writers, graphic arts specialists, photographers, and editors

Subject-matter experts who contributed their knowledge

Individuals who were consulted on some aspect of course design or implementation

When showered with the exhilarating aura of program success, it perhaps is only human nature to bask in the warmth of the praise offered. It's wonderful for the ego and provides a soothing balm for any discomforts suffered along the way. But sharing the success spotlight with others does not diminish one's own role. In fact, just the reverse holds true. Giving appropriate credit to others actually *enhances* one's position within the organizational structure. Moreover, giving credit where credit is due is not only a fundamental rule of good supervision but of personal integrity as well.

These five STARS principles are not an absolute guarantee of success, but they will certainly start the training director down the right road. Success will never come easily or happen magically overnight. Liberal doses of patience, understanding, and empathy, along with personal integrity are needed. In the end, however, the results obtained will more than compensate for the effort expended. A fair bargain, don't you think?

SUMMARY

1.   In most organizations, there is a direct correlation between the perceived value of training and the vitality of the training-organizational relationship.

2.   The strength of an effective training partnership rests heavily on the following principles:

Never take the organization's commitment to training for granted.

Never rely on a successful track record.

Do not use the influence of a training mentor as a shield to protect an image.

Never assume that training is indispensable.

Admit failure when you have failed.

3.   To insure a successful training partnership with the line, the STARS principles should be employed:

Stay close to the line.

Travel to the client base.

Always stick to the training objectives.

Remain faithful to principles.

Share success with others.

4.   A strong training partnership with the parent organization is never established easily; it requires a great deal of time, perseverance, and effort. However, in the long run, the benefits of the strong union developed will be well worth the effort.

CASE STUDY: "SO, WHAT ARE FRIENDS FOR?"

From just about any perspective, Hal Bradford had been in an enviable position for several years. As director of training for Jan Cosmetics, Ltd., he was responsible for a department of eight specialists with a training population of slightly over 700 employees throughout the world.

Originally hired after graduating from a prestige college, Hal's first job in the organization was as a sales representative in the highly successful fashion line of the cosmetics group. Advancement followed quickly, and within three years (after two successive promotions) he was promoted to regional sales manager for the northwest sales area. It was at that juncture that Hal was offered the job of training director by Jim Raleigh, a senior vice-president of marketing for the cosmetic group.

Although it was a bit unusual to promote a sales manager into the lead training slot, Jim Raleigh was confident that Hal was the best person for the job. He felt that Hal would be a "natural" for the position since his undergraduate degree was in psychology and the primary thrust of training during the next few years would be in the sales and marketing effort.

At first, Hal was reluctant to accept the offer. He finally consented after Jim convinced him of two things. The first was that the existing staff of eight training specialists were well versed in their assigned jobs and therefore would need very little managing. The second factor was Jim's personal guarantee of training support. Since Jim Raleigh was a strong advocate of training, Hal felt secure in the knowledge that a high-placed mentor would always supply the needed back-up if and when required.

Hal accepted the job, and for the first six months everything went well—so well, in fact, that Hal became increasingly pleased that he had accepted this new assignment. Jim was right. The training staff required very little guidance; within a few weeks a major program was introduced and met with immediate success. What pleased Hal even more was Jim's constant encouragement and support, both verbally and in several very flattering memorandums.

Looking back, it was difficult for Hal to recall precisely when things started to turn sour. No one event stood out in his mind. He was reasonably certain, however, that whatever had caused the problem, it was really not his fault. He did recall some resentment from the staff when he took the major credit for the new training program—but after all, as head of the department, he saw no reason not to. Also, he remembered a few times when certain key members of his staff tried repeatedly to see him and had to be shunted off. That was unfortunate, but they just had to realize that he was extremely busy and simply did not have the time to worry about every "little decision" of the staff.

The problem probably came to a head when he reprimanded Susan Farley for not teaching her assigned class in product knowledge training. At the last minute she had called in sick, and it was difficult for him to get another instructor. Granted, when Susan did appear early the next morning, he probably should not have yelled at her, especially in front of several others who were in the room at that time. But he really had no choice, especially when her tone became sarcastic.

As Hal was mulling over these events, his thoughts were interrupted by a telephone call. It was Jim Raleigh's secretary who reported that Mr. Raleigh wanted to see him immediately.

As Hal entered Jim's office, the following dialogue took place:

Jim: Sit down, Hal. We have some serious matters to discuss.

Hal: Sure. Hope you can make it fast though. I have lots of things to do this morning.

Jim: Well, whatever your schedule is, what I have to say will take priority.

Hal: [*puzzled*] Okay. What's on your mind?

Jim: It's about an unofficial visit I had today from one of your people on the training staff, and I'm really upset about it.

Hal: [sarcastically] I'd like to know who it was who came to see you. Guess they find it hard to keep pace with me. By the way, who was this person?

Jim: [a bit annoyed] That's unimportant. What *is* important, however, is *what* was said. This person told me that she was appointed to represent your *entire* staff, and they were very upset with the way that they were being managed. Frankly, this really troubles me.

Hal: Specifically, what is their "problem"?

Jim: There are several. For one, you never seem to have time to meet with them. For another, they feel you always take full credit for projects done mainly by your staff. And worse of all, you have become less tolerant of your key people, which has now created a difficult work environment for all concerned.

Hal: Regarding the tolerance thing, I guess you are referring to the ridiculous incident with Susan yesterday. I'm sorry that I yelled at her, but there was simply no excuse for her not making it to class that day. Besides, I didn't like her tone of voice. No reason for anyone to get sarcastic, *especially* to the boss.

Jim: Well, it may interest you to know that before this absence she had a perfect record of attendance. On the day she called in sick, she had a 102° temperature—and actually tried to get out of bed so as not to disappoint you. How's that for a good reason to be upset with her boss?

Hal: Well, how was I to know?

Jim: [angrily] Perhaps you should have asked her!

Hal: Look, Jim, I'm sorry about that, but as long as we are talking, I have a concern of my own. I've been getting a few complaints lately from the line about the "attitude" of training towards some participants. Frankly, I've been too busy to look into it, so it would sure help if you would put in a "good word" for me in the right places. Know what I mean?

Jim: Yes.

Hal: [relieved] So you'll do it for me?

Jim: No. And as long as we are on the topic, let's review a few things you must do immediately, if you want to stay in your job!

Hal: [*shocked*] Hey, wait a minute. That's unfair! I get in a little bit of
          trouble, and now you want to talk about my career being threatened?

Jim: Exactly.

Hal: But why can't you just put in a few good words for me? After all,
          when you think about it, *what are friends for*?

CASE STUDY DISCUSSION POINTS

1.   In your opinion, is Hal *entirely* wrong in both his attitude and management style? In what respect might Jim be at fault?

2.   Everything considered, should Jim now support Hal (even to a degree)
for the good of the training department?

3.   Should Hal's staff have come to him first, before expressing their griev-
ance to Jim? Since they did not do this, do they have the same right in
expecting matters to straighten out quickly?

CHAPTER QUESTIONS

1.   In any organization, how much support can one really expect from a
mentor? Over what time frame can one count on this sphere of influence?

2.   Would the STARS principle apply to *any* training-organizational relationship and under *any* circumstance? Can you identify which of these principles are the easiest to obtain? Conversely, which are the most difficult to
accomplish?

3.   In your opinion, even with the strongest of a training-organizational
partnership, wouldn't the training function be one of the first to be reviewed
in anticipated periods of economic business downturn? If you don't agree,
why not?

THE NEXT STEP

With the completion of this chapter, we have concluded the full learning
cycle for instructional skills in modern-day organizational environments.
While opinions may differ on a few of the principles outlined throughout
the book, there should be no disagreement on the fact that teaching today is
not an exact science, and that it continually demands a wide array of skills
by the instructor. Unlike the disciplines of mathematics and science, teaching has no standard set of formulas to make the task of teaching easier, and

that in itself creates one of the exciting challenges for those that have the honor of calling themselves instructors.

Over the years, many questions have arisen on all facets of the instructional skills process. The next chapter answers a variety of commonly asked questions in a logical, orderly sequence.

12

QUESTIONS FREQUENTLY ASKED ABOUT TRAINING

LEARNING OBJECTIVES

The following series of dialogues represent a cross section of commonly asked questions about the broad area of training. For ease in reading, each question along with its corresponding answer has been grouped in numeric chapter sequence.

TRAINING AND THE ORGANIZATION

Question: Regarding the securing of management commitment for training, you appear to give a great emphasis to the need for mutual trust and respect, which must be earned. Isn't this a rather obvious requirement for training to be successful?

Answer: Yes, it should be obvious to everyone involved in the training function, and therein lies the problem. Perhaps due to the sheer

303

simplicity of the statement, some trainers could take this for granted, and that could be the start of a dangerous mistake. The building and maintaining of high levels of mutual trust and respect are core ingredients for successful implementation of training within the organization. Such a relationship generally takes a long time to build, yet it can be destroyed overnight. One should never take something so important lightly, nor can the principles involved ever be overemphasized.

Question: You state that there is no ideal number of people required to carry out a training and development function within an organization. Could you amplify further on this?

Answer: The size of the department is really determined by a multitude of factors. Certainly the size of the organization being serviced is important, but the true test is really determined by the size of the training budget *averaged over several years*. This is directly influenced by the organization's training expectations and *long-term* commitment to this specialized effort.

Question: I note that you have recommended that the head of training report directly to the line—in this case, to the marketing director. Isn't that a bit unusual? I believe that in most organizations training reports directly to personnel. What's wrong with that?

Answer: I'm aware that my recommendation has probably stirred up some controversy. A common thread throughout my book is that, in order to be successful, training must respond to line needs, in effect becoming part of the line organization. While I certainly have nothing against the personnel function, I believe that the personnel group (for whatever training services requested) should be considered as a *client* of training, similar to any other group within the total organization. My reasoning here is based on the sincere belief that there is a direct ratio between training's involvement with the line and its ultimate credibility throughout the company.

Question: While I respect your opinion, I'm still not sure that I agree with you.

Answer: And I respect your thoughts, but still hold to my opinion.

Question: You mentioned that the needs-analysis process consists of five distinct steps. Can you think of any situation where any of the elements in the process can be combined?

Answer: Certainly. Depending upon the complexity of the needs-analysis task, coupled with the degree of skill reflected by the analyst, various steps can be merged. For example, during the fourth step, summarizing data, an easy transition could be made to the final step of recommending areas of training required. Once again, the merging of steps within the process depends on the complexity of the assigned task.

ADULT LEARNING METHODOLOGIES

Question: I agree completely that lack of time due to other job pressures is a formidable barrier to adult learning. But what can be done about it?

Answer: That's a difficult question to answer since every case is a bit different. A clear danger signal here would be a situation where an organization overtly supports training but demands that every class be held after working hours or on weekends. While there *may* be a valid reason for this, the training director has the responsibility of acquainting senior management with the pitfalls involved and perhaps working out some sort of compromise. However, employees should never be made to feel "guilty" about attending a class instead of working at their desks. I would hope that that type of company philosophy went out prior to the 1940s.

Question: You emphasize the point that learning is greatly enhanced from stimulation to the senses. Isn't learning also greatly affected by the sheer skill of the instructor?

Answer: Of course. But if you carefully study the platform techniques of highly effective instructors, I'm sure that you'll find that they naturally draw on stimulation of the senses. For example, highly skilled teachers will *never* lecture for over 10 minutes, relying on *voice alone*. In addition, they will employ a range of techniques—use of hands, facial gestures, and voice modulation, to name just a few. Where appropriate, they will use audio-visual aids.

Question: I like the idea of positive reinforcement as a direct aid to the learning process. But isn't this technique more effective with children, or perhaps young adults, than with adults?

Answer: That misconception is somewhat common. The technique of positive reinforcement works equally as well with preschool children and with senior citizens; age has no effect at all on the efficiency of the learning process.

Question: Well, then, wouldn't you agree that the use of a role play to display a positive model could be viewed as more threatening to adults than to children?

Answer: Yes. And in this respect, the instructor must always take great care that the role play is perceived and conducted in a non-threatening environment.

Question: What happens when participants gain a higher skill level through the use of positive reinforcement, but then receive no "on-the-job" support?

Answer: Not only will the new skill level rapidly dissipate, but there is also a good chance that the individual will experience strong feelings of frustration and resentment.

INSTRUCTIONAL COMMUNICATION SKILLS

Question: Honestly now, do you think an instructor with sound knowledge of the subject, teaching in a well-equipped class-room with a good learning environment, can fail simply because adequate levels of feedback aren't obtained?

Answer: Absolutely.

Question: Regarding room environment, I've heard that in Europe it would be unthinkable, all things being equal, to have a class-room without windows, yet in the United States that is not unusual. Am I correct?

Answer: I have no statistics on this, but I believe that you are correct. Take heart in the fact, however, that this condition seems to be improving with each passing year. Placing participants in a classroom without windows—especially when programs run over several days—can easily subtract from the total learning experience one hopes to obtain.

Question: I like the idea of the components within the communication cycle but am confused over your opinion that even *negative* feedback can be considered worthwhile in the communication process. Care to elaborate?

Answer: The point here is that even though the other person may be disagreeing with you (hence, negative feedback), you at least have the opportunity to respond with an appropriate answer. In a sense, negative feedback is far more useful than *neutral* feedback where *no response is obtained.*

Question: I question your emphasis on the environment that surrounds the communication process. If a speaker is really stimulating, very little else should really matter.

Answer: Have you ever sat in a room during midsummer when the air-conditioning has broken down and the temperature has risen to over 90°?

Question: Your review of frame of reference has a special significance for the instructor who is facing a classroom of students for the first time. But how does the teacher know what is on the participants' minds when they enter the classroom?

Answer: The teacher has no way of knowing at that moment. However, through discreet class probing plus careful observation of body language, especially during the first few minutes of the program, the instructor can learn a great deal about the participants' attitudes.

Question: If effective listening is such a critical skill in the total communication process, don't you agree that *every* instructor should receive training in it *before* beginning teaching as a career?

Answer: I agree completely. Unfortunately, as with many other elements in the communication process, some people (including many instructors) believe that they are already skilled listeners and therefore need no specialized training. Nothing could be further from the truth.

Question: I agree that maintaining eye contact is a definite aid to effective listening. However, wouldn't you agree that there sometimes is a fine line between maintaining a steady fixed gaze on the speaker and *staring* at someone? What's the guideline here?

Answer: Common sense. One should always attempt to maintain a continued gaze at the speaker, but every so often to glance at
something else. In any event, if one had to err, it's better to err
on the side of a stare than to be accused of never having looked
at the speaker at all!

Question: Can a truly professional speaker reach a point where he or she
achieves a 95 percent perfection rate in effective communication? In other words, can a speaker become so proficient that
continued training in communication is no longer needed?

Answer: Perhaps. But surely such a speaker would want to work on the
5 percent that still needs improvement.

DEVELOPING THE INSTRUCTOR'S GUIDE

Question: I can understand your point about tailoring the instructor's
guide to suit an individual's teaching style. However, isn't there
an inherent danger in allowing this? If the same course were
taught by three different instructors, wouldn't there be a
chance of "unevenness" in the learning process from the participant's viewpoint?

Answer: Not really. By *tailoring*, I am referring to a slight customization
of the basic instructor's guide to suit the individual style of the
instructor. In no way would this change course content; rather,
it would allow each instructor some latitude in platform techniques while retaining program integrity. For example, in a goal-
setting module, the guide could state that the instructor should
list and discuss the four criteria for setting effective goals. A
slight tailoring here could mean the addition (or embellish-
ment) of one or more of the criteria involved, perhaps bridging
it to a personal experience that the instructor has encountered
on the job or in previous classes.

Question: I don't agree completely with your "two-phase instructor cycle"
prior to the teaching of a class for the first time. I can understand the importance of instructor training, but is it really
necessary for an otherwise experienced instructor to have to sit
through a class as a participant? In all due respect, isn't that a
waste of time—especially for a seasoned teacher?

Answer: Absolutely not. In fact, just the reverse holds true. Without first experiencing the course as a participant, the instructor would stand a good chance of wasting valuable instructional time during the first session in attempting to judge how each of the course components are "hinging together." Any way viewed, it's a definite plus at least to have had exposure to a course *as a student* before attempting to teach others as the instructor.

Question: I like the idea of having each page of the guide arranged with sequential teaching notes on the left and suggested flip charts on the right. But aren't many guides prepared with the teaching notes on one page and the required charts listed in a separate book?

Answer: Yes, I have seen and used both versions. I personally prefer the former since everything the instructor needs is contained in the *one* guide. The less one has to be concerned with on the platform, the better!

Question: I agree with most of the instructor's guide traps that you mentioned, but not with your recommendation that the guide never be shipped with the conference material but always carried by the instructor. I prefer to travel with a minimum of baggage and have *always* shipped my instructor's guide ahead with the rest of the material. For your information, nothing has ever gone wrong. Care to comment?

Answer: I wish you continued good luck.

PRECLASS LOGISTICS

Question: All things being equal, I would always prefer holding a class in a bona fide conference center rather than a hotel. What are your thoughts on this?

Answer: That's a tough one to answer due to the many variables involved. For example, as a general rule, it's usually more reliable to hold a seminar in a conference center since that is their only business. In most cases a center can accommodate last-minute requests for additional flip charts or overhead projectors, for example. In a hotel audio-visual equipment is generally rented from a local dealer, and advance notice is required. Granted' that I am generalizing a bit here, I do find that a good hotel facility has a definite advantage over conference centers in the general ambiance and more relaxed atmosphere. In the final analysis, the decision on site selection must take in all of these factors, plus the personal experience obtained from the holding of previous programs in both places.

Question: I'm amazed at the rather voluminous number of categories and specific questions contained in the *Meeting Checklist*. Why was the form designed in this manner?

Answer: After *many years* of experience in being responsible for meetings, coupled with liberal doses of mistakes due to the absence of just such a checklist, this form was created. But a word of caution is appropriate here. Extensive as this checklist is, it is *never* a substitute for good common sense on the part of the meeting planner. I believe that one readily complements the other—they work in tandem.

Question: All things being equal, are there any specific room arrangements that you personally prefer over others?

Answer: Yes. In the majority of teaching assignments, I would always choose the standard U-shaped arrangement. Properly used, it brings the instructor in close proximity with each participant, creates a feeling of class togetherness, and gives the instructor a high degree of control in conveying information.

Question: When conducting an off-site session, I like the idea of giving the class at least two to three hours for recreation and "time off" at noon. However, when the class has to stay until 6:30 instead of breaking at 5:00 fatigue becomes a big problem—especially in the late afternoon. How do you handle that?

Answer: No easy answer can be given. I also like the idea of a long break at lunch, especially when the program is held at a resort. But it then becomes imperative to plan the afternoon schedule very carefully, placing the "heaviest" activities as early after the break as possible. Also, make certain that additional coffee and soda are introduced—especially in the late afternoon.

AND WHAT DO YOU SAY, AFTER YOU SAY "HELLO"?

Question: I'm a bit surprised at your heavy emphasis on the ice breaker activity required of the instructor *prior* to the class start. Doesn't this place too much emphasis on social aspects? After all, the instructor's role is to teach. not to play the part of a social director.

Answer: I assume from your question that you believe that meeting participants beforehand is in some way slightly demeaning for the instructor. Frankly, nothing could be further from the truth. Let's look at this from a participant's point of view. If I were scheduled to attend a class over several days, I would feel more comfortable meeting the instructor *beforehand* in a less formal atmosphere. Wouldn't you? Conversely, the teacher would also benefit, getting to know the class a bit better prior to taking the platform. In no way can this be viewed as condescending on the instructor's part—unless of course, the instructor perceives it that way, which would be unfortunate for all concerned.

Question: I agree that during class introductions the instructor's task includes matching participants' expectations to stated program objectives. However, isn't there a built-in danger here? What happens if there is a very wide discrepancy between the two? Doesn't that spell trouble?

Answer: Very much so, but such a situation should never happen. Before enrolling in *any* class, the participant should receive both a course description *and* an overview of individual program components. Also included should be the general learning objectives of the course in simple, straightforward terms. Informing participants about the course *in advance* of enrollment greatly reduces the chances of mismatched expectations.

Question: You seem to favor the use of teams and small-group assignments as teaching vehicles. While this sounds quite feasible, isn't there a danger that (1) one person will dominate the others in the team, and (2) one team will be visibly stronger (more experienced) than the other? How do you handle that?

Answer: By carefully selecting both individuals and team members *in advance of the program.*

Question: I completely disagree with your view that an instructor should have direct experience in the subject being taught. After all, a well-grounded formal education in a particular field is certainly of some value, and many instructors have far more education than most participants have. What's your view on that?

Answer: Certainly, having a sound educational educational in the subject being taught is vital to success. However, to be effective in front of a class, the instructor still requires a reasonable degree of teaching skill, plus some *practical experience*. Let's put it this way. An instructor may have a comprehensive educational background on the skill of applied coaching, but unless he or she has *actually coached someone*, a definite degree of teaching effectiveness has been lost.

EFFECTIVE PRESENTATION SKILLS

Question: You have probably heard this many times, but aren't some people natural public speakers—terrific on the platform, even though they have had *no* formal training in presentation skills?

Answer: I will answer this in two ways. To begin with, there *are* people who bring a high degree of command and public speaking skills without any type of platform training whatsoever. At the same time, however, I would also state that these *same people* would improve even further with exposure to formal public speaking techniques.

Question: No one can argue the fact that room environment and physical layout are important to a presentation, and accordingly should be reviewed by the speaker *in advance*. However, aren't there times when this is simply not possible for the speaker to do?

Answer: It can happen, but it should be avoided at all costs. At the very least, if the speaker knows that this will occur, he or she should make every effort to have someone at the conference site check the arrangements personally and report back to the speaker. A little preplanning at this stage can go a long way in avoiding some unexpected and unpleasant surprises later on.

Question: I've attempted your recommended deep-breathing exercise just prior to speaking, and it didn't work. I was just as nervous as before. What happened?

Answer: Don't be discouraged if this method does not show visible results right away. It takes a lot of practice and patience to minimize the discomfort that you feel. *Keep trying*, for it will work!

Question: You seem to place high emphasis on the use of audio-visual aids as an effective teaching technique. While I generally agree, don't you think that this technique can be overdone in a classroom?

Answer: Perhaps, but I have never seen it happen. On the other hand, I have witnessed many mediocre presentations that could have been greatly enhanced by just a few well-positioned slides, flip charts, or a film. Certainly, the instructor should control the graphics used (and *not* vice versa), but as a general rule, the more audio-visuals used, the more effective the presentation will be.

Question: When answering questions from an audience, must *every* question be rephrased? Admittedly, it allows everyone in the room to understand thoroughly what has been asked, but can't the whole process get redundant—or perhaps even boring?

Answer: Although there could be a slight chance of that I would err on the side of rephrasing. Bear in mind, however, that not every question has to be fully rephrased. Sometimes a concise partial paraphrasing is more than sufficient, yet still accomplishes the basic objective of keeping everyone on track.

Question: The "Question-and-Answer Strategy" section within the *Presentation Planner* looks like it might have value for speakers. But, I wonder if it can prepare a speaker for *all* anticipated questions from an audience. What do you think?

Answer: You are correct in the sense that one cannot anticipate *every* question that may be raised after the presentation. But this section will at least get the speaker to think about possible questions and therefore become better prepared to answer them.

The mere exercise of anticipating questions in advance always gives the speaker a competitive edge on the podium.

CLASSROOM GAMES THAT WORK

Question: You specify that in order to be meaningful, a game should be highly participative. Does this mean that during the playing of the game, *everyone* must be involved? Would you clarify, please?

Answer: Let's look at it this way. A successful game conducted in front of a room with only two players can be very participative since the entire class gets involved in the game scenario. As just one example of this, each of the players in the game could be *team captains* who are representing their *team players* (the participants who are viewing this from their seats). Naturally, to be effective, the game must have some type of action, excitement, or competitiveness built in; otherwise, it will be perceived as boring.

Question: Frankly, I never use a game given to me by another instructor. My own experience has shown that unless you are thoroughly familiar with every facet of it, it can backfire and truly become demotivating for the participants. Has this ever happened to you?

Answer: Yes, it has, and for the same reason that you experienced. On the other hand, I am always on the lookout for appropriate games developed by other instructors, and with their permission, would not hesitate in using them in the classroom. The key, of course, is exactly what you mentioned—*not using a game unless you are thoroughly knowledgeable in every facet of it.*

Question: Over the years, I've encountered some strong pros and cons regarding the awarding of a prize to a game winner. Some say it cheapens the entire exercise, even to the point of making it demeaning. Other instructors hold to the exact opposite point of view. What's your opinion?

Answer: Personally, I like the idea of awarding prizes to game winners.

It definitely heightens the excitement of the competition, thereby adding value to the game. However, a caution to note is that *the prize must always be appropriate to the game.* In other words, a prize of high perceived value can actually detract from the true purpose of the game! It is not uncommon for instructors to fall into this trap.

Question: The effective listening game certainly appears to have potential for a powerful learning experience for participants. However, I have a sense that unless properly controlled by the instructor, the game could prove demotivating—perhaps even dangerous. Am I correct?

Answer: Yes. My suggestion is that you *do not* attempt this game without first observing an experienced instructor who is very familiar with the game conduct it. Done well, however, it truly is a powerful way to illustrate the difficulties experienced in attempting to listen effectively to others.

TEACHING STRATEGIES

Question: I like the section "Use of a Facilitator," but need clarification on one point. Are you saying that a good facilitator, once trained, can rather easily become a good instructor? Is there a fine line of distinction here?

Answer: Yes, there is a definite line of distinction involved. A good facilitator is crucial to the successful conduct of a given program. The difference between an instructor and facilitator lies in the *degree* of teaching skill required for each role. Whether a good facilitator can *eventually* (not easily) become an effective instructor is a moot point, since every case is different. As a general statement, however, one could say that with the proper *coaching* and *support*, a facilitator stands a good chance in progressing towards a satisfactory level of the advanced instructional role.

Question: Are you then saying that it's the *responsibility* of the instructor to further develop a facilitator who is part of the instructional team?

Answer: Absolutely.

Question: Isn't it true that no matter how it is positioned by the instructor, a role play will almost always be viewed as threatening by some class members? If so, what can be done about it?

Answer: Yes, it certainly can be looked upon as threatening by some participants. While there is no absolute guarantee against this unfortunate occurrence, the responsibility to *minimize* this wherever possible falls on the instructor. This can be accomplished in several ways, including talking to the participant *privately* prior to the role play and carefully watching the "action" during the role play, being ready to gently "step in" without being obvious to the rest of the role-play team. Finally, if a participant is extremely apprehensive, I would make certain that this individual played the role of an observer for the first round. Note the fine line of distinction here. At all times, the instructor must guide the reluctant participants through a nonthreatening experience, yet somehow give them the actual interaction of role playing with another person. It's not an easy task!

Question: Regarding the handling of class disruptions, you seem to imply that an instructor should *never* ask a disruptive participant to leave the room. Isn't that taking a rather soft approach to troublemakers? What can you do when all else fails?

Answer: The sending of a participant out of the room should only be taken as a last resort, and even then, it must be handled with extreme caution. If this type of unfortunate situation ever does occur, the cardinal rule is: *never institute the request in front of the class*. Rather, wait until the coffee or lunch break and talk to the participant *privately*. Most problems can be resolved via this one-to-one talk. If that also fails, then the participant has the option of *not* returning to class at the completion of the break. In all cases, however, it is far better to have a participant return to the session, where the instructor can continue to attempt problem resolution, than to have a conspicuously empty seat in the classroom after the recess.

Question: Handling a problem participant who is of a much lower rank than the instructor seems difficult enough. But how in the world do you handle the same situation when the problem participant is of much higher rank than you?

Answer: With great care!

EVALUATING TRAINING RESULTS

Question: It's always been our practice *not* to send the completed evaluation summary to participants. The problem is that one risks the chance of a participant's *misinterpreting* the summary, thereby receiving a false impression of the results obtained from the program. Besides, one doesn't expect the participant to respond to the summary, so why take the chance?

Answer: First, it's a matter of common courtesy. After completing a training program, participants have a *right* to know the results. You *are* correct, however, in not anticipating a formal response from them. But, so what? Rest assured that, if handled properly, sending a summary will usually draw some type of verbal feedback from class members, and that in itself is *always* valuable.

Question: Can an experienced instructor actually "hype" the class ratings during the closing moments of the course?

Answer: Yes, to an extent. However, if a program is poorly designed or completely fails to meet the stated learning objectives, the negative class reaction via the written evaluation will be clearly evident.

Question: I still can't decide whether it's better to ask a class to complete the evaluation *before* leaving the room, despite time pressure, or to allow them to fill the form out back on the job or at their leisure. What is your preference?

Answer: Wherever possible, I ask participants to complete the evaluations *before* they leave the classroom. However, I make it a rule to leave sufficient time in the course schedule so participants do not feel rushed. My own opinion is that the written feedback is far more accurate when the experience is "fresh" in people's minds rather than several days later when the classroom experience has been reduced to a lingering memory.

Question: And the participants never object to this procedure?

Answer: Sometimes they do. However, when I explain the reasoning behind the request, most participants readily cooperate.

Question: In our company training programs, it is mandatory that all participants complete the evaluation and *sign their name*. The facilitator collects these at the door, and no one is allowed to leave the room without handing in the evaluation. This must be an excellent system, since we always get a 100 percent response, and the great majority of our courses are rated quite favorably. What's your reaction to that?

Answer: I have a mixed reaction. While it must be gratifying to always receive a 100 percent response (with most of these being quite favorable) you might want to question the *validity* of their responses.

THE TRAINING/ORGANIZATION PARTNERSHIP

Question: I agree that training, *properly directed*, is an essential component of an organization, but isn't it also true that the training department is the first to be curtailed in times of a prolonged economic slump?

Answer: I'm not certain if training would always be the *first* to be reviewed, but yes, it would most likely fall under this category. Whether we care to recognize it or not, in times of a business slowdown, *nonrevenue-producing units* will usually be looked at in terms of possible expense reduction. It's a fact of life we have to recognize. But, this is precisely where a well-run, relevant training department will outlast those that do not measure up to the standards set by senior management.

Question: It is quite obvious that having a senior executive as a mentor of training is highly desirable. But how does one go about securing this relationship?

Answer: No easy response can be made to your question. Generally, a high-ranking individual will at some time indicate an interest in the training function, and this could be a natural starting point in the mentor relationship. Always bear in mind, however, that this type of relationship can *never* be forced, but seems to grow and further solidify over time. Like any other type of relationship, it will enhance itself naturally if the ingredients of trust and mutual respect are ever-present.

Question: You continually refer to the importance of "staying close to the line." But, in attempting to do this, isn't there a danger of line management's perceiving training as a pure staff function that is exceeding its authority?

Answer: Definitely not. As a matter of fact, the more that training is recognized as an *extension of the line*, the easier it will be for this function to build and maintain a high degree of relevancy in its output.

Question: A final question on line involvement: In our organization, all our instructors are from line management positions, and we find that they make ideal subject-matter experts in front of a class. During the past eight months, our firm has practically doubled in size, and as a result we expect to triple the number of training programs within the next few weeks. This means that instead of relying on the three line instructors who were carrying the teaching load, we now have to recruit at least five or six more. I have two questions. Do you think that we should begin some type of formal instructor training for line management? And if so, when should we start?

Answer: Yes. Yesterday.

13

EPILOGUE

In a broad sense this chapter can be compared to the experience an instructor has accumulated by gathering knowledge prior to teaching a formal program in an industrial or commercial setting. It's now time for each instructor to apply or reinforce the principles outlined in this book in actual classroom teaching.

It should be an exciting time indeed, for throughout the book I've attempted to transfer an array of feasible teaching ideas and concepts in the most practical form possible—both to the novice instructor and to those with several years of experience. Each chapter was carefully designed to present the latest in platform techniques so as to give the instructor a comprehensive grounding in both basic and advanced skills. Yet, I caution readers not to be lulled into any false sense of security by the mere act of reading the previous twelve chapters. In order to be truly effective as an instructor, you must constantly *reinforce* your current knowledge and *expand* into higher skill levels. If this book has provided any degree of stimulus for that worthwhile objective, then the time spent in writing same will have been well worth it.

This juncture is an ideal time to consider the broad field of teaching in a business environment and its ramifications for those engaged in this highly specialized field of endeavor.

THE OPPORTUNITY

Regardless of the organization or the type of industry one is associated with, the opportunity for teaching has never been more promising. Along with this challenging opportunity comes the heavy responsibility of being the very best teacher that one is able to be—in spite of changing economic conditions and the ever-swinging business environment pendulum.

And the task will not be easy. In today's fast-paced environment, both individuals and the organizations they are associated with face highly complex and continual changes. Established ways of teaching considered quite satisfactory only a few short years ago are now being reevaluated. Every business organization operating in the current volatile business climate must either adapt successfully to change or face the very real danger of failing as an organization. And in adapting to change, new concepts, fresh ideas, and better ways of doing things must be transmitted from those who create them to those who must carry them out, making the role of teacher more important to the organization than at any other time in history.

As a result, teaching provides a rewarding benefit for those who have both the motivation and aptitude to transmit information to others in a classroom setting. With the challenge comes the almost certain built-in frustration of instructing classes in environments that are not always ideal, working with participants who are not really motivated to learn (for whatever the reason), and teaching skills that may be in vogue one day and obsolete the next.

Over the years the professional instructor has been highlighted as one who always retains a high degree of flexibility, continues to build on his or her knowledge base, and readily accepts new challenges as they arise. For those instructors who have not been exposed to any formal classroom training. I hope that this book will be a realistic first step in the climb toward professionalism. The challenges involved in teaching others are more critical and important than ever before—therefore, this book should be viewed as just the *first* stepping stone in the long journey toward becoming a first-rate instructor.

THE BENCH MARK

An author can never be absolutely certain as to the existing knowledge base that readers will bring to a book. It's a safe bet, however, to assume that many of you will have at least several years of platform experience, and some perhaps are even highly seasoned teachers. For those with experience, this book should provide an additional benefit: By reviewing your own teaching techniques and comparing them with the principles woven throughout these chapters, you should have a worthwhile bench mark for evaluating your own platform techniques.

In the final analysis, any organization providing a product or service to the end user is only as good as the caliber of people who represent it. Increasing the effectiveness of these people is a direct responsibility of the training function—with the transmission of the task falling heavily on the instructor. It's an awesome responsibility indeed, but one that is borne by the enviable breed of individuals called teachers.

PARTING GUIDELINES

If one were to survey the various professions, certain fundamental guidelines would emerge and act as basic cornerstones for success. The business of teaching others in a classroom is no exception, and in fact, the need for guidelines possibly applies even more directly to the platform instructor. Going a bit further, I'm reasonably certain that these same guidelines will be just as valid 100 years from now as they are today. Let's quickly review each one, noting not only their good sense on an individual basis, but the close relationship each one has to the next.

Keep Your Role in Perspective

Always remember that as a teacher you automatically assume a mantle of authority. This authority, or the control that you have over the class, should always be kept in the proper perspective, never wavering in face of uncertainty nor used as a weapon for those that you may hold in disregard. In the final analysis, it is a sacred trust given to those who impart knowledge to others, and one that must be used wisely at all times.

Always Be Conscious of the Individuality of Participants

Regardless of your length of time as a teacher, never forget that each student is unique and has a right to be recognized as such. The class participants will vary in their ability to absorb what is being taught and will bring with them a wide array of motivations, frustrations, and diverse perceptions of the value received from the instruction given. Never make the mistake of taking a participant for granted or of lumping several individuals together into preconceived categories.

Admit Your Mistakes

Instructors are only human and can make a mistake on the platform just as easily as a participant can make a mistake in the classroom. Admitting to an error in front of the class is interpreted by others not as a sign of weakness but rather as a mark of personal integrity and strength.

Keep Building Participant Self-Esteem

To recognize and reinforce achievement in the classroom is a powerful motivator for participant learning. This can never be accomplished through deception or false praise, but only via *well earned* praise for those who deserve it. Depending on the actions of the teacher, a participant's sense of self-esteem can be either reinforced or slowly destroyed—even in a few hours.

Be Firm, but Fair

Students do not expect to be perfect in the classroom and rely on you to be fair with them at all times. Being firm takes delicate balance: Teachers have to walk the fine line of maintaining flexibility where called for, yet never wavering in judgment when a decision is required.

Strive for Team Synergism

Keep striving for the beneficial effects of team synergism and its built-in thrusts to achieving ever-higher levels. While participants expect to be treated as separate entities, they also appreciate the positive benefits of being productive team members, working with others to reach a common objective.

Develop Your Replacement

Begin recruiting for your successor from your first day on the platform. Once found, start developing this person's potential and ability with an aim to make him or her *as good as or better than you*. No one is indispensable, but you may not get promoted until a suitable successor has been both selected and trained. Clearly, it's a fundamental management practice to have someone on your staff who can take over for you at a moment's notice.

Never Stop Learning

Effective teaching techniques rely on innovative methods that are both cost efficient and learning effective. Regardless of our number of years as teachers, we are never too old to absorb new techniques and therefore put ourselves in a better position to impart knowledge in a rapidly changing environment. Learning is truly a lifelong process, starting from the moment of birth and concluding only with the termination of life itself. Don't let yourself become cheated prematurely.

Be Yourself

Probably the most important guideline of all is to be yourself. Each instructor brings to the platform all of the unique characteristics and qualities he or she possesses as an *individual*. Never try to emulate someone or something that you are not. Never form yourself into a false mold in order to reach a stated objective. In the long run, this practice will rarely work. Participants will either accept you for what you are, or they will not accept you at all. No compromise will ever take place in this regard.

FINALE

This book started with a quotation from Ruffini, who stated, *"The teacher is like a candle which lights others in consuming itself."*

In my view, this simple statement contains the entire overview of teaching as a profession. But one should never be lulled into complacency with the sheer beauty of the phrase itself. Always keep in mind that in lighting the way for others, a part of you is also given freely.

In the end it's a very small price to pay for the priceless gift of knowledge imparted to those who seek it from you.

SELECTED READINGS

Apps, J. W. *Improving Your Writing Skills*. Chicago: Follett, 1983.

Argyle, M. *The Psychology of Interpersonal Behavior*. Gretna, LA: Pelican, 1978.

Bair, M., and Bry, A. *Visualization: Directing the Moves of Your Mind*. New York: Barnes & Noble, 1979.

Bell, C. R. "The High Performance Trainer." *Training and Development Journal*, June 1983.

Berne, E. *Games People Play*. New York: Grove Press, 1964.

Berne, E. *What Do You Say After You Say Hello?* New York: Grove Press, 1972.

Bligh, D. A. *What's the Use of Lectures?* New York: Penguin, 1972.

Bullard, J. W., and Mether, C. E. *Audio-Visual Fundamentals*. Dubuque, IA: Brown, 1974.

Bullock, D. H. *Programmed Instruction*. Englewood Cliffs, NJ: Educational Technology Publications, 1978.

Burger, R. E., and Addeo, E. G. *Ego Speak*. Radnor, PA: Chilton, 1973.

Burley-Allen, M. *Managing Assertively: How to Improve Your People Skills*. New York: Wiley, 1983.

Craig, R. L., ed. *Training and Development Handbook*, 2d ed. New York: McGraw-Hill, 1976.

Davies, I. K. *The Management of Learning*. New York: McGraw-Hill, 1971.

Deegan, A. X. *Coaching*. Reading, MA: Addison-Wesley, 1979.

Deming, B. S. *Evaluating Job-Related Training*. Englewood Cliffs, NJ: ASTD/Prentice Hall, 1983.

Denova, C. C. *Test Construction for Training Evaluation*. Washington, DC/New York: ASTD/Van Nostrand Reinhold, 1979.

327

Engel, H. M. *Handbook of Creative Learning Experiences*. Houston: Gulf, 1973.

Freeman, G. L., and Taylor, E. K. *How to Pick Leaders*. New York: Funk & Wagnalls, 1950.

Hyman, R. T. *Improving Discussion Leadership*. New York: Teachers College Press, 1980.

Gagne, R. M. *The Conditions of Learning*, 2d ed. New York: Holt, Rinehart & Winston, 1970.

Goldstein, I. L. *Training: Program Development and Evaluation*. Monterey, CA: Brooks-Cole, 1974.

Goudket, M. *An Audio Visual Primer*, Rev. ed. New York: Teachers College Press, 1974.

Gronlund, N. E. *Stating Behavioral Objectives for Classroom Instruction*. New York: Macmillan, 1970.

Gross, R., ed. *Invitation to Lifelong Learning*. Chicago: Follett, 1983.

Hamblin, A. C. *Evaluation and Control of Training*. New York: McGraw-Hill, 1974.

Harris, T. A. *I'm O.K.—You're O.K.* New York: Harper & Row, 1969.

Howe, M. J. A., ed. *Adult Learning—Psychological Research and Applications*. New York: Wiley, 1977.

Hudson, L. *Human Beings: The Psychology of Human Experience*. New York: Doubleday, 1975.

James, M., and Jongeward, D. *Born to Win*. Reading, MA: Addison-Wesley, 1971.

Kemp, J. E. *Planning and Producing Audio Visual Material*. New York: Harper & Row, 1980.

Kirkpatrick, D. L., ed. *Evaluating Training Programs*. Washington, DC: American Society for Training & Development, 1975.

Knowles, M. *The Adult Learner—A Neglected Species*, 2d ed. Houston: Gulf, 1978.

Knowles, M., and Knowles, A. *Introduction to Group Dynamics*. New York: Associated Press, 1972.

Laird, D. *Approaches to Training and Development*. Reading, MA: Addison-Wesley, 1978.

Leech, T. *How to Prepare, Stage and Deliver Winning Presentations*. New York: Amacom, 1983.

Linver, S. *Speak and Get Results*. New York: Summit Books, 1983.

Lynch, A. F., and Newman, P. J. *Behind Closed Doors: A Guide to Successful Meetings*. Englewood Cliffs, NJ: Prentice-Hall, 1983.

Maier, N. R. F., Salem, A. R., and Maier, A. A. *The Role Play Technique*. San Diego: University Associates, 1975.

Margolis, F. H., and Bell, C. R. *Managing the Learning Process*. Clearwater, FL: Lakewood Publications, 1983.

Maslow, A. H. *Motivation and Personality*. New York: Harper & Row, 1954.

McGehee, W., and Thayer, P. W. *Training in Business and Industry*. New York: Wiley, 1961.

McLagen, P. A. *Helping Others Learn: Designing Programs for Adults*. Reading, MA: Addison-Wesley, 1978.

McLarney, W. J. *Management Training*. Homewood, IL: Richard D. Irwin, 1955.

Moore, M. L., and Dutton, P. "Training Needs Anaysis: Review and Critique," *Academy of Management Review*, July 1978.

Mumford, A. *The Manager and Training*. Marshfield, MA: Pitman, 1971.

Murray, S. L. *How to Organize and Manage a Seminar*. Englewood Cliffs, NJ: Prentice-Hall, 1983.

Newstrom, J. W., and Lilyquist, J. M. "Selecting Needs Analysis Methods," *Training and Development Journal*, October 1979.

Newstrom, J. W., and Scannel, E. E. *Games Trainers Play*. New York: McGraw-Hill, 1980.

Nichols, R. G., and Stevens, L. A. *Are You Listening?* New York: McGraw-Hill, 1957.

Oppenheim, A. N. *Questionnaire Design and Attitude Measurement*. Portsmouth, NH: Heinemann, 1966.

Otto, C. P., and Glaser, R. O. *The Management of Training*. Reading, MA: Addison-Wesley, 1970.

Peters, T. J., and Waterman, R. H. *In Search of Excellence*. New York: Harper & Row, 1982.

Sager, A. W. *Speak Your Way to Success*. New York: McGraw-Hill, 1968.

Sarnoff, D. *Speech Can Change Your Life*. New York: Dell, 1970.

Saunders, N. *Classroom Questions: What Kinds?* New York: Harper & Row, 1966.

Smith, H. *Developing Your Executive Ability*. New York: McGraw-Hill, 1946.

Steil, L. K., Summerfield, J., and DeMare, C. *Listening: It Can Change Your Life*. New York: Wiley, 1983.

Tead, O. *The Art of Leadership*. New York: McGraw-Hill, 1935.

Theobald, J. *Classroom Testing: Principles and Practice*. New York: Longman, 1974.

Tracey, W. R. *Designing Training and Development Systems*. New York: American Management Association, 1971.

Xerox Learning Systems. *Managing for Motivation*. Stamford, CT: Xerox Corporation, 1973.

Yankelovich, D. *New Rules: Searching for Self-Fulfillment in a World Turned Upside Down*. New York: Random House, 1981.

Zemke, R., and Kramlinger, T. *Figuring Things Out—A Trainer's Guide to Needs and Task Analysis*. Reading, MA: Addison-Wesley, 1982.

Zivan, M. S. *Transactional Analysis for Managers*. New York: American Management Association, 1975.

INDEX

Active feedback, 169
Activity schedule, 167
Adult:
  defined, 30
  learning guidelines, 42–45
Audio-visual aids:
  audio recordings, 204
  overhead projector, 202–203
  16mm films, 203
  slides, 203
  videotape, 204–205

Barriers to learning:
  fear of failure, 34
  lack of time, 33
  motivational level, 31–32
  no perceived need, 33
  resistance to change, 34–35
Behavior modeling, 220–221
Billing arrangements, 129
"Burn-out," 155

Catalyst, 52
Cause and effect relationships, 16–17
Checkout procedures, 129
Coaching procedures, 39
Commitment (defined), 4
Communication:
  components, 55–63
  cycle, 53
  levels, 51–52
  vehicles, 51
  game, 223–228
  guidelines, 226–227
Cross introductions, 160

Daily activity planner, 129–133
Defense mechanisms, 67

Effective listening:
  active listening principles, 75–79
  key word selection, 76–77
  roadblocks involved, 70–75

Evaluating training results:
  biases, 272–275
  perceptions, 274
Evaluation techniques:
  cautions to be observed, 282–284
  sample criteria, 276–282
Examination guidelines, 96–97
Expectation iceberg, 5
Experiential exercises, 220

Facilitator:
  characteristics of, 243–244
  duties required, 248–249
  functions, 243
  roles, 9
  skills, 245–246
Facilities:
  assumptions involved, 110
  review, 110–128
Feedback, 60–61
Flash cards, 179
Flip charts:
  pre-printed, 158–159
  uses, 179
Frame of reference:
  defined, 63–64
  stages involved, 65–66
  syndrome, 67

Games:
  basic characteristics, 221–222
  cautions, 222–223
  defined, 220
  four classroom games that work, 223–239

Halo effect, 283, 289
Handling class disruptions, 258, 265
"Herding instinct," 148

"Ice-breaker" technique, 150–154
Instructional writer, 8
Instructor:
  defined, 173
  duties required, 9, 247
  training cycle, 86
Instructor's Guide:
  benefits of, 84
  common sense guidelines, 101–102
  pitfalls involved, 98

relevant assumptions, 85–86
  sequential components, 87
Introducing program content, 165–166
Introductions/expectations, 160–163
Introductory remarks booster, 182

Job analyst, 21

Learning:
  bridge, 150
  defined, 36
  fundamental principles, 36–37
  objectives, 159
  positive reinforcement process, 37–42
  receptivity, 84
  sequence, 90
Listening game, 228–231

Management commitment, 3–6
Marketing oriented company (defined), 13
Media specialist, 8
Meeting, management of, 126
Meeting checklist, 111–117, 128
Mind sets, 148
Motivation (defined), 31
Motivational self-discovery game, 231–236
Murphy's law, 111, 244

Needs analysis, 20–26
Negative characteristic syndrome, 283
New skill proficiency steps, 175
Non-verbal communication game, 236–239

Organizational training relationships, 11
Overhead projector transparencies, 179

Participant's profile, 160–161
Perceptions, 22
Performance criteria, 159
Practical knowledge, 155–156
Pre-class logistics, 134–135
Presentation elements:
  bridge, 184–185
  close, 186–188
  main body, 185–186
  opener, 184
Presentation framework:
  cycle 1: pre-talk logistics, 177–180
  cycle 2: the presentation, 180–188

cycle 3: question and answer strategy, 188–189
cycle 4: critique, 190–192
four cycle model, 177
Presentation notes, 192–193
Presentation planner:
  benefits involved, 201–202
  section 1: pre-talk checklist, 200
  section 2: presentation outline, 200–201
  section 3: question and answer strategy, 201
  section 4: critique, 201–202
Prizes/awards, 128
Problem participants:
  type 1: "I'm too busy, but I'm here," 260
  type 2: "I know better than you," 260–261
  type 3: "I'm in charge here," 261–262
  type 4: "I need your help," 262–263
  type 5: "everything is wrong, as usual," 263–264
  type 6: constant talker, 264–265
Program:
  administrator, 9
  description, 90
  design, 15–16
  designer, 8
  development, 85
  objectives, 89–90, 157–159
Progress segmentation chart, 166

Recommended training relationship structure, 13
Recreational facilities, 126–128
Relaxation technique, 181
Resistance to change syndrome, 35
"Reverse procedure" technique, 163
Role-play:
  advantages of, 250
  conducting, 254–257
  debriefing, 257–258
  disadvantages, 250
  objectives, 92–93
  organizing, 252–254
  positioning, 251–252
  strategy steps, 251
Room arrangements:
  auditorium style, 123–125

conference table, 122–123
interactive team, 120–121
standard "U-shaped," 121–122

Sample criteria, 276
Sequential teaching steps, 150
16mm film, 180
Stars principle, 291
Successful public speaking:
  interrelated traits, 175–176
  stimuli produced, 176
Synergism, 168–169

Task analyst, 8
Teaching excellence guidelines, 323–325
Teaching notes, 93–97
Team assignments, 168–169
35mm slides, 179
Trainer:
  defined, 2
  specific responsibilities, 2–3
Training:
  functional structure, 7–8
  fundamental elements, 2
  management commitment, 3–6
  origins, 2
  status quo maintenance, 6
  unwarranted assumptions, 5–6
Training and development manager:
  functions involved, 8–10
  position objective, 14
  principal responsibilities, 14–15
  responsibility for control, 10
Training objectives:
  long term, 294
  short term, 294
Training/organization partnership, 288–290
Training process, 7

Video presentation guidelines, 205–206
Videotapes, 180

Welcoming class:
  bridging technique, 156
  instructor introduction, 155
  strategy, 154–155